The Post-Soviet Potemkin Village
Politics and Property Rights in the Black Earth

The Post-Soviet Potemkin Village addresses the question of why the introduction of private property rights sometimes results in poverty rather than development. Most analyses of institutional change emphasize the design of formal institutions, but this study of land privatization in the Russia–Ukraine borderlands shows instead how informal practices at the local level can drive distributive outcomes.

Amidst widely differing institutional environments and reform pathways, local officials in Russia and Ukraine pursued strategies that produced a record of reform, even as they worked behind the scenes to maintain the status quo. The end result in both countries was a facade of private ownership: a Potemkin village for the post-Soviet era. Far from creating new private property rights that would bring development to the rural heartland, privatization policy deprived former collective farm members of their few remaining rights and ushered in yet another era of monopoly control over land resources.

Jessica Allina-Pisano draws on her extensive primary research in the Black Earth region conducted over a period of nine years to reach this surprising conclusion and uses extensive evidence from interviews, participant observation research, and documentary sources.

Jessica Allina-Pisano is an Associate Professor in the School of Political Studies at the University of Ottawa and an Associate of the Harvard University Davis Center for Russian and Eurasian Studies. She received her Ph.D. in political science from Yale University.

April 2008
New York

For Tim,
With thanks for your
encouragement, intellectual
companionship, and above all,
inspiration — Jessica

• "evidence"
  ↓ (p. 23)
language of confid
and testing

• style of documentation of direct quotes (vs. Vitebsky)
• microscopic focus to explain similarities rather than differences. (16)
• ethnography and the study of informal practices
   how do you recognize, with less study, informal (22) practices.

• Treatment of people — thin (p 38 "one of two sisters")

The Post-Soviet Potemkin Village

Politics and Property Rights in the Black Earth

→ p. 23 - what does ethnography have to offer?
p. 24 - language skills ← russian ukranian surzhyk

→ tethered cows (conclusion)

p. 186 - implications for a social science that sees from above, through the eyes of the state

p. 11 - potential variation in local responses, set A - A chooses two similar outcomes

JESSICA ALLINA-PISANO

University of Ottawa

intro → discussion of interview vs observation

p. 3 - "In reality...."

p. 4 → ethnographic methods are particularly suited to uncover the gap between de jure and de facto

what needs to be explained (gap) → bureaucratic resistance to supplying land
→ economic constraints that suppressed demand for land

p. 14 - "small, out of the way places" — cf. TSING
→ p. 22 "ossification of inequalities and creation of inflexible property rights that benefitted the elites at the expense of most other participants."

p. 59 - national directive, local control (unlike prior eras) [version of the principal-agent problem: "officials charged with implementing post-Soviet land privatization were rural insiders with broad legislated and de facto power in implementing policy reform."
   bureaucratic weapons of the weak.

* interviews &
p. 62 - evaluating overt verbal justification: "...ideas served mainly as rhetorical justification for actions driven mainly by more practical concerns."

CAMBRIDGE
UNIVERSITY PRESS

p. 73 - head of L'viv district state administration: "...retain the enterprises ...just in another form - a private form."

p. 79 - invokes rationality: "it would have been 'irrational'" → by what measure?
p. 84 - privatization a mechanism of dispossession.

CAMBRIDGE UNIVERSITY PRESS
Cambridge, New York, Melbourne, Madrid, Cape Town, Singapore, São Paulo, Delhi

Cambridge University Press
32 Avenue of the Americas, New York, NY 10013-2473, USA

www.cambridge.org
Information on this title: www.cambridge.org/9780521879385

First published 2008

Printed in the United States of America

A catalog record for this publication is available from the British Library.

Library of Congress Cataloging in Publication Data
Allina-Pisano, Jessica.
The Post-Soviet Potemkin village : politics and property rights in the black earth /
Jessica Allina-Pisano.
    p.   cm.
Includes bibliographical references and index.
ISBN 978-0-521-87938-5 (hardback) – ISBN 978-0-521-70931-6 (pbk.)
    1. Land reform – Russia (Federation)   2. Land reform – Ukraine.   3. Right of property –
Russia (Federation)   4. Right of property – Ukraine.   I. Title.
HD1333.R9A45   2008
333.3'147–dc22   2007010054

ISBN   978-0-521-87938-5 hardback
ISBN   978-0-521-70931-6 paperback

p. 20 - private farming entailed a risk few rural people were willing to accept.

chpt. 3 → private farmers were elites → some tell a behavioralist story → people were not entrepreneurial enough = but Allina's story is about availability of resources and connections.

decentralization to local elite-level control =

chpt 4. → decreasing support + increasing regulation.
Black Earth bureaucrats used their discretion to regulate in ways that allowed them to harass, intimidate, etc. in ways that allowed them to reshape social geography of land use. → goal: repossession of land by state institutions. private ownership an interim condition rather than irrevocable right. public shaming.

chpt. 5 → Politics of Payment → form of compensation changed dramatically. (less pay)

chpt 6 → Facade →
p. 187 "... many Black Earth villagers ... understood privatization as a conspiratorial fraud of massive proportions."

Contents

p. 185 - "... land ownership provided a legitimizing facade that proclaimed to the world and, importantly, to international lending institutions, the existence of alienable private property in the Black Earth countryside, even as ownership threatened ruin for some Black Earth villagers."

too weak

p. 185 - parchment institutions do have the potential to matter → they can contain rights which may serve as the basis for future reconfigurations of power.

List of Maps, Illustrations, and Tables

Maps

Illustrations

Tables

Acknowledgments

This book is the product of many people's labor. It is also the result of a decade of work in cities and villages in five countries: the United States, Russia, Ukraine, Mozambique, and, most recently, Canada. In each place, the generous advice, experience, and labor of colleagues and friends smoothed the task.

The community at Harvard University's Davis Center for Russian and Eurasian Studies, where I was fortunate to spend two years in residence at the beginning and end of this project, provided a collegial, challenging, and supportive environment that made writing a pleasure. I am particularly grateful to participants in the Post-Communist Politics and Economics Workshop, the Economics Seminar, and the Historians' Seminar for valuable feedback at various stages. A semester at the Kennan Institute in Washington, DC, provided an opportunity for sustained interaction with other scholars conducting research in rural areas of post-Soviet space, as well as with scholars and policy makers based in Russia and Ukraine. The Harvard Ukrainian Research Institute provided a lively community within which to complete the final stages of the book.

At various points in this project, I presented my research to colleagues at a number of institutions, including the Leibniz-Institut für Länderkunde in Leipzig, McGill University in Montreal, the Moscow School of Social and Economic Sciences, Princeton University, University College London, and the University of Toronto. The comments and questions I received in those venues helped sharpen the argument of the book. The Program in Agrarian Studies at Yale University was an intellectual home during the early stages of the project. Conversations with colleagues there as I completed the manuscript were a pleasure as well as a great help in thinking through broader comparative dimensions of the problems discussed here.

At Colgate University, my institutional home for four years as I worked on this project, conversations with Anne Pitcher and Michael Johnston were an ongoing source of intellectual stimulation. Members of the History Department read and commented upon early drafts of chapters. Kira Stevens in particular made very helpful suggestions as to how I might improve the argument. Nancy Ries, in the Department of Sociology and Anthropology, has been unfailingly generous with her time and insight, providing patient and invaluable guidance. Suzanne Slomin and Aaron Locker of Green Rabbit Farm in Madison, New York, kept me in mind of what it means to do agricultural work.

Several colleagues generously gave of their time to read and comment on the manuscript, in part or in whole. They are Jeffrey Burds, Timothy Colton, David Cameron, Anna Grzymała-Busse, Yoshiko Herrera, Atul Kohli, Martha Lampland, Pauline Jones Luong, Alexandr Nikulin, Timothy Pachirat, Pauline Peters, and James C. Scott. Conversations with other colleagues pushed me to think in new ways. Those colleagues include Dominique Arel, Nancy Bermeo, Kate Brown, Valerie Bunce, Jane Burbank, Sue Cook, Keith Darden, Andrea Graziosi, Halyna Hryn, Grigory Ioffe, Esther Kingston-Mann, Stephen Kotkin, Alena Ledeneva, John LeDonne, Peter Lindner, Ruth Mandel, Charles Mironko, Margaret Paxson, Jesse Ribot, Blair Ruble, Ed Schatz, Oxana Shevel, Sherrill Stroschein, Lynne Viola, Lucan Way, David Woodruff, Deborah Yashar, and Tat'iana Zhurzhenko.

At Cambridge University Press, Lewis Bateman was consummately helpful and responsive in shepherding this book through the writing stages. I am particularly grateful for the careful review and helpful comments on the manuscript provided by the anonymous readers at the Press.

I had the great fortune to work with manuscript editor Ronald Cohen, whose meticulous work, deft touch, effective guidance, and unfailing graciousness made the editing process a pleasure. Scott Walker at the Harvard University Map Collection worked patiently to produce the maps in this book, and I am grateful to him and the Collection for giving me permission to use the maps. André Simonyi provided generous and tireless assistance in revising the index and proofreading. Yaryna Yakubyak ably proofread the Russian and Ukrainian text in the footnotes. Mark Beissinger, Benedict Carton, Frederick Cooper, Anna Grzymała-Busse, Yoshiko Herrera, Jeannette Hopkins, and Nancy Ries all provided valuable advice about navigating the publishing process.

A number of organizations provided generous financial support for this project. Post-doctoral fellowships from the Eurasia Program of the Social Science Research Council, the Davis Center at Harvard University, the Kennan Institute for Advanced Russian Studies, and the Harvard Ukrainian Research Institute made possible three semesters of leave from teaching, without which this book would have been much longer in coming. At Colgate, a faculty grant supported work on the project. The National Science Foundation, the Social Science Research Council, the International Research and Exchanges Board, a Fox International Fellowship, and the Yale Center for International and Area Studies supported more than two years of research in Russia and Ukraine for this book.

I have had the opportunity to develop earlier versions of the arguments presented here in previous publications. I am grateful to the following publications and publishers for kindly granting me permission to use their material:

The Johns Hopkins University Press, for permission to reprint (1), in substantially revised form, material from my article "Sub Rosa Resistance and the Politics of Economic Reform: Land Redistribution in Post-Soviet Ukraine," *World Politics*, 56:4 (July 2004), and (2), pages 308–317 of my essay "Reorganization and Its Discontents: A Case Study in Voronezh *oblast'*," in O'Brien, David J. and Stephen K. Wegren, eds. *Rural Reform in Post-Soviet Russia*, Woodrow Wilson Center, 2002. This material appears in Chapter 2.

The Journal of Peasant Studies, for material used in Chapter 3 that originally appeared in my article "Land Reform and the Social Origins of Private Farmers in Russia and Ukraine," *Journal of Peasant Studies*, 32:4 (July 2004).

*International Labor and Working Class His*tory, for evidence used in Chapter 5 that originally appeared in my article, "The Two Faces of Petr Arkad'evich: Land and Dispossession in Russia's Southwest," *International Labor and Working Class History*, 2007.

Vitaly Zhikharev, editor-in-chief of the Voronezh newspaper *Kommuna* for permission to reprint visual material, 17 March 2006, No. 38 (24674).

In Russia, many people gave of their time, energy, and knowledge to assist me, at times spending their social capital on my behalf and patiently helping me through the complicated enterprise of establishing contacts and conducting research in rural areas. I cannot mention them all by name here, but they were instrumental in making this project possible. This book could not have been researched without the friendship of Mikhail Savin, who introduced me to Voronezh politics in the summer of 1996 and subsequently helped me in more ways than I can count. In Voronezh, T.I. and the entire Rassoulovy family provided true homes away from home and helped me resolve so many of the challenges of everyday existence that characterized life in provincial Russia in the 1990s. Ioulia Rassoulova provided valuable assistance in tracking down newspapers and transcribing interviews. The villagers of Chayanovksoe tolerated my mistakes with good humor, and the Ritunsky family, K. Udovina, V. Shcherbakova, and the grandmothers' folksong ensemble-drinking club helped me feel at home. My hosts in the town of Pavlovsk were generous to a fault, and respondents in the districts of Anna, Liski, and Verkhniaia Khava took time away from busy work lives to educate me in the subtleties not only of land reform, but also of local banking and credit regimes, the challenges of grain elevator operation, and dozens of other subjects. The staff of the division of regional studies at the Nikitin Regional Public Library in Voronezh was particularly helpful in locating and obtaining local press materials published in the early 1990s.

In Ukraine, many people provided intellectual or logistical support, gave generously of their time, and made research a genuine pleasure. In Kharkiv, they include V. P. Burda, A. V. Galaka, N. F. Osipova, and V. P. Lemishchenko. Members of the regional farmers' association consistently offered their hospitality and cheerfully accepted my presence at their meetings. V. I. Belins'kyi, V. A. L'vov, and O. V. Babenko were particularly patient and helpful interlocutors. Lilia Kim and her colleagues in Kharkiv women's organizations were a source not only of logistical support, but also of inspiration. M. Kamchatnyi and L. Kulik provided useful insight and logistical support during a research trip in 2006. Valentin Kulapin helped me in many ways. His knowledge of the region and personal acquaintance with local producers opened the door to many farm directors' offices. I also benefited tremendously from many hours of conversations with his colleagues in land tenure offices in the region.

People in the national capitals likewise provided valuable assistance. I am grateful to a number of people in Kyiv for writing letters of introduction that opened doors to state offices in Kharkiv. They are Anatoliy Yurchenko, who was also a source of good-natured conversation, advice, and research material; Viktor Pryvalov, Donald Van Atta, and Volodymyr Dem'ianchuk. In Moscow, a number of people assisted me in thinking about how to get this project started – Moshe Lewin, Gennady Bourdiugov, Irina Koznova, Aleksandr Nikulin, Valery Vinogradsky, and the agricultural economics division of the Department of Economics at Moscow University.

This project was born fifteen years ago at a small kitchen table in a five-story Soviet apartment bloc, after a weekend hauling sacks of potatoes from a garden plot near Novgorod overland by foot, truck bed, and fourth-class train to St. Petersburg. Although neither the Kirsanov family nor I realized it at the time, my conversations with them in 1991, and their subsequent willingness to share their space and their lives with me during the following, difficult year, started me down this path, and I thank them for it.

I owe a great deal to the close friends who have been a constant source of support and happiness along the way. They include Adil Baizhumanov, Laina and Sarah Bay-Cheng, Jarrett Barrios and Doug Hattaway, Fr. Robert Bowers, Elizabeth Cohen, and Elaine Goldenberg. Thanks are also due to the Allina family for their support and interest. Several generations of women in my family worked long hours at hard jobs so that their daughters might have better opportunities than they themselves had. I hope my efforts serve the memory of Catherine Tobin and Rose Spitz well.

Eric Allina-Pisano has been my greatest friend and has contributed to this project in more ways than I can possibly articulate. His love, support, and intellectual companionship made this book possible.

I owe my most grateful thanks to my interlocutors in the Black Earth, who generously shared the details of their work lives with me. I hope that their willingness to participate in this project will result in a more accurate understanding of the challenges rural people faced at the end of the twentieth century. I would like to think I have their story right. I'll have done my job well if they find something in this book that they recognize as their own.

Note on Transliteration

In footnotes and in the text, I have largely used the Library of Congress system of transliteration for Russian and Ukrainian words. For reader comfort, I have abbreviated some transliterations of proper names in the text: Moskovsky rather than Moskovskii. Unless otherwise noted, all translations are my own.

Note on Sources and Methodology

To avoid repetition and to allow the reader readily to identify geographical locations, I have used the following abbreviations in the notes: unless otherwise specified, "Voronezh" and "Kharkiv" refer to the regions, rather than the cities.

Abbreviations of District Names in Footnotes

Voronezh Region, Russian Federation		Kharkiv Region, Ukraine	
AV	Anninskii district	BK	Bohodukhivs'kyi district
LV	Liskinskii district	CK	Chuhuivs'kyi district
PV	Pavlovskii district	DK	Derhachivs'kyi district
SV	Semilukskii district	KK	Krasnokuts'kyi district
VV	Verkhnekhavskii district	LK	Lozivs'kyi district
	(Khava, in text)	MK	Kolomats'kyi district
		NK	Novovodolaz'kyi district
Lipetsk Region, Russian Federation		PK	Pecheniz'kyi district
DL	Dankovskii district	VK	Vovchans'kyi district
		XK	Kharkivs'kyi district
		ZK	Zolochivs'kyi district
		Zakarpats'ka Region, Ukraine	
		UZ	Uzhhorods'kyi district

In order to preserve the anonymity of my respondents, in no case do I identify specific villages or other rural settlements. Names that appear in the text, except where I quote press reports, are pseudonyms, as are the names of the Voronezh agricultural collective "Chayanovskoe" and other collectives where I conducted interviews, the district in Kharkiv I have called "L'viv" district, and the names of private farmers. Interviews with state officials identify the offices or divisions of administration, but not the titles of my respondents. The latter choice required some compromise of analytical precision in describing the reconfiguration of state power in the Black Earth countryside, but any other approach would have revealed too much about the identity of my interlocutors.

Newspapers and Statistics

A variety of perspectives are represented in the newspapers used in this study. For about ten years following the Soviet collapse, district and regional newspapers in both Russia and Ukraine covered a range of responses to land reform. During the 1990s, with local budgets stretched to the breaking point, newspapers were a luxury, and public libraries suspended subscriptions for months or years. District and regional newspapers were therefore not readily accessible. I read them in public libraries when they were available, borrowed back issues from editorial offices, and salvaged bound issues from state offices that had no space to store them.

District newspapers were successor institutions to party publications and were often owned or managed by local governments. They covered both pro- and anti-Moscow and Kyiv positions, reflecting local governments' often ambivalent stance toward reform policy. For example, in Voronezh, the Liski paper ran a number of stories about attempts to reclaim land that had belonged to local families prior to collectivization. Despite the absence of legislation providing for restitution, the stories were sympathetic to the claimants, who consistently faced a wall of bureaucratic indifference. At the same time, the Liski press also ran stories by farm chairmen who were critical of land privatization, advocated for buying produce locally, and positioned themselves as protectors of rural interests.[1]

In addition to using state-published statistical data, this study uses unpublished numerical evidence. I gathered this evidence from regional and district state offices, village councils, and individual enterprises. Statistical data, like much of the other information I collected during two years of research, was not easy to obtain. I collected it in the context

---

[1] For example, Leonid Vybornov, "Zybkoe ravnovesie," *LI*, 13 January 1998, 2.

Abbreviations of Newspaper Titles in Footnotes

Russia		Ukraine	
AV	*Anninskie vesti* (Anna)	DP	*Dneprovskaia pravda* (Dnepropetrovsk)
KO	*Kommuna* (Voronezh)	DU	*Delovaia Ukraina*
KR	*Krest'ianskaia Rossiia*	KP	*Kyiv Post* (Kyiv)
KV	*Krest'ianskie vedomosti*	NZ	*Novyny Zakarpattia* (Zakarpattia)
LI	*Liskinskie izvestiia* (Liski 1991–)	SK	*Slobid'skyi krai* (Kharkiv)
LZ	*Leninskoe znamia* (Liski–1991)	TT	*Trybuna trudiashchykh* (Kharkiv district)
MP	*Maiak Pridon'ia* (Pavlovsk)	UK	*Uriadovyi kur'er*
NG	*Novaia gazeta*	ZN	*Zerkalo nedeli*
RV	*Raionnyi vestnik* (Khava)	ZoP	*Zoria Poltavshchyny* (Poltava)
SZ	*Semilukskaia zhizn'* (Semiluki)	ZaP	*Zaporiz'ka pravda* (Zaporizhzhia)
VR	*Verkhnekhavskie rubezhi* (Khava)	ZH	*Zhytomyrshchyna* (Zhytomyr)

of ongoing relationships built over a period of months or years. This often required weeks of visiting state functionaries in their offices, exchanging – in an unacknowledged quid pro quo – stories about life in America for a page of economic data. In some cases, my initial visits were made possible only by a letter of introduction or telephone call from a high-ranking member of the national government. Much of the data I was able to collect was made available to me only after six or more months of ethnographic research. In district offices and on individual collective farms, I copied statistical material by hand, as photocopiers often were not available. In many instances, information ostensibly in the public domain was simply off-limits. For example, my attempts to review the public records of court cases involving private farmers – many of whom had to sue to receive physical access to land to which they held formal title – were consistently thwarted. In Kharkiv, I asked a senior faculty member at the National Law Academy to inquire about these records at the office of her acquaintance, the chief prosecutor for the region. The answer to her inquiry was a flat refusal to grant access to these "public" records.

Interviews and Ethnographic Research Techniques

A thorough discussion of the nuances of conducting interviews and ethno-graphic research in the post-Soviet countryside would require another complete book. I have noted a few points in order to explain how the evidence I have presented in this book was produced.

Researching a book about land privatization required that I learn a great deal about Black Earth agriculture. Over time, as I accumu-lated knowledge about the nuances of sugar beet seeding, the differences between tractors produced in Kharkiv and those manufactured in Minsk, and how to manage canning vegetables using a hot plate and a bathtub, my interlocutors were more forthcoming in conversation. The sequence of my research thus shaped the type and quality of the evidence I was able to collect. I conducted my research in Russia before I began my research in Ukraine, returning once again to Voronezh near the end of my field research in Kharkiv. The interviews I conducted then proved to be among the most fruitful of my time in the Black Earth. Additionally, my field sites for extended ethnographic research were qualitatively different on each side of the border, with a farm site in Russia and a state office and a farmers' organization in Ukraine. I have cited evidence from that research in the text as field notes or oral testimony (using the abbreviation "OT"), which refers to statements made to me or in my presence outside the context of interviews.

The accidental fact that I physically resemble people in the Black Earth, combined with hard-won language skills and cultural knowledge culti-vated over a period of seventeen years, helped me blend in and acquire not only "outsider" but also "insider" perspectives in research. Those "insider" perspectives were not unproblematic, however. My more or less successful efforts to acquire local accents in Voronezh and Kharkiv, after first having been trained in literary Russian and Ukrainian, meant that I often was called upon to provide an explanation of my identity. Most people began by asking how long I had been living in the United States; this assumption placed me in the socially and politically dubi-ous category of, as several people put it to me, "former Russian." Oth-ers used different cues to decide "who stood behind me" and what I was really after: Soviet-trained ethnographers work in teams, rather than singly, and there was no recent tradition of foreigners poking around asking questions for any reason other than matters of state. This meant that most rural people approached me with a measure of suspicion.

On more occasions than I could count, my interlocutors, drawing upon decades of experience of state surveillance, articulated the belief that I was collecting information for a government or agricultural firm. Another respondent remarked that I couldn't be a foreigner because I drove a small Russian vehicle. An American, after all, "would drive something fancier."

While a few private farmers and local state officials whom I interviewed had visited the United States on Department of Agriculture exchange programs, the majority of my interlocutors had never before met an American or other foreigner from the "far abroad." In some cases, this meant that the scripts people drew upon in interview and conversational narratives were everyday scripts, familiar to me from years of previous social interaction with people in and from Russia and Ukraine, rather than, necessarily, practiced liturgies of "what we tell the foreigners." In the course of my research, I came to conclude that the most important aspect of my outsider status was my urban identity and educational level, rather than my foreignness as such. The fact that my grandparents had been farmers helped bridge the divide somewhat, and on some occasions I was privy to village gossip and deprecation about city folk who summered in the countryside – even as I was the subject of it on other occasions.

Most interviews took place wherever my interlocutors happened to be working. On a few occasions, they occurred in respondents' homes. Some were individual interviews, while others were structured conversations that included small groups of people who knew each other. The latter tended to be especially revealing, as they often included both joking and heated arguments. I selected some of my interlocutors randomly, speaking with whomever agreed to speak with me. There are multiple selection biases implicit in this or any other approach: this method favored people who either had free time or were engaged in tasks for which my presence would not be a distraction. Thus, it was easier to find pensioners willing to speak with me than people of my own age, who were busy with farm and household labor. A few people with a specific complaint against a farm director or state official sought me out for conversation in places I frequented, sometimes requesting that I bring their story to an international audience. On some occasions, a member of officialdom would introduce me to a farm director or other local leader, who then spoke with me or directed me to others. Still other interviews came about as people whom I met in the course of research introduced me to their acquaintances. The resulting narratives tended to vary primarily according to who was present when the interview or conversation took place, rather than according to who made the introduction.

Interviews tended to last about an hour and a half, though they ranged from twenty minutes to five hours. I spoke with some people only once, while in other cases I interviewed people I saw regularly over the course of a year or more. A small number of rural people have been longer-term interlocutors, with conversations spanning seven years or more.

The mechanics of note-taking and recording posed a significant challenge. As the chairman of Chayanovskoe put it to me, "people here have respect for the written word" because text written about them, in the hands of the authorities, had the power to ruin their lives. Most people refused to speak in the presence of a tape recorder or other recording device, and some even asked that I put down my pen. Higher-status people generally were more willing to be recorded; for this reason, longer passages in the text tend to come from private farmers or farm directors. In cases where I could use neither notebook nor tape recorder, I wrote up my notes immediately after the conversation. Because of most people's wish to speak off the record, I have avoided quoting unpublished direct statements of lower-level employees in the text. Instead, I used those interviews and conversations to help me interpret the statements of local officials, farm directors, and other more powerful figures in the Black Earth countryside.

My research also included an ill-fated survey, with a very small sample size including only a few respondents. The reason for this is that the directors of collectives whom I approached would not allow survey questions to be asked of their workers. Survey questions were concrete, straightforward, and not explicitly political – for example: "What is the size of your land share?" and "Did you receive a land share certificate?" One farm director "categorically objected" because he did not want members of his collective to "get any ideas." It should be noted that when the Ukrainian or Russian governments or international lending institutions conducted surveys, directors were compelled to allow participation and were in a position to instruct some employees as to "correct" responses.

In the text, I have emphasized what my interlocutors said they thought they were doing. Their statements are valuable not because they necessarily bear any intrinsic truth (social scientists are not yet in the business of measuring sincerity) but because of what they reveal about the expectations of people in rural communities and provincial governments. In using this evidence, I have, however, compared their statements with what I have come to learn about the practice of agriculture in the region and the incentives people faced both in their professional capacities and as members of rural and provincial communities.

Glossary

Terms are given only in the language(s) in which they appear in the body of the text. For words associated primarily with the Soviet period, only the Russian terms appear: thus, *kolkhoz* (Russian), but not *kolhosp* (Ukrainian).

AKKOR	Association of Private Family Farmers and Agricultural Cooperatives of Russia
blat	A non-monetary exchange mechanism based on personal favors
chastnik	Private owner – here, a farm head
chudak	An eccentric
dacha	Summer cottage, often modest
gostorg	State trade office under communism
hospodar	Owner, master (Ukrainian)
iz"iatie	Seizure (here, of land)
khoziain	Owner, master (Russian)
kolkhoz	Collective farm
kolkhoznik	Member of a collective farm
kottedzh	Luxury home, often in the countryside (from English, "cottage")
krest'ianskoe (fermerskoe) khoziaistvo	Private farm (Russian)

kulak	Rich peasant (*lit.* fist), persecuted under Stalin in the 1930s
mitingovshchina	Rule by demonstrations
naturoplata	In-kind payment
oblast'	Administrative region of Russia or Ukraine
pai (also *dolia*)	A share in land or non-land farm assets
prodnalog	In-kind tax
razbazarivanie	Squandering, often by selling off
selians'ke (fermers'ke) hospodarstvo	Private farm (Ukrainian)
sotka	A unit of area: one-hundredth of a hectare (1 hectare = 2.47 acres), or 100 square meters
sovkhoz	State farm
tiapka	Garden hoe suitable for cutting plant roots

MAP 1. Two regions of the Black Earth, Voronezh and Kharkiv *oblasti*, 1991–present. Copyright © 2006, Harvard University Map Collection/Scott Walker. Reprinted with permission.

MAP 2. Voronezh *oblast'* in the twenty-first century. Copyright © 2006, Harvard University Map Collection/Scott Walker. Reprinted with permission.

MAP 3. Kharkiv *oblast'* in the twenty-first century. Copyright © 2006, Harvard University Map Collection/Scott Walker. Reprinted with permission.

The Post-Soviet Potemkin Village
Politics and Property Rights in the Black Earth

Introduction

Land Reform in Post-Communist Europe

In December 1991, as the flag of the Soviet Union flew its last days over the Kremlin, a small crowd armed with crutches and wheelchair wheels stormed the regional state administration building in an eastern Ukrainian city. The city, Kharkiv, lies fifty miles from the Russian border.[1] The protesters were a group of senior citizens and disabled people from the Saltivka housing development in Moskovsky district, an area of the city named for its location on the road to the Soviet metropolis. The group had gathered to demand land for garden plots.

The protesters had specific land in mind. The land lay at the eastern edge of the city, bordering the Saltivka housing development to the west and the fields of one of the most successful agricultural collectives in the region to the east. That farm, named Ukrainka, was among the biggest dairy producers in the area. Food supplies in city markets, however, had become unpredictable and expensive. Residents of Saltivka wanted land to grow produce for themselves and their families.

In response, the Kharkiv district executive committee ordered that Ukrainka relinquish nearly 300 hectares of land for garden plots, in addition to 75 hectares already alienated for that purpose the previous spring. Members of the Ukrainka collective objected to the proposed plan,

---

[1] This account is based on a series of newspaper articles about the incident in a Kharkiv regional paper: M. Mel'nyk, "Pole rozbratu mozhe nezabarom staty arenoiu spravzhnikh boiv mizh horodianamy i selianamy. Chy vystachyt' im hluzdu unyknuty 'zemel'noi viiny'?" *SK*, 11 December 1991, 1; N. Hlushko, "Khto zupynyt' Popykina?" *SK*, 8 February 1992, 2; and A. Bondar, "Grabezh sredi bela dnia. Zemliu – po zakonu," *SK*, 10 December 1991, 1.

arguing that the proximity of the housing development already caused problems for the farm. Residents of the development walked their dogs in the fields, trampling down seedlings and ruining crops.

In the face of rising conflict between residents of the housing development and members of Ukrainka, the district leadership decided on a compromise. It would allot the land adjacent to the high rises for garden plots and give Ukrainka 500 hectares of fallow land in a neighboring state farm named "Red Army." This solution, it was thought, would both satisfy the protesting constituencies and provide a buffer zone between the housing development and the fields of Ukrainka.

Members of the Ukrainka collective refused to accept such a compromise. Instead, they took to their tractors to defend the land of their farm. Ukrainka tractor operators planned to bulldoze the low picket fences between garden plots in the fields alienated from the collective. Saltivka residents, meanwhile, threatened to battle the collective with Molotov cocktails.

The Paradox of Ownership

This book is about conflict surrounding the privatization of a natural resource, and how that conflict shaped property rights for millions of people. The privatization in question involved the partition and distribution of millions of acres of public land in an expanse of the Eastern European steppe known as the Black Earth. The book addresses a central question in the study of institutional development and the politics of economic transformation: Why do programs of property rights development sometimes fail to deliver on their initial promise? And why, despite the efforts and intentions of reformers and participants in the process, does an ownership society at times produce poverty rather than development?

After the collapse of the Soviet Union, and amidst a global context of accelerating enclosure movements, states in Eastern Europe and Eurasia embarked upon the most far-reaching privatization projects of the twentieth century. Among the sharpest political battles surrounding commodification and privatization were those concerning land. This book focuses on Russia and Ukraine, where land transfers of previously unimaginable scale occurred twice during the twentieth century – first during the collectivization drives of the 1920s and 1930s that consolidated land holdings in collective and state farms, and then in the privatization efforts that followed the collapse of Soviet power and sought to undo collectivization.

Ordinarily, such massive transfers of land occur only in the course of imperial conquest or in the aftermath of war. But in the decade after the fall of the Soviet Union and before the turn of the new millennium, 700 million hectares of land in the Russian Federation, an expanse as large as all of Australia, were privatized. Fifty-five percent of the total land mass of Ukraine, an area larger than Germany, was transferred from state ownership into the hands of individuals. In both Ukraine and Russia, land privatization drew upon global boilerplate policies and was accompanied by intense anxiety regarding questions of local and national sovereignty and territorial integrity. As politicians struggled to maintain stability amidst the deep uncertainties of empire's end, rural people worried about outsiders buying vast tracts and making them "slaves on our own land."[2]

A central feature of institutional change in these states is the superficial character of the property rights that resulted from over a decade of privatization. Liberal economic policies and local politics combined to produce a facade of rural ownership – a modern Potemkin village. Like the wooden facades that, according to legend, were constructed along Crimean roads to impress and mislead Tsarina Catherine the Great during her travels at the end of the eighteenth century, post-Soviet Potemkin villages convinced Moscow and Kyiv of local state officials' loyalty and international lending institutions of the Russian and Ukrainian governments' commitment to property rights reform. In Russia and Ukraine, the documentary record shows the creation of millions of new landowners through titling. On paper, rural capitalists arose, like Minervas, fully formed from fields recently emptied of socialist forms of production. State records in both countries show the allocation of millions of hectares of land to erstwhile members of collective farms and workers on state farms.

In reality, although a few individuals benefited from reform, privatization was a process through which most agricultural laborers *lost* the means to extract value from the land.[3] Few of these private owners came to have either access to or profit from their land: land privatization resulted in the individuation and transfer of property rights without, in most cases, actual partition. Today, many rural shareholders hold only a sheet of paper declaring their ownership of a few hectares on the usually vast territory

---

[2] This refrain of the post-Soviet countryside is also noted by Caroline Humphrey, *The Unmaking of Soviet Life: Everyday Economies after Socialism*. Ithaca: Cornell University Press, 2002, 168.

[3] Katherine Verdery observes a similar problem in Romania. Verdery, *The Vanishing Hectare: Property and Value in Postsocialist Transylvania*. Ithaca: Cornell University Press, 2003.

of a former collective. The range of options for making meaningful use of that ownership is narrow, and leasing land back to the former collective is often the only option available. As payment for the use of their land, owners receive, at best, a few sacks of grain, a compensation of lesser value than the entitlements they received during the last decades of collectivized agriculture.

Privatization's evident failure to improve material life has led some observers to categorize post-Soviet land reform as cosmetic or illusory – a view widely shared by those who labor in the fields and farms of the Black Earth.[4] The hollow character of new property rights should not be understood to mean, however, that no change has occurred.[5] Even as current conditions mean most villagers cannot use land ownership rights to generate capital, private property rights now exist in the world of bureaucracy and law. Land may change hands legally, and future political and economic actors strong enough to prevail in local battles over land may find it easy to persuade shareholders to divest themselves of rights that have had little practical meaning.

The existence of new ownership rights on the books, combined with a landscape populated by dispossessed peasants, presents an analytical as well as a practical problem. The existence of such an unusually broad fissure between *de jure* and *de facto* property rights regimes requires explanation, and this book provides one. The explanation presented here hinges upon two sets of factors, both of which operated at the local level: bureaucratic resistance to supplying land, articulated through a set of informal political practices and explained by a combination of discretion, norms, and incentives; and economic constraints that suppressed demand for land, explained in large part by the effects of the simultaneous implementation of privatization and other elements of structural adjustment programs.[6] Here, the complementary interaction of structural economic parameters and causally proximate political mechanisms explains the

[4] Max Spoor, "Agrarian Transition in Former Soviet Central Asia: A Comparative Study of Kazakhstan, Kyrgyzstan and Uzbekistan," ISS Working Paper No. 298, 1999 quoting Stephen K. Wegren, "The Land Question in Ukraine and Russia," *The Donald W. Treadgold Papers* 5 (February 2002), Jackson School of International Studies, University of Washington, 13.

[5] Stephen K. Wegren, "Change in Russian Agrarian Reform, 1992–1998: The Case of Kostroma Oblast" in Kurt Engelmann and Vjeran Pavlakovic, eds. *Rural Development in Eurasia and the Middle East: Land Reform, Demographic Change, and Environmental Constraints.* Seattle: University of Washington Press, 2001.

[6] Lawrence King, "Shock Privatization: The Effects of Rapid Large-Scale Privatization on Enterprise Restructuring," *Politics and Society* 31:1 (March 2003) 3–30.

development of the modern Potemkin village.[7] The hidden character of bureaucratic resistance created an official record of distribution where none or little actually had occurred, while economic constraints limited rural people's desire and capacity to convert paper rights into actual allocation of land in the fields.

Land privatization in the Black Earth is not a case of underfulfillment of a plan, or of local state institutions that lacked the ability to carry out a policy. Instead, local state officials, with the help of farm directors, deliberately constructed a facade of *de jure* rights while pursuing an entirely different and demonstrably contrary set of goals – namely, the preservation of large-scale agriculture, in which farm directors would control land resources and local state oversight would continue to play an important role.[8]

Privatization Globally and in the Black Earth

Land reform in post-Soviet Russia and Ukraine occurred in the context of both post-communist change and a global rush to privatization. Across industrialized countries and those areas of the globe that have come to be known as the developing world, states and private interest groups are redefining common pool resources as commodities.[9] Water tables, ports, coastal fisheries, forests, and even the genomes of plants and animals are the targets of new enclosure movements whose underlying purpose is capital accumulation.[10] Redefinition is a political process, and interest groups

---

[7] Herbert Kitschelt, "Accounting for Postcommunist Regime Diversity: What Counts as a Good Cause?" in Grzegorz Ekiert and Stephen E. Hanson, eds. *Capitalism and Democracy in Central and Eastern Europe*. Cambridge: Cambridge University Press, 2003, 74.

[8] Such deliberate construction of facades was widespread in Soviet life, where bureaucrats responded to the pressures of economic planning by manipulating the record of results. An example from housing construction is Aleksandr Vysokovskii, "Will Domesticity Return?" in William Craft Brumfield and Blair A. Ruble, eds. *Russian Housing in the Modern Age: Design and Social History*. Washington, DC: Woodrow Wilson Center Press, 1993.

[9] By definition, common pool resources such as pasture are, in contrast to pure public goods, subtractive and excludable, even as the costs of exclusion are high. For a useful summary of definitional issues concerning property rights, see Elinor Ostrom, "Private and Common Property Rights," in Boudewijn Bouckaert and Gerrit De Geest, eds. *Encyclopedia of Law and Economics*. Cheltenham: Edward Elgar Publishers, 2000.

[10] Michael Goldman, ed. *Privatizing Nature: Political Struggles for the Global Commons*. New Brunswick, NJ: Rutgers University Press, 1998, and Verdery and Caroline Humphrey, eds. *Property in Question: Value Transformation in the Global Economy*. Oxford: Berg, 2004.

positioned to profit from enclosure may mobilize to spur redefinition of commons even as local communities resist the transformation of common pool resources into privately owned commodities from which they are unlikely to benefit.

As the incident in Saltivka illustrates, battles over redefinition formed a central tension in programs to privatize land in Russia and Ukraine. Land privatization involved conflicts that cohered around social status, access to state-centered networks, and a host of material concerns that mark differentiation within subordinate groups in rural areas. As in other cases of privatization, the rules governing those distributive battles were the rules of power and political hierarchy, not of market competition. For this reason, privatization of the commons often has not resulted in efficient allocation of resources: new property rights arrangements come to reflect status quo ante power relationships rather than generating economically optimal distribution of resources.

Even where policy dictates the distribution of common pool resources among all current individual users of those resources, large numbers of those users may be excluded from the privatization process for reasons that do not reflect their desire or long-term capacity for productive resource use and ownership. This is particularly likely to be the case in the privatization of agricultural land.[11] The natural vagaries of agriculture leave farmers narrow margins of error, and the economic risks involved in making major changes to cultivation patterns are substantial.[12]

The creation of private, individual rights to property, and the conflicts over resources it engenders, can result in efforts to protect common pool resources from redistribution.[13] Economic ideas underpinning

[11] The matter of how to classify, amidst changing property regimes, collectively managed agricultural land that includes cultivated fields as well as pasture, is thorny indeed. This book conceptualizes such land in the terms that seem most similar to the way most rural people in the Black Earth see it: as a common pool resource.

[12] James C. Scott, *The Moral Economy of the Peasant: Rebellion and Subsistence in Southeast Asia*. New Haven: Yale University Press, 1976. On the role of risk in Russian decollectivization, see Erik Mathijs and Johan Swinnen, "The Economics of Agricultural Decollectivization in East Central Europe and the Former Soviet Union," *Economic Development and Cultural Change*, 47:1 (October 1998) 1–26.

[13] For example, Marc Edelman, *Peasants against Globalization: Rural Social Movements in Costa Rica*. Stanford: Stanford University Press, 1999; Jacqueline M. Klopp, "Pilfering the Public: The Problem of Land Grabbing in Contemporary Kenya," *Africa Today*, 47:1 (2000) 7–26; Miles Larmer, "Reaction and Resistance to Neo-Liberalism in Zambia," *Review of African Political Economy* 103 (2005) 29–45.

privatization efforts emphasize efficiency as a primary outcome of property rights creation, but the hidden costs, both human and institutional, of such processes sometimes claim only a marginal place in analysis. However, those costs can and do shape the development of property rights in practice. Where privatization of common pool resources contradicts local normative commitments regarding resource allocation, and where privatization is not accompanied by positive short-term economic incentives for participants in the process, political and economic obstacles may result in specific, predictable distortions of policy blueprints. Amidst such obstacles, attempts to create property rights may subvert the putative goals of privatization, impoverishing rather than enriching and, in cases of large-scale land redistribution, creating a basis for contesting control over territory.

Within the Black Earth, which stretches from east-central Ukraine to southwest Russia, the regions (*oblast*) of Voronezh and Kharkiv form part of the rural heartland of Soviet-era iconography. At harvest time, combines roll through fields of golden wheat below a deep blue sky. The Black Earth possesses some of the best soil in the world for agriculture, and topsoil in places is two meters thick, soil "so rich you could spread it on bread."[14] The land is capable of producing higher crop yields than the non-Black Earth regions of Russia and Ukraine,[15] and the ground so readily coaxes life from underfoot that, in a mad hope of replicating the region's fertility at home, Hitler is believed to have ordered invading soldiers of the Third Reich to ship trainloads of Black Earth soil from the *Lebensraum* to wartime Germany.

After the fall of the Soviet Union, the prospect of private land ownership held great promise in the area. Unlike many other parts of post-socialist Eastern Europe and Eurasia that had adopted similar programs of land privatization, Black Earth farms possessed natural and technological resources conducive to successful agricultural production. Agricultural collectives in the Black Earth enjoyed a longer growing season than farms to the north and in the Far East, and the natural environment freed farms from many of the usual risks of agricultural work. Collectives accessed markets through extensive rail links and road networks,

---

[14] The phrase is in common use in the Black Earth.
[15] Grigory Ioffe and Tatyana Nefedova, *Continuity and Change in Rural Russia: A Geographical Perspective*. Boulder: Westview, 1997 and Grigory Ioffe, *Sel'skoe khoziaistvo Nechernozem'ia: territorial'nye problemy*. Moscow: Nauka, 1990.

and by the 1980s, many farms in the region had begun to install modern machinery and introduce leasing brigades. In the Black Earth, reformers had every reason to believe that peasant labor, freed from the dulling harness of state socialism, would produce bountiful harvests and return the area to its pre-Revolutionary status as the breadbasket of Europe. If land privatization had a chance to improve production efficiency and labor incentives anywhere in the former Soviet Union, it would be in the Black Earth.

The modern history of the Black Earth likewise provided favorable ground for the introduction and development of new property rights. Unlike much of Eastern Europe, most Black Earth fields had no prior single owner. After the abolition of serfdom in 1861, peasant land communes governed agriculture, periodically redistributing narrow strips of land cultivated by individual households. The Stolypin-era reforms of the early twentieth century led some peasants to request the permanent allotment of their current land holdings. The vast majority of households in the Black Earth, however, did not.[16] In the 1930s, collectivization drives consolidated fields but did not assign land to particular individuals. Instead, the Soviet state held land on behalf of "the people." When post-Soviet states introduced programs of land privatization, policy makers were able to sidestep the "war between competing social memories" that characterized the restitution programs of post-socialist Eastern and Central Europe.[17] Post-Soviet states returned land to the tiller through distribution, rather than restitution. Under privatization policy, the entire steppe would, for the first time in living memory, be enclosed and every field would have an owner.

The Black Earth was dizzy with success in the formal development of property rights, and the paper record of privatization shows the creation of million-strong armies of landowners. On both sides of the border, the formal reorganization of collective and state farms was complete within the first decade of reform, as regional and local officials seemed to follow reform legislation to the letter. Regardless of the political orientation of local leaders or district state administrations, farm reorganization was carried out relatively quickly. By January of 1994, 95 percent of Russian agricultural enterprises subject to reorganization had undergone the

---

[16] David Kerans, *Mind and Labor on the Farm in Black-Earth Russia, 1861–1914*. Budapest and New York: Central European University Press, 2001.

[17] Verdery, "The Elasticity of Land: Problems of Property Restitution in Transylvania," *Slavic Review* 53:4 (1994) 1086.

process.[18] When Ukraine finally completed the process, state institutions achieved nearly 100 percent compliance with the reform policy.[19]

Agricultural collectives successfully completed their transformation on paper, but the fields of most farms were not partitioned.[20] By the end of the 1990s, private farmers in both countries still consisted of a very small group of rural producers, and people who claimed land for such farms constituted less than 1 percent of the rural population. Private farmers emerged earlier in Russia than in Ukraine, but in both countries they occupied less than 10 percent of agricultural land during the 1990s.[21] According to official national figures, in 1994, by which time most of the private farms that would survive into the next decade had already been established,[22] private farmers provided only a 2 percent share of total agricultural production in Russia even as they sowed 6 percent of cultivated land.[23] In Ukraine during the same year, private farmers produced only one-third of 1 percent of the value of gross agricultural output in the country.[24] By the middle of the decade, there was broad consensus among observers in both countries that private farming had not fulfilled the reformers' expectations.[25]

On each side of the border, members of agricultural collectives who were to be the primary beneficiaries of privatization had little to show for their ownership of land and asset shares in reorganized collectives. The economic environment in which reformed enterprises operated contributed to low or negative firm profits; consequently, land rents were

---

[18] *Sel'skoe khoziaistvo Rossii. Statisticheskii sbornik.* Moscow: Goskomstat Rossii 1995, 49.

[19] *Informatsiinyi biuleten' shchodo reformuvannia zemel'nykh vidnosyn v Ukraini.* Kyiv: Derzhkomzem, 1999. Reorganization policy in Ukraine was formulated early in the 1990s, but there was a major push to complete the process at the end of the decade.

[20] Throughout the text, I use the terms "agricultural collective" and "reorganized collectives" to refer to collective and state farms and their successor enterprises, respectively. Where the organizational form is relevant to the analysis, I have noted it in the text.

[21] *Ukraina u tsyfrakh 2002: Korotkyi statystychnyi dovidnyk.* Kyiv: Konsul'tant, 2003: 104, 118; *Sel'skokhoziaistvennaia deiatel'nost' khoziaistv naseleniia v Rossii.* Moscow: Goskomstat Rossii, 2003: 12, 41.

[22] A round of reorganization in Ukraine in 2000 added to the ranks of private farmers, but many of those were collectives reregistered as private farms.

[23] At that time, agricultural collectives contributed 60 percent of total production and household cultivation 38 percent. *Sel'skoe khoziaistvo Rossii 1995*, 47, 52.

[24] *Sil's'ke hospodarstvo Ukrainy 1997*, 9.

[25] Stephen K. Wegren, "The Politics of Private Farming in Russia," *The Journal of Peasant Studies* 23:4 (July 1996) 106–40, and Donald Van Atta, ed. *The Farmer Threat: The Political Economy of Agrarian Reform in Post-Soviet Russia.* Boulder: Westview Press, 1993.

negligible, wage arrears frequent, and benefits thin. Where privatized collectives were successful, farm directors' local power freed them from adhering to contracts with worker-shareholders. Meanwhile, in the absence of appropriate machinery, access to credit, and cadastral services, few worker-shareholders could choose to work the land shares themselves. Without a robust private farming sector to compete with former collectives for land, former collectives could continue to pay a pittance for the use of land shares. Rather than generating a new class of peasant-owners, land privatization in Russia and Ukraine led to the proletarianization of the countryside.

An international border divides the Black Earth, and after the fall of Soviet power, different types of state institutions developed on the two sides of that border. In Ukraine, the representatives who populate regional legislatures, as well as many of the bureaucrats who walk the halls of local administrative offices, serve at the pleasure of the President. Under the increasingly authoritarian rule of Leonid Kuchma (1995–2004), officials' loyalty to the center better predicted the stability of their positions than their ability to achieve positive economic change.[26] Across the border, during the second half of the 1990s, some of their Russian counterparts gained their positions through local elections. Even in later years, when regional governors and officials again were selected in Moscow, Russia's federal structure allowed local state officials relatively greater autonomy than their counterparts exercised in unitary Ukraine.

Furthermore, the newly independent Ukrainian and Russian governments chose diametrically opposed transitional pathways with respect to the speed and sequencing of political and economic reforms.[27] The Russian Federation initiated a program of rapid economic liberalization less than one month after the formal collapse of the Soviet Union, before actively developing democratic political institutions. Ukraine delayed economic liberalization until the mid-1990s, choosing instead to devote initial attention to political reform. The language of land reform legislation in the two countries was virtually identical, but privatization was

[26] Kimitaka Matsuzato, "All Kuchma's Men: The Reshuffling of Ukrainian Governors and the Presidential Election of 1999," *Eurasian Geography and Economics* 42:6 (2001) 416–439.

[27] Rather than using speed as a barometer for reform success, as was common in the 1990s, this study treats it as an independent variable. See János Kornai, "Ten Years After 'The Road to a Free Economy': The Author's Self-Evaluation," conference paper, Annual Bank Conference on Development Economics. World Bank, Washington, D.C. April 2000, 24.

implemented at different times in the decade, with greater or less dispatch, and amidst varying institutional environments.

Conditions within Voronezh and Kharkiv regions varied as well. The two regions together cover an area the size of Austria, and within them, the initial economic strength of agricultural enterprises, the existence of favorable growing conditions, access to urban markets, the condition of social and material infrastructure, and local attitudes toward privatization varied widely from village to village within the Black Earth. Today, local economies range from ramshackle ghost town collectives to massive agricultural enterprises that provide reliable social services for their employees.[28] Likewise, districts in which local commercial elites favored the development of private sector agriculture sit side by side with districts in which Soviet-style forms of management continue to prevail even today (2007).

Amidst decades of heated debates about the effects of institutional design and the speed of reform on economic development, one would expect property rights to have developed differently in Russia and Ukraine.[29] The surprising result was that, instead, reform affected most rural people on both sides of the border in highly similar ways, with virtually identical levels of apparent success and similar results in the actual allocation of land.[30] Even as outcomes varied among individual villages, most villagers were dispossessed of rights and revenue they had previously enjoyed. In both countries, battles over land privatization produced a system of limited *de facto* property rights that bore little resemblance to the paper rights trumpeted by the two governments.

The mechanisms that produced these results were similar across the Black Earth. Parchment institutions served as a facade behind which

---

[28] Tatiana Zhurzhenko, "Becoming Ukrainians in a 'Russian' Village: Social Change and Identity Formation in Udy (Kharkiv oblast', Ukraine)." Paper presented at the Danyliw Seminar in Contemporary Ukrainian Studies, University of Ottawa, 29 September 2005.

[29] The literature on this topic is vast. See, for example, M. Steven Fish, "The Determinants of Economic Reform in the Post-Communist World," *East European Politics and Societies* 12:1 (Winter 1998); Stephan Haggard and Robert R. Kaufman, *The Political Economy of Democratic Transitions*. Princeton: Princeton University Press, 1995; and Haggard and Steven B. Webb, eds. *Voting for Reform: The Political Economy of Adjustment in New Democracies*. Oxford: Oxford University Press, 1994.

[30] Efforts to establish private farming were marginally more successful in Voronezh than in Kharkiv, and in Russia as a whole compared to Ukraine. For example, by 2002 private farms occupied approximately 10 percent of farmland in Voronezh and 7 percent of farmland in Kharkiv. However, given outcomes that fell so far short of reformers' expectations, as well as imprecision in and obstacles to collection of surveying data, the difference is not meaningful in any practical sense.

those charged with distributing land pursued other goals entirely. In both Kharkiv and Voronezh, the formal design of governance and reform policy did not drive land reform outcomes; rather, local politics made all the difference, and in the world of the post-Soviet Black Earth, it appeared that all roads led to Rome.

Alternative Explanations

What explains the existence of post-Soviet Potemkin property rights across this expanse of the Black Earth? Much of the literature on postcommunist transformation has emphasized the problem of institutional capacity in states pursuing economic reform, and some scholars have argued that degrees of state weakness explain variation in reform outcomes across post-communist settings.[31] The cross-national similarity of property rights development in the Black Earth could lead to the inference that the Russian and Ukrainian states were both weak in implementing reform.

Such an assessment would not capture the full range of causes that produced Potemkin property rights in the Black Earth. Although the Soviet collapse left centralized command structures weakened and disrupted, key state institutions in Russia and Ukraine remained strong relative to most elements of rural society. Even as the central state withdrew from the provision of social services under the terms of structural adjustment programs, urban bias, which reflected the weakness of rural society in relation to the state, intensified during the post-Soviet period.[32] Poverty, deterioration of transportation infrastructure, and a lack of privately owned meeting space made organized political opposition to reform a rarity in the countryside. In implementing land privatization policy, the state set the terms of state–society relationships.

---

[31] For example, Shu-Yun Ma, "Comparing the Russian State and the Chinese State," *Problems of Post-Communism* 47:2 (March-April 2000) and Ilya Prizel, "Ukraine's Lagging Efforts in Building National Institutions and the Potential Impact on National Security," *The Harriman Review* 10:3 (Winter 1997).

[32] On state withdrawal from social services provision, see Mark G. Field, David M. Kotz, and Gene Bukhman, "Neoliberal Economic Policy, 'State Desertion,' and the Russian Health Crisis," in Jim Yong Kim, Joyce V. Millen, Alec Irwin, and John Gershman, eds. *Dying for Growth: Global Inequality and the Health of the Poor.* Monroe, Maine: Common Courage Press, 2000. On urban bias, see Robert H. Bates, *Markets and States in Tropical Africa.* Berkeley: University of California Press, 1981; Michael Lipton, *Why Poor People Stay Poor: Urban Bias in World Development.* Cambridge: Harvard University Press, 1976; Aushutosh Varshney, "Urban Bias in Perspective," *Journal of Development Studies* 29:4 (July 1993); and Wegren, "Democratization and Urban Bias in Postcommunist Russia," *Comparative Politics* 34:4 (July 2002).

Furthermore, rural people almost certainly did not experience the state as weak.[33] As the following chapters show, local state institutions did not release their grasp as communism took its last breath. Instead, privatization provided an opportunity for the state to reassert its power at the local level. In Moscow and Kyiv before the Soviet fall, land codes and presidential decrees granted broad discretion to regional, district, and village officials charged with implementing land reform; devolution was not a function of state collapse, but a conscious decision by central authorities. Local officials used this discretion, actively intervening to obstruct the individuation and privatization of land: "The deputy head of the region called: 'We're doing this so that there won't be any changes.'"[34] Precise specification of the relationship between state capacity and policy outcomes thus requires distinguishing between state officials' ability and their willingness to implement policy.[35] Even as some land reform initiatives in post-Soviet space were largely unfunded mandates, the bureaucratic – or, in Mann's terms, infrastructural – resources they marshaled were considerable, and officials used those resources to oppose the individuation of land rights.[36]

Finally, there are conceptual reasons not to rely upon state weakness as a primary explanation for Potemkin land rights. First, some assertions of state weakness derive from the claims of political actors involved in the reform process. Hough suggests that Russian reformers repeatedly made reference to state weakness in order to deflect blame for policy failures. He writes, "From early 1992, the Russian government proclaimed it was powerless vis-à-vis other actors both to avoid responsibility for economic difficulties and to justify strengthening its power."[37] Second,

---

[33] I thank Eric Allina-Pisano for this formulation.

[34] Interview, department of agricultural management, NK, 21 July 2006.

[35] Some observers have noted a lack of will on the part of state elites, as well as low capacity. Graeme Gill, "Russia's Weak State: What Is to Be Done?" *Australian Slavonic and East European Studies* 14:1–2 (2000). In Ukraine, in policy areas where regional elites were willing to cooperate with the demands of the center, the state has demonstrated relative strength. Matsuzato, "All Kuchma's Men: The Reshuffling of Ukrainian Governors and the Presidential Election of 1999," *Eurasian Geography and Economics* 42:6 (2001) 416–439.

[36] Michael Mann, "The Autonomous Power of the State: Its Origins, Mechanisms and Results," in *Archives européennes de sociologie* 25 (1984). Shifts in regime type during the reform period are not decisive here. Atul Kohli argues that both democratic and authoritarian regimes can develop the administrative capacity necessary for supporting industrial development. Kohli, *State-Directed Development: Political Power and Industrialization in the Global Periphery.* Cambridge: Cambridge University Press, 2004.

[37] Jerry F. Hough, *The Logic of Economic Reform in Russia.* Washington, DC: Brookings, 2001, 19.

weak state capacity was both a stipulation and a product of reform policy. Sachs provided among the most forceful statements of this component of liberalization, urging governments in Eastern Europe to "get the planners out of the process."[38] Because a central aim of privatization was to reduce the state's role in economic life, an analytical framework that relies primarily upon the causal role of state capacity risks confounding explanation and explanandum. Finally, as Wegren notes, assessments of the post-communist state as weak often confuse incomplete reform implementation with the poor economic performance that may result from reform.[39]

The Russian and Ukrainian regions of the Black Earth occupy the same corner of the former Soviet Union, and it may be tempting, alternatively, to regard the dismal results of land privatization as a direct consequence of Leninist legacies, or of historical trajectories over the *longue durée* in a part of Eastern Europe formerly under Romanov rule.[40] Such an explanation would cast obstacles to property rights development in the Black Earth chiefly in terms of local ideological landscapes, the terrain of which, conditioned by seventy years of Soviet governance, was hostile to the seeds of liberalism that privatization would bring. Viewed through such a lens, the tractor drivers of Ukrainka were communist reactionaries who resisted the march of progress by preventing the individuation of land rights.

But Potemkin villages in the twenty-first century do not constitute simply one more chapter in a long book of policy failures explained by the specific conditions that inhered in southwestern Russia and eastern Ukraine at the end of the twentieth century. Villagers in western Ukraine with a recent history of private land rights also fared poorly in late twentieth-century land privatization.[41] In post-Soviet Zakarpattia, a land-poor region in western Ukraine governed by Austro-Hungary early in the twentieth century and incorporated into the Soviet Union only after the end of World War II, former members of collective farms face limitations on property rights similar to those encountered by their counterparts in the

---

[38] Jeffrey Sachs, *Poland's Jump to the Market Economy*. Cambridge: MIT Press, 1991, 46.

[39] Wegren, *Agriculture and the State in Soviet and Post-Soviet Russia*. Pittsburgh: University of Pittsburgh Press, 1998.

[40] Ken Jowitt, *New World Disorder: The Leninist Extinction*. Berkeley: University of California Press, 1992; Stephen E. Hanson, "The Leninist Legacy and Institutional Change," *Comparative Political Studies* 28:2 (July 1995) 306–314.

[41] Mykhailo Rushchak and Mykhailo Sharha, "Kontseptsiia ahrarnoi reformy na Zakarpatti," *NZ* 28 December 1995, 4.

Black Earth. There, despite the labor and trade opportunities afforded by the nearby borders with Slovakia, Poland, and Hungary, economic constraints and farm directors' strategies to consolidate their own control prevent many villagers from demanding land, and land share ownership generates few financial benefits for worker-shareholders. Even as collective forms of agriculture dissolved more quickly into the poorer soil of western Ukraine, many rural people found private ownership of farmland an unrewarding prospect. As one villager put it, "We didn't take [land] because at the time we had no machinery. If you have no machinery, there's no point in taking it."[42]

In Central and Eastern Europe, where land privatization involved restitution rather than distribution, new parchment institutions likewise do not predict the actual disposition of private, individual property rights. In her magisterial study of post-socialist land reform in Transylvania, Verdery found that villagers encountered dwindling opportunities to establish and realize value from their land and that "obtaining rights proved far less important than controlling the context in which those rights could be exercised." In Vlaicu, the village at the center of her study, rural participants in land privatization encountered the individualization of risk and liability rather than the individualization of assets.[43] Meanwhile, in Bulgaria, where collectively farmed land was returned to its post-war owners during the 1990s, Meurs showed that rural people, responding to high transaction costs and social norms, slowed agricultural restructuring and maintained agricultural cooperatives as a hedge against risk and a repository of value, rather than establish private family farms.[44]

Imperial Russian history likewise provides little guide in explaining contemporary outcomes. The link is tenuous between contemporary privatization processes and collectivist or egalitarian traditions associated with pre-Revolutionary land tenure practices.[45] While disjunctures between official policy and unofficial practice are a longstanding feature of Eurasian governance, the Potemkin property rights of the present are

[42] Interview, former collective farm worker, UZ, 19 May 2004.

[43] Verdery, *The Vanishing Hectare: Property and Value in Postsocialist Transylvania*. Ithaca: Cornell University Press, 2003, 20 and 24.

[44] Mieke Meurs, *The Evolution of Agrarian Institutions: A Comparative Study of Post-Socialist Hungary and Bulgaria*. Ann Arbor: University of Michigan Press, 2001.

[45] Peter Lindner and Aleksandr Nikulin, "'Everything Around Here Belongs to the Kolkhoz, Everything Around Here Is Mine' – Collectivism and Egalitarianism: A Red Thread through Russian History?" *Europa Regional* 12:1 (2004).

not part of a long shadow cast by a primordial past. Recent work by Jane Burbank has shown that pre-Revolutionary peasants routinely engaged in contestation in local courts over land – an indicator of robust rights – and that the distance between customary law and official policy was not as wide as previously had been thought.[46]

Explaining Convergence

A large body of scholarship is devoted to explaining political and economic variation in post-communist societies, emphasizing divergence in outcomes among individual states, the distinctiveness of national pathways, and variation within states.[47] Land privatization demands a different approach. Whatever the variety in experience among individual members of farming communities in post-Soviet space, and however the allocation of property rights may differ across regions and states, there remains for rural people a common outcome: knowing that they are legally entitled to a set of rights, and experiencing significant limitations on using those rights. Here, the first task for the social scientist is not to focus on relatively small degrees of variation in outcomes, but to explain how strikingly similar phenomena arose from different situations.[48]

The regularity of land privatization outcomes across the Black Earth is linked in large part to the global economic context in which land reform is implemented. That context includes subsidies for agricultural production in North America and the European Union, trade barriers and debt for

[handwritten margin notes: "rather than differences"; "explain similarities"]

[46] Jane Burbank, *Russian Peasants Go to Court: Legal Culture in the Countryside, 1905–1917*. Bloomington: Indiana University Press, 2004.

[47] For example, Valerie Bunce, "The Political Economy of Postsocialism," *Slavic Review* 58:4 (Winter 1999) 756–793; Grzegorz Ekiert and Jan Kubik, *Rebellious Civil Society: Popular Protest and Democratic Consolidation in Poland, 1989–1993.* Ann Arbor: University of Michigan Press, 2001; Chris Hann, *The Skeleton at the Feast. Contributions to East European Anthropology.* Canterbury: University of Kent, 1995; Yoshiko Herrera, *Imagined Communities: The Sources of Russian Regionalism.* Cambridge: Cambridge University Press, 2005; Anna M. Grzymala-Busse, *Redeeming the Communist Past: The Regeneration of Communist Parties in East Central Europe.* Cambridge: Cambridge University Press, 2002; Pauline Jones Luong, *Institutional Change and Political Continuity in Post-Soviet Central Asia: Power, Perceptions, and Pacts.* Cambridge: Cambridge University Press, 2002; Jeffrey Kopstein and David A. Reilly. "Geographic Diffusion and the Transformation of the Postcommunist World," *World Politics* 53:1 (October 2000) 1–37.

[48] Theda Skocpol, *States and Social Revolutions: A Comparative Analysis of France, Russia, and China.* Cambridge: Cambridge University Press, 1979; Mark Beissinger, *Nationalist Mobilization and the Collapse of the Soviet State.* Cambridge: Cambridge University Press, 2002.

poorer countries, and the price scissors that serve as a perennial obstacle for farmers. The exigencies of the world economic environment thus play an important, if relatively neglected role in determining local distributive outcomes in post-communist states.[49]

Despite differences in institutional design on the two sides of the border, the local state officials who implemented reform policy in Russia and Ukraine faced a single set of practical challenges as they attempted to manage economic crisis. The removal of price controls and tariffs in Eastern Europe amidst continuing subsidy regimes in the West created similar incentives for local agricultural economies in Voronezh and Kharkiv. Furthermore, both regional economic crisis linked to the Soviet collapse and the simultaneous withdrawal at the national level of budgetary support for many social services (a condition, like land privatization, for IMF loan disbursement) heightened the importance of collectives as social institutions across the Black Earth. In that context, preservation of status quo property relations was a more rational short-term choice for local elites than privatization and individuation of land.[50]

Local state officials developed a repertoire of informal practices in response to economic liberalization, bypassing formal institutions and curtailing distribution. These practices included a tacit rule of hidden resistance to decollectivization; a post-Soviet version of *blat* (a non-monetary mode of exchange embedded in personal relationships and characterized primarily by favors of access),[51] which limited the circle of possible beneficiaries of land privatization; and a set of regulatory norms that maintained state control over privately owned assets, ultimately leading to the repossession of privately held land.

These were not uniquely post-Soviet responses; covert actions may be taken in response to any contested policy, and such resistance is not limited to the state offices of rural Russia and Ukraine. People are likely to express resistance obliquely wherever strong hierarchies prevail, and the production of diverging public and private narratives, or "transcripts," has been observed in multiple contexts.[52] Post-Soviet forms of *blat* are

[49] Ellen Comisso, "Prediction versus Diagnosis: Comments on a Ken Jowitt Perspective," *Slavic Review* 53:1 (Spring 1994).

[50] Meurs, *The Evolution of Agrarian Institutions: A Comparative Study of Post-Socialist Hungary and Bulgaria*. Ann Arbor: University of Michigan Press, 2001.

[51] J. S. Berliner, *Factory and Manager in the USSR*. Cambridge: Harvard University Press, 1957, and Alena Ledeneva, *Russia's Economy of Favors: Blat, Networking and Informal Exchange*. Cambridge: Cambridge University Press, 1998.

[52] James C. Scott, *Weapons of the Weak: Everyday Forms of Peasant Resistance*. New Haven: Yale University Press, 1987; Scott, *Domination and the Arts of Resistance: Hidden*

cousin to China's *guanxi* and related to a multitude of informal distributional practices elsewhere.[53] Finally, the persistence of old regulatory
relationships and institutions amidst new property rights regimes has frustrated reform across transitional settings, sometimes entrenching political
interests rather than depoliticizing economic activity.[54]

Here, the origin of these practices lies not in direct recapitulation of
Soviet traditions (which they may resemble) but rather in their reminis-
cence and recycling – just as cadres in China, Hungary, and the Czech
Republic have found new uses for previously developed social capital and
knowledge.[55] The machinery of Soviet politics and society did not persist
in the Black Earth countryside as before. Rather, local state officials used
pathways laid in the Soviet era to produce new norms and rules for distribution. Soviet institutional legacies thus functioned as a resource for
overcoming information asymmetries, uncertainty, moral hazard, and a
host of other challenges. However, instead of reproducing Soviet institutions, state officials renovated them for use in a new environment. As
Verdery has observed, "what might look like legacies are better seen as
responses to quite contemporary processes."[56]

Local officials in Kharkiv and Voronezh thus drew upon a common vocabulary of backroom practices developed during the Soviet era.
The shared *habitus* of previous decades allowed renovated informal
rules, practices, and norms to become routinized and integrated into the
operation of formal state institutions.[57] These practices emerged in the

Transcripts. New Haven: Yale University Press, 1990; Jacob S. Hacker, "Privatizing Risk
without Privatizing the Welfare State: The Hidden Politics of Social Policy Retrenchment
in the United States," *American Political Science Review* 98 (May 2004).

[53] Mayfair Yang, *Gifts, Favors and Banquets*. Ithaca: Cornell University Press, 1994;
Thomas Gold, Doug Guthrie, and David Wank, eds. *Social Connections in China: Institutions, Culture, and the Changing Nature of Guanxi*. Cambridge: Cambridge University
Press, 2002; Ming-cheng M. Lo and Eileen M. Otis, "Guanxi Civility: Processes, Poten-
tials, and Contingencies," *Politics and Society* 31 (2003).

[54] M. Anne Pitcher, *Transforming Mozambique: The Politics of Privatization, 1975–2000*.
Cambridge: Cambridge University Press, 2002.

[55] Jean C. Oi, "Fiscal Reform and the Economic Foundations of Local State Corporatism
in China," *World Politics* 45:1 (October 1992); Oi, *State and Peasant in Contemporary
China: The Political Economy of Village Government*. Berkeley and Los Angeles: University of California Press, 1989; David Stark and László Bruszt, *Postsocialist Pathways:
Transforming Politics and Property in East Central Europe*. Cambridge: Cambridge University Press, 1998; Grzymala-Busse, *Redeeming the Communist Past*. Cambridge: Cambridge University Press, 2002.

[56] Verdery, *Vanishing Hectare: Property and Value in Postsocialist Transylvania*. Ithaca:
Cornell University Press, 2003, 11.

[57] Oleg Kharkhordin, *The Collective and the Individual in Russia: A Study of Practices*.
Berkeley: University of California Press, 1999.

Black Earth in response to precipitous political change and acute economic crisis rather than as a direct bureaucratic legacy of the communist past: the motivation for some state officials' resistance to decollectivization emanated from practical concerns about global economic pressures, but the mechanism for achieving that end was the construction of new forms of governance along the byways of the old.[58]

Across the Black Earth, local officials acted to preserve collective institutions that would maintain social services and provide food for the population, farm directors sought to maintain large-scale production and, in many cases, consolidate their own control over labor and land resources, and rank and file members of agricultural collectives sought to minimize their own risk amidst economic crisis.[59] All the while, state and farm elites created a formal record of change in land ownership. The combination of these strategies produced property rights that were paper thin in practice; as Johnson has found in Russia's banking sector, Potemkin property rights were the results of the interaction between national economic policy and local institutional response.[60]

→ *Tsing's phrase!*

Local Politics and Political Theory

The research presented here is grounded in small, out of the way places: farms, villages, and towns in the Black Earth. Its theoretical implications, however, are linked to broad, overarching questions in social science: the effects of social and institutional context on policy implementation, how rights that exist on paper operate in practice, and how formal institutions and informal practices shape distribution of social goods.

First, land privatization outcomes in the Black Earth shed light upon a long standing, but unresolved disagreement in the study of politics. In the wake of communism's demise in Europe at the end of the twentieth century, Burke once again battled Rousseau as proponents of gradual reform and "shock therapy" debated the proper pace of institutional change.[61]

---

[58] Herbert Kitschelt, Zdenka Mansfeldova, Radosław Markowski, and Gábor Tóka. *Post-Communist Party Systems: Competition, Representation and Inter-Party Cooperation.* Cambridge: Cambridge University Press, 1999.

[59] Also see Judith Pallot and Tatyana Nefedova, "Geographical Differentiation in Household Plot Production in Rural Russia," *Eurasian Geography and Economics* 44:1 (2003) 40–64.

[60] Juliet Johnson, *A Fistful of Rubles: The Rise and Fall of the Russian Banking System.* Ithaca: Cornell University Press, 2000.

[61] For example, Peter Murrell, "What Is Shock Therapy? What Did It Do in Poland and Russia?" *Post-Soviet Affairs* 9 (1993) 111–140; Kazimierz Z. Poznanski, *Poland's Protracted Transition: Institutional Change and Economic Growth, 1970–1994.*

The empirical record has shown that advocates of rapid privatization were mistaken in some of their expectations regarding distributional outcomes, but in the case of land privatization, neither school of thought predicted the similarity of outcomes in states pursuing different reform pathways. In important respects, neither approach focused sufficient attention on the institutional mechanisms that would drive change at the local level. Even alternatives to this dichotomous analytical framework, such as Burawoy's concept of involution, largely address outcomes rather than the causal mechanisms that produce them.[62]

This book focuses on precisely such mechanisms. In so doing, it shows how local responses to economic incentives were more important in driving privatization outcomes than rapid or gradual reform pathways or the design of formal institutions.

The essential teleology of the transition paradigm included widespread agreement about the aims of reform, but diverse views on how to achieve them. The question was never whether to privatize, but how fast and in what relationship to political change.[63] Likewise, resistance to privatization was predicted on the part of both "losers" and "winners" in the electoral realm and on the part of elites seeking to capture the reform process. Such resistance, however, was conceptualized primarily in relationship to the sequencing and timing of reform rather than as a response to policy content.[64] Those who objected to reform on practical grounds had no place in the narrative.

Cambridge: Cambridge University Press, 1996; Sachs, *Poland's Jump to the Market Economy*. Cambridge: MIT Press, 1991.

[62] Burawoy et al. write, "[u]ndoubtably there has been a transition to a market economy but its consequence was not the *revolutionary* break-through anticipated by the prophets of neoliberalism, nor the *evolutionary* advance found in other countries such as China but an economic primitivization we call *involution*," 46. Michael Burawoy, Pavel Krotov, and Tatyana Lytkina, "Involution and Destitution in Capitalist Russia," *Ethnography* 1:1 (2000) 43–65. Also see Burawoy, "Transition without Transformation: Russia's Involutionary Road to Capitalism," *East European Politics and Societies* 15:2 (Spring 2001) 269–290 and Burawoy, "The State and Economic Involution: Russia through a Chinese Lens." *World Development* 24 (1996) 1105–17.

[63] John Marangos provides a critique of the neo-liberal foundations of both gradualist and "shock therapy" strategies. Marangos, "A political economy approach to the neoclassical model of transition – New Perspectives on Transition Economics: Europe," *The American Journal of Economics and Sociology* 61:1 (January 2002).

[64] Adam Przeworski, *Democracy and the Market: Political and Economic Reforms in Eastern Europe and Latin America*. New York: Cambridge University Press, 1991; Joel S. Hellman, "Winners Take All: The Politics of Partial Reform in Postcommunist Transitions," *World Politics* 50 (January 1998).

Second, the book addresses the way rights in law are enacted in practice. It builds upon existing literature on property rights development in
post-communist states by examining not only the bundles of rights found
in post-Soviet rural society, but also the relationship of those legal rights
to economic activity. This connection is vital for addressing a major analytical gap in the study of political economy, in which the relationship
between private property rights and more effective engagement with markets, widely understood by policy makers to be the ultimate goal of privatization, is theoretically unspecified and under-researched.

The conceptual distance between *de jure* and *de facto* property rights
emphasized here differs from the mixed, "fuzzy," or "recombinant" property rights in the literature on privatization in other post-communist
states.[65] There, distortions in ownership regimes generally concern complexity or lack of clarity in the allocation of rights. The focus of this book
is the systematic disjuncture between legal categories of rights, however
those bundles of rights are constituted, and the ways in which those rights
practically are used. Formal property rights in rural Russia and Ukraine
did not appear to predict the forms enterprises took or their capacity to
participate in market economies. Contrary to reformers' promises and
expectations, labor incentives generated by the creation of formal property rights were, for most rural people, tied neither to efficiency nor to
profits. The new property rights regimes of the 1990s left rural producers
in Russia and Ukraine with formal claims to the disposition of land but
no practical agency in the disposition of their own labor.

Scholars of post-communist property rights development have observed that adaptation to market-oriented economic policies has led in
some cases to innovation and flexible property rights regimes.[66] This literature, as well as recent research on land rights in Africa, emphasizes
that flexibility in rights allocation grants latitude or "negotiability" to
rights holders.[67] Emphasis on flexibility provides a welcome corrective to

[65] Oi and Andrew Walder, eds. *Property Rights and Economic Reform in China*. Stanford:
Stanford University Press, 1999; Verdery, "Fuzzy Property: Rights, Power, and Identity
in Transylvania's Decollectivization" in Burawoy and Verdery, eds. *Uncertain Transition:
Ethnographies of Change in the Postsocialist World*. Lanham, MD: Rowman and Littlefield, 1999; Stark and Bruszt, *Postsocialist Pathways: Transforming Politics and Property
in East Central Europe*. Cambridge: Cambridge University Press, 1998.
[66] Stark, "Recombinant Property in East European Capitalism," *American Journal of Sociology* 101: 4 (1996) 993–1027; Verdery, "The Elasticity of Land: Problems of Property
Restitution in Transylvania," *Slavic Review* 53: 4 (1994) 1071–1109.
[67] Sara S. Berry, "Debating the Land Question in Africa," *Comparative Studies in Society
and History*, 44:4 (2002) 638–68.

analytical frameworks that rob local actors of historical agency, but such a vantage point also has the potential to obscure the view of inequalities produced by the process of privatization. As Peters argues, it may occlude the ways in which new institutions empower some individuals at the local level but disempower others, or how the capacity to produce certain types of change may be limited to the already privileged and powerful.[68]

In explaining how land privatization resulted in limited *de facto* distribution of resources, this book shows how a combination of state oversight and market forces made possible mechanisms of capital reproduction for elites, and impoverished most participants in the process. Repeated iterations of land privatization, rather than producing flexible rights, led to the ossification of inequalities and the creation of inflexible property rights regimes that offered producers weaker labor incentives than existed before reform.

Finally, this book is part of a growing body of research that examines the role of informal practices in shaping political and economic outcomes in the post-communist world.[69] Numerous studies of policy implementation have shown that state and societal actors in the periphery may reshape policies emanating from the center, and recent work has analyzed the role of local bureaucrats in shaping economic policy implementation.[70] Here, systematic observation of informal practices clarifies how unwritten rules drive the operation of formal institutions.[71]

In the Black Earth, the character of *de facto* property rights was shaped in part by the existence of their parchment counterparts. Informal

---

[68] Pauline E. Peters, "Inequality and Social Conflict Over Land in Africa," *Journal of Agrarian Change* 4:3 (July 2004).

[69] For example, Gerald Easter, *Reconstructing the State: Personal Networks and Elite Identity in Soviet Russia*. Cambridge: Cambridge University Press, 2000; Keith Darden, "Blackmail as a Tool of State Domination: Ukraine under Kuchma," *East European Constitutional Review* 10 (Spring/Summer 2001); Grzymała-Busse and Pauline Jones Luong, "Reconceptualizing the State: Lessons from Post-Communism" *Politics and Society* 30:4 (2002) 529–54; Gretchen Helmke and Steven Levitsky, "Informal Institutions and Comparative Politics: A Research Agenda," *Perspectives on Politics* 2 (December 2004); Alena V. Ledeneva, *Russia's Economy of Favors*. Oxford: Oxford University Press, 1998; Lucan Way, "The Dilemmas of Reform in Weak States: The Case of Post-Soviet Fiscal Reform," *Politics and Society* 30 (December 2002).

[70] Joel S. Migdal, State *in Society: Studying How States and Societies Transform and Constitute One Another*. Cambridge: Cambridge University Press, 2001. Pradeep Chhibber and Samuel Eldersveld, "Local Elites and Popular Support for Economic Reform in China and India," *Comparative Political Studies* 33:3 (April 2000) 350–373.

[71] Alena V. Ledeneva, *How Russia Really Works*. Ithaca: Cornell University Press, 2006.

practices that prevented substantive allocation of land could not have developed outside of the context of official state structures: the informal regimes governing privatization worked within formal political institutions to generate outcomes that were themselves obscured from outside view. But it is precisely the hidden outcomes of property rights reform – the actual disposition of rights, as opposed to the existence of parchment institutions – that ultimately will drive economic performance.

The Evidence

[handwritten margin note: comparative logic of the study → comparative inquiry built into the study]

[handwritten margin note: cf. Scott]

The study of border areas such as the Black Earth holds a number of advantages for comparative analysis, allowing the researcher to hold constant environmental variables while testing the effects of political and social institutions.[72] This strategy, combined with a most different cases, most similar outcome design, permits deductive elimination of a number of explanations for the development of Potemkin property rights across an expanse of Eastern European steppe.[73]

Having established that the divergent reform pathways in Russia and Ukraine did not themselves drive privatization outcomes, the book builds theory on the basis of close, direct observation of the mechanisms of transformation. It examines the process of property rights development as it unfolded at the local level in order to identify the causal mechanisms that explain how and to whom land was distributed. This method not only can serve as a corrective to existing mid-level theory about the politics of economic transformation, in which nationally aggregated outcomes may obscure the direction of political change, but it also allows one to ask questions other methods would not suggest.[74]

The finding of fake property rights to land was not itself observable, and documentation of the existence of the post-Soviet Potemkin village was not possible, except through ground-level research. Identifying the explanation for this outcome required the use of a variety of sources,

---

72 See, for example, Seymour Martin Lipset, *Agrarian Socialism: The Cooperative Commonwealth Federation in Saskatchewan.* Berkeley: University of California Press, 1950; Juan J. Linz, *Conflicto en Euskadi.* Madrid: Espasa-Calpe, 1986; Peter Sahlins, *Boundaries: The Making of France and Spain in the Pyrenees.* Berkeley: University of California Press, 1989.

73 Adam Przeworski and Henry Teune. *The Logic of Comparative Social Inquiry.* New York: Wiley-Interscience, 1970.

74 Richard Snyder, "Scaling Down: The Subnational Comparative Method," *Studies in Comparative International Development* 36:1 (Spring 2001).

many of which were not easily accessible to the researcher. Data collection for this study involved long trips over unpaved country roads far from telephones, Xerox machines, and Internet connections. Amidst the infrastructural decay of the post-Soviet period, the offices, farms, and county libraries that housed information about land privatization were often without basic utilities. In some places, obtaining numerical data meant copying tables into a notebook by hand. In all cases, data collection involved the gracious cooperation of people struggling to make ends meet amidst crushing physical demands and minimal compensation.

In the course of twenty-five months of research in Russia and Ukraine between 1997 and 2006, I conducted structured and open-ended interviews with over 300 people involved in the privatization process in the two countries: local bureaucrats, private farmers, directors of reorganized collective and state farms, worker-shareholders in those farms, and others. Field interviews in the Black Earth are complemented by interviews I conducted with farmers, collective farm administrators, and villagers in the western Ukrainian region of Zakarpattia, where environmental, cultural, and historical conditions differed significantly from Voronezh and Kharkiv.

Many of my interlocutors wore more than one "hat" – the private farmer who was also a member of a village council, the collective farm worker–shareholder who commuted to a second job in a nearby city, the district land tenure official who farmed a two-hectare plot of land. The identities of those individuals resisted easy classification and complicated the task of compiling neatly categorized lists of "private farmers interviewed," "pensioners," "collective farm machinists," and so on. In the notes, I have provided information about the relevant work identity, as I understood it, of each person I have cited. Where necessary, I have included additional details in the text. Some interviews took place in the offices of collective farms or village councils. Many others occurred in sunflower and sugar beet fields, in farm warehouses, and in any number of the other places where my interlocutors happened to be working. I communicated with each respondent directly in his or her own native language – in this case Russian, Ukrainian, or Surzhyk, a local Creole.[75]

---

[75] Most people began our conversation in Russian, the language they believed I would know best. In Kharkiv, interviews and conversations moved into Ukrainian or Surzhyk only after I had introduced a word or phrase in that language or dialect. In a few cases, a single flattened vowel or soft consonant was sufficient to cue a shift.

In the politicized environment of the post-Soviet Black Earth, my identity as an urban, educated foreigner with connections in Moscow and Kyiv routinely elicited responses that ranged from litanies of economic distress to statements of improbably high harvest yields.[76] When using interview data and records of conversations, therefore, I have read "against the grain." While avoiding the use of evidence that seemed outlying, and that appeared only once or twice in the course of my research, I assign greater analytical weight to statements that depart from established narratives than to those that echo official scripts. When speaking with state officials and directors of agricultural collectives, this meant listening for comments that emerged in the interstices of conversation. My efforts were aided by speech forms that signal counter-hegemonic discourse, such as a device common in post-socialist environments that follows a current slogan with a more personal view, as in "I am for the equality of all forms of land tenure, but collective farms are our future."[77] Above all, it required constant alertness to statements that my interlocutors may have believed a researcher from North America would want to hear. Over time, apparently frank assessments by my interlocutors moved from the periphery to the center of conversations, as I learned to insert cues into conversation that showed some knowledge of the situation: the cost of plowing a garden plot in a particular year, the optimal distance between sunflower seedlings, the market price of a fattened pig.

Still, formal interviews did not tell the entire story. Interlocutors on sensitive subjects engage in careful filtering of what they do and do not want the researcher to know, or what they do or do not want to be on record as having said. To address this problem, I observed the process of privatization through ethnographic research in three different field sites, each of which afforded a different view onto how the process unfolded. I lived on a collective farm in August and September 1998 while it was undergoing privatization; I attended weekly meetings of a regional private farmers' association over the course of a year; and over a period of months, I observed land transactions in a local government surveying office, sitting in on conversations between local state officials and collective farm managers and watching as pensioners argued with local officials about

---

[76] See Note on Sources and Methodology, xx–xxi. See also Nancy Ries, *Russian Talk: Culture and Conversation during Perestroika*. Ithaca: Cornell University Press, 1997.

[77] See Scott, *Domination and the Arts of Resistance: Hidden Transcripts*. New Haven: Yale University Press, 1990, ch. 4.

paperwork for their land shares. This on-site research provided access to meetings closed to the press and general public. The observations gathered in those settings provide greater contextual detail for, and in some cases, a corrective to statements made in interviews.

Written documentation complements interviews and participant-observation research. The evidentiary base for this book includes thousands of articles from the district and regional press in Voronezh and Kharkiv; accounting records of individual enterprises in both regions; published and unpublished statistical data at the regional, district, and enterprise level; and material from national newspapers in both Russia and Ukraine. District newspapers constitute a particularly rich, if largely unmined, source of information about rural governance and agrarian change. These newspapers chronicle the daily challenges faced by private farmers and privatized collective farms in their struggle to wrest a living from the soil; publish the accomplishments of exceptional farm employees; provide a forum for villagers concerned about infrastructural decay and crime in their communities; and enumerate weekly production and other data for individual enterprises.

Discrepancies often exist between farm statistics produced for internal use and the data reported to the national government or international lending organizations. Such discrepancies can be the product of public relations efforts, but they also can be due to problems of data transmission in the context of deteriorating public infrastructure. Electricity in Kharkiv region, for example, was unavailable for several hours each day during the winter months of 1999–2000. During one afternoon, I listened as a district dispatcher received, calculated, and recorded quarterly production figures over a scratchy telephone line from a local collective farm where the farm accountant had no light and no way to power a calculator. Local state offices had to do the best they could with scarce resources to meet broad institutional mandates. Because of resulting irregularities in statistical data, and the occasional, but troublesome to identify unreliability of an individual datum, I have either used data gathered as close as possible to the source or have obtained and compared multiple sources of the same indicators.

I begin the analysis of land relations in the months just before the fall of the Soviet Union. The choice of 1991 as a starting point may appear obvious: the end of empire, the rebirth of two independent states, and the initiation of separate reform programs in Russia and Ukraine are political events that mark a discrete period in contemporary history. However, the events that bracket this study must be considered in the context of the rural societies under consideration, in which the degree and character of social and economic change does not necessarily vary according to the punctuated timelines of political transformation. [From this perspective, 1991 is merely the year in which we join the story of ongoing processes of change in agriculture and agrarian society.]

The Argument

The book opens with a discussion of the environment into which reformers introduced new property rights. Chapter 1 sets the stage for privatization in the Black Earth. It documents the economic and political changes that had begun to take place in the Black Earth before the collapse of Soviet power, and that subsequently shaped local responses to land privatization policy. The rest of the book is devoted to explaining how and why the facade of property rights developed. Chapters 2, 3, and 4 show how local bureaucrats restricted the supply of land through the development of informal practices. Chapter 5 explains how the politics of payment on former collectives suppressed villagers' demands for land both initially and in subsequent iterations of distribution. Chapter 6 shows how, after over a decade of privatization, forms of legal ownership predicted neither modes of production nor the actual disposition of property rights.

The creation of formal rights without substantive material benefit has resulted in a dangerous situation for rural communities. Land privatization in the Black Earth generated optimal conditions for the eventual development of a landless peasantry and brought no noticeable real improvements for rural people, but it did introduce formal institutional change. Impoverished populations now hold documents entitling their holders to unspecified plots of land, and where more powerful actors choose to step in and lease (and, as national legislatures allow it, purchase) large tracts of land, rural people will have little practical choice but to relinquish their rights in exchange for whatever small sum may be offered. The former *kolkhoznik* thus will continue to labor even as he slowly loses any claim on the soil he tills, finally becoming, as W. E. B. DuBois wrote a century ago of former slaves in the post-bellum American South, even less than a "tenant on shares, in name, but a laborer with indeterminate wages in fact."[78]

---

[78] W. E. B. DuBois, *The Souls of Black Folk*. Chicago: A. C. McClurg and Co., 1903.

I

Things Fall Apart

On a Friday morning in April 1991, B. D. Mostovoi faced a problem. A refrigeration unit had broken down in the livestock section of the state farm he directed. The unit stored milk, one of the chief sources of income for the farm. The emergency was reported right away to the district agricultural services office, but no repairman was available until the following afternoon. By Monday, it had become clear that the necessary spare part was not available in the district. One had been located in a neighboring district – and another, one journalist dryly noted, in the far-off Chuvash republic. Meanwhile, the state farm sent its usual delivery of milk, now already half-spoiled, to the local dairy processing plant. By the fourth day of the emergency, the head veterinarian of the farm, A. G. Oprishchko, had gone to the media with the story. As the days and hours wore on, Mostovoi worried about who would pay for the substantial losses that continued to accumulate as long as the refrigerator remained out of service.[1]

Mostovoi's problem was absolutely typical of its time. People across the Black Earth faced challenges at the dawn of the post-Soviet era that had little to do with ownership of land. Instead, collective and state farms contended with material and personnel shortages: inputs became increasingly scarce as inter-enterprise networks broke down, infrastructure of all kinds deteriorated, and price scissors made agriculture unprofitable, feeding further disintegration. Rapidly changing village populations left farms with new social problems but fewer skilled workers.

Local responses to these problems focused on decentralization and market development. Before the formal introduction of post-Soviet market

[1] A. Khokhlov, "Ostryi signal. ChP v Liptsakh," *TT* 18 April 1991, 3.

reforms, directors of agricultural collectives concentrated on local labor pools, outsourced production to households, and pulled away from the demands of state buyers, choosing instead to seek private outlets for the sale of their goods.[2] Meanwhile, widespread political and economic insecurity attending the Soviet collapse increased the importance of agricultural collectives as social institutions, only months before reformers in Moscow and Kyiv would demand the privatization of agricultural land.

Our Heavy Cross

The year of the death of Soviet power brought massive shortages in consumer goods and agricultural and industrial inputs to communities across Eurasia. The broad sweep of these problems distinguished them from previous shortages in the Soviet republics, which, though serious, generally had been narrower in both scale and the number of goods affected at a given time.[3] In Voronezh region, the Khava district newspaper lamented, "...the shortage of many goods is being felt more and more in commerce. Practically all types [of goods] have disappeared from store shelves."[4] Townspeople in nearby Liski district, a major center of cattle husbandry, noticed lines forming in the morning for dairy products. As in Leningrad and other Soviet cities, district executive committees in Black Earth towns attempted to regulate demand by introducing ration coupons.[5]

The origin of the problem was not a decline in production levels as such but the breakdown of distribution networks.[6] It was not an absolute lack of raw materials within Soviet borders that drove consumers to spend

---

[2] On "public functions in the family sphere" under socialism, see Hans Buechler and Judith-Maria Buechler, "The Bakers of Bernburg and the Logics of Communism and Capitalism," *American Ethnologist* 26:4 (2000) 799–821.

[3] For a discussion of the urban social meanings of such shortages, see Nancy Ries, *Russian Talk: Culture and Conversation during Perestroika*. Ithaca: Cornell University Press, 1997. Earlier shortages and the ways people found to circumvent them are discussed in Elena Osokina, *Our Daily Bread: Socialist Distribution and the Art of Survival in Stalin's Russia, 1927–1941*. Trans. Kate Transchel and Greta Bucher. London: Sharpe, 2001 and Alan Ball, "Private Trade and Traders during NEP," in Sheila Fitzpatrick, Alexander Rabinowitch, and Richard Stites, eds. *Russia in the Era of NEP: Explorations in Soviet Society and Culture*. Bloomington: Indiana University Press, 1991.

[4] V. Venevtsev, "Ekonomika raiona: itogi i prognozy," *RV* 28 February 1991, 2–3.

[5] V. Ivanov, "Chrezvychainye obstoiatel'stva. Ekh, liudi, liudi...I vy eshche khotite 'bol'shogo moloka'..." *LZ* 14 November 1991, 1.

[6] The character of the predicament was not unusual. Amartya Sen, *Poverty and Famines: An Essay on Entitlement and Deprivation*. Oxford: Oxford University Press, 1984.

long hours standing on lines and farms to scramble for fuel, seed, and fertilizer.[7] Agricultural production in the Black Earth was embedded in an intricate web of raw goods and transportation suppliers: each enterprise depended on a broad network of other enterprises and institutions, and any break in the chain of production had immediate and wide-ranging effects on production cycles. As one collective farm chairman in Liski described the problem, "Goods have been produced, but we can't realize them."[8]

By the late 1980s, the system of forced accountability among contracting enterprises had weakened, and with the spiraling decentralization of power within the Soviet state, distribution networks began to disintegrate. Distributors frequently contracted for produce and then refused to accept and pay for it.[9] In Kharkiv, business partnerships dissolved despite an executive order to preserve existing ties, and the lack of oversight of partnership relationships threw many collectives into crisis.[10] Commentators in Liski lamented the difficulty for agricultural producers "when shortages are felt for everything in the country, when chaos and confusion reign in all spheres, when all enterprise ties are destroyed, when contract obligations very often are not honored, when there is no proper order in the formation of prices ... "[11] The nature of the problem was well known in Moscow and Kyiv, and a high-ranking Ukrainian official at the time complained of political disorder created by *mitingovshchina*, or "rule by demonstrations," that a relatively small number of producers – in this case, coal miners – were able to generate by virtue of their place in production networks.[12]

Input shortages plagued both ends of the production cycle. Some shortages resulted from breaks in supply chains that had grown increasingly frequent since the first years of *perestroika*, when the director of one enterprise in Kharkiv had remarked that "what has happened with material-technical supply is our heavy cross."[13] In 1991, the perennial shortage

---

7 For a literary account of the social organization of and activity associated with Soviet lines, see V. Sorokin, *Ochered': Roman*. Paris: Sintaksis, 1985.

8 N. Petrenko, "Rabotat' na sklad? Eto sovsem plokho? ... " *LZ* 6 August 1991, 1.

9 A. Reshetov, "Kakie semena, takie i vskhody," *TT* 18 April 1991, 2.

10 "Takie nenadezhnye partnerskie sviazi," *TT* 18 May 1991, 2.

11 "Budem zarabatyvat' valiutu? Budet ne po-khoziaiski, esli ustupim takuiu vozmozhnost'," *LZ* 27 July 1991, 1.

12 Timofeev, A. "Obrasti konkretikoi na mestakh," *TT*, 12 May 1991, 1–2.

13 Ibid. Also see Stephen K. Wegren, "Democratization and Urban Bias in Postcommunist Russia," *Comparative Politics* 34:4 (July 2002).

of spare parts for agricultural machinery was particularly acute.[14] The head engineer of a collective farm in Khava described that shortage that year as "problem number one,"[15] while a collective farm member in Liski observed:

What more than anything else currently arouses the concern of those who work the land of the district? The worthless supply of a whole range of parts and spare parts for combines and harvesters. We seem to lack in small things, but the troubles those very "trifles" cause is more than sufficient. Everything must be "procured," selected, even bartered so as not to leave grain in the field.[16]

A shortage of parts meant that machinists were unable to repair tractors on time to seed crops promptly, and seeding even one week late could dramatically reduce yields.[17] In 1990, the harvest season in parts of the Black Earth had stretched almost to the New Year, leaving cadres insufficient time to prepare for the following growing season.[18] A string of small catastrophes followed, as winter crops went unsown and some fields were left for spring plowing. Empty fields became overgrown with weeds, which spread to neighboring fields. Without prompt attention to aggressive varieties of weeds, crop yields would be diminished for years to come.[19]

Deteriorating infrastructure accompanied collapsing distribution networks, and high loads on combines and other machinery led to frequent breakdowns and harvesting delays.[20] Machinery in poor repair required more diesel than new equipment, and work on many agricultural collectives came to a standstill at the height of the growing season due to a lack of fuel.[21] Problems in the fields were reflected on livestock farms: heating on livestock farms often failed, leaving animals cold and in poor health.[22] Even as milk production in some areas increased, the quality of dairy

---

[14] A. Reshetov, "V zharu s prokhladtsei..." *TT* 29 June 1991, 1; "Nuzhnye neotlozhnye mery," *RV* 26 March 1991, 1–2; "Kak budem ubirat' urozhai?" *LZ* 22 June 1991, 1.

[15] A. Kalutskii, "Bez problem ne obkhoditsia," *RV* 12 November 1991, 1.

[16] "Na starte – zhatva-91. Takie seminary nuzhny," *LZ* 6 July 1991, 1.

[17] The chief agronomist of a collective in Khava provides a detailed description of this problem in N. Skudnev, "Vesennii den' god kormit. Vyshli v pole khleboroby," *RV* 13 April 1991, 1.

[18] V. Zavarin, "Ispol'zovat' vse rezervy," *RV* 2 February 1991, 1.

[19] "Na boga nadeisia..." *RV* 11 July 1991, 1, 3.

[20] For example, "Kak budem ubirat' urozhai?" *LZ* 22 June 1991, 1; "Nuzhny neotlozhnye mery," *RV* 26 March 1991, 1+2.

[21] A. Sashin, "Kak s goriuchim?! ili Doloi 'chernuiu tetrad'!" *TT* 2 April 1991, 1.

[22] V. Chikunov, "'01' preduprezhdaet. V rezul'tate bezotvetstvennosti," *RV* 28 February 1991, 3; N. Zamiatin, "Chto pokazali vzaimoproverki. Za shchitom prichin" *RV* 16 February 1991, 1, 3.

products decreased as a result of "catastrophic" shortages in disinfecting and cleaning agents.[23] Workers on some farms added water to milk in order to increase apparent yields.[24]

Input shortages meant that some collectives had difficulty bringing the harvest in from the fields.[25] A lack of trucks to transport grain from the fields to silos, grain elevators, and markets was a common problem, but some agricultural enterprises faced even more mundane obstacles. In Liski, a vegetable and fruit processing plant filled its warehouse with finished goods but could not find a way to ship them to consumers in Voronezh, Perm, and other industrial centers: the supplier of wooden pallets in Kursk had not delivered the containers, and seemed to have no intention of doing so. The director of the processing plant noted that "Our supplier, as they say, doesn't give a damn (*i v us ne duet*)... This is what we've lived to see: an ordinary container has become a stumbling block."[26]

The shortage of packing material was not an isolated incident. Such problems were endemic in the broader crisis of distribution and inter-enterprise trade. Fieldworkers on one state farm in Kharkiv complained of spending hours waiting in the fields for containers in which to pack harvested vegetables, while a vegetable processing plant in Liski had sent representatives to "all corners of Russia" in search of glass jars and tin lids.[27] Growing irregularities in supply chains required extraordinary advance planning: a reserve of parts could make or break a harvest, but stockpiling spare parts required time, labor, connections, and money or tradable resources. Even with a great deal of thought and planning, some building materials, such as reinforced concrete, could not be stored.[28]

Post-production distribution networks suffered as well. In Kharkiv district, 1991 brought unprecedented bounty in the vegetable harvest, but state vegetable stores in the district were virtually empty.[29] A local newspaper devoted a series of articles to the problem, asking why, in a district that produced 50,000 to 70,000 tons of vegetables yearly, there was

[23] A. Lomaza, "Ot chernoi korovki da beloe molochko," *TT* 7 May 1991, 2.
[24] V. Golomedov, "Vyshe kachestvo – bol'she pribyli s seminara spetsialistov na Shukavskom molokozavode," *RV* 18 May 1991, 1.
[25] "Kak budem ubirat' urozhai?" *LZ* 22 June 1991, 1.
[26] N. Petrenko, "Rabotat' na sklad? Eto sovsem plokho?..." *LZ* 6 August 1991, 1.
[27] V. Ivanov, "Interv'iu po povodu... A trudnosti... Kogda ikh ne bylo?" *LZ* 2 July 1991, 1; A. Khokhlov, "Kapusta i fol'klor," *TT* 19 October 1991, 1.
[28] A. Khokhlov, "Perestroika po-'Kutuzovski'," *TT* 1 October 1991, 2.
[29] "Mestnye Sovety: radius deistviia. Reshat' kollegial'no," *TT* 5 September 1991, 2.

such a widespread shortage of vegetables in stores.[30] The answer matched accusations leveled against farms in other post-socialist countries[31]: low purchase prices for agricultural goods did not always meet the cost of production, so farms and manufacturers were withholding goods from the market in hopes of higher prices.[32]

Low purchase prices from manufacturers and producers thus did not always translate into low prices for consumers. Price increases sometimes led to more goods on store shelves and market counters, but this change was not always linked to an improved supply; some goods remained in stores because few people could afford to buy them.[33] Meanwhile, private buyers purchased goods and resold them at high prices in urban markets. If Soviet state institutions had once drained food from the countryside in order to provide for cities, now mixed market forces replicated the process: as food left collective and state farms for urban markets, city dwellers rushed into the countryside to cultivate cheaper food for themselves in victory gardens.[34]

"Vikings" and Hutsuls

In the new decade of the 1990s, local identities coalesced in opposition to increasing numbers of city people, ethnic Russians from central Asia and the Caucasus, and nomadic people in Black Earth villages.[35] Despite

[30] V. Danilenko, "Ovoshchi: ot polki – k prilavku. Razve tol'ko tseny kusaiutsia?" *TT* 17 August 1991, 2. A. Timofeev, "Pochemu ovoshchi – ostryi defitsit v 'ovoshchnom' prigorode?" *TT* 15 August 91, 2.

[31] Gerald Creed, "The Politics of Agriculture: Identity and Socialist Sentiment in Bulgaria," *Slavic Review* 54:4 (Winter 1995) 863.

[32] V. Dukhno, "Ovoshchi: ot griadki do vashego stola. Chto diktuet rynok?...Glazami potrebitelia," *TT* 24 January 1991, 3.

[33] V. Pleshkov, "Snova o vermikul'ture, ili Est' delo dlia nastoiashchego khoziaina," *LZ* 6 August 1991, 3.

[34] Village stores were still managed by *gostorg*, and although a mix of state and market forces were at work, prices on produce in these stores remained under state control. It would be easy to blame continuing state control for the supply crisis in rural areas, but it does not require a great deal of imagination to imagine what might have happened had price controls been lifted: prices in village stores would have risen, and the direction of travel for purchase might have changed, with urbanites flooding villages in search of better bargains than private city markets. In either case, the supply crisis *for rural consumers* would have remained: stores would be better stocked, but consumers would not have been able to afford the goods. This, of course, is precisely what did happen when price controls were lifted in Russia in January 1992.

[35] For a discussion of urban-rural migration within Russia and from former Soviet Republics, see Yuri Medvedkov and Olga Medvedkov. "Turning Points and Trends

mortality rates that far surpassed and often doubled birth rates, both Kharkiv and Voronezh regions saw positive population growth during that time.[36] Much in-migration was to provincial capitals, but some people made their way to villages, where life appeared relatively more insulated from the vagaries of political and economic change. The movement toward the countryside contrasted with both previous and subsequent trends, as the more dramatic upheaval and uncertainty in near and distant Soviet cities led urbanites to seek refuge in the periphery.[37]

At the same time, the food crisis led urban Black Earth residents to seek land for kitchen gardens. Local government responded to the demand, and the pages of district newspapers were filled with articles addressed to urbanites new to growing food.[38] Rural readers repeatedly encountered information meant for others, elementary advice on topics about which villagers had a lifetime of expertise: how to seed a small plot to feed a family, how to transport and prepare potatoes with minimal waste, and fundamental rules for vegetable gardening.[39]

The expansion of city dwellers' garden plots led in many places to incursions on villagers' land and growing resentment among agricultural workers.[40] Such change, while rooted in common hardship, foreshadowed the higher degree of social differentiation that would arrive with privatization and the other economic reforms of the 1990s. Garden plots allowed urbanites to gain a foothold in the countryside: those allotments would remain when the height of the crisis subsided, and they laid a foundation for land distribution to those who eventually would establish "country estates" on land that previously had been used for agriculture, hunting and trapping, and foraging.

---

in Russia's Urbanization," in George J. Demko, Grigory Ioffe, and Zhanna Zay-onchkovskaya, eds. *Population Under Duress: The Geodemography of Post-Soviet Russia.* Boulder: Westview, 1999.

[36] See *Goroda i raiony Voronezhskoi oblasti.* Voronezh: Voronezh regional committee on state statistics, 1996, 4–9; *Statystychnyi shchorichnyk,* 1997 excerpted in M. L. Chmykhalo, ed. *Upravlinnia zvedenoi informatsii ta rehional'noi statystyky,* 194.

[37] Zhores Medvedev, *Soviet Agriculture.* New York: Norton, 1987, 318–322.

[38] V. Pleshkov, "Snova o vermikul'ture ili Est' delo dlia nastoiashchego khoziaina," *LZ* 6 August 1991, 3.

[39] The author of one piece, identified in the byline as "a housewife," noted that that year, every family in the district center had its own garden. Ye. Yevtiukhina, "Khoziaike na zametku. Ne kartoshka – ob"edenie..." *LZ* 4 June 1991, 3. In Kharkiv, see "Sovety ogordniku. Ovoshchi na uchastke," *TT* 27 April 1991, 3, and "Sovety ogorodniku. Bor'ba s koloradskim zhukom," *TT* 7 May 1991, 3.

[40] For example, N. Solontsevoi, "Konfliktnaia situatsiia. Skazka v...tsisterne," *TT* 16 May 1991, 3.

Urban incursion into rural life was not limited to land transfers. People who had labored all of their lives in cities sought not only gardens in rural areas but also work and produce directly from agricultural collectives. The head of Liubotinsky state farm in Kharkiv district remarked in fall 1991 that it was not only beautiful scenery that had attracted city dwellers to the farm's apple orchards: some were drawn by advertisements for harvest-time labor, while others from a nearby town came to pick apples for themselves.[41] Visitors did not always wait for the harvest to take produce, so Liubotinsky managers hired workers whose specific task was to protect the apples from "envious eyes and grabbing hands." A guard and dog rid the orchard of "mechanized crooks" who escaped to their cars to "save themselves, running from the sharp cuspids, shedding plunder on the run and holding up torn designer jeans."[42]

Urbanites' practice of helping themselves to crops in the fields, while arguably rooted in Soviet understandings of collective production and ownership, undoubtedly irritated farm workers, who viewed those harvests as their own. Such transgressions were widespread and could spell serious losses for collective and state farms. When the director of Kharkiv Tractor Factory state farm complained that outsiders were carrying off the farm's highest quality produce, he noted that "during the harvest season the problem practically grows to the dimensions of a natural disaster."[43] In autumn of 1991, the disappearance of produce from Tsirkunovsky state farm in Kharkiv became so acute that its director decided to regulate and profit from, rather than stop, the theft. He had scales set up next to vegetable fields, offering pick-your-own tomatoes for forty kopeks per kilogram. On Saturdays, this arrangement yielded so much cash that it looked like "sacks of ballots on election day," and the director began to advertise on local television.[44]

Farm managers walked a political tightrope when outsiders sought jobs in the countryside. In Liski, one local collective farm hired fifty new families in 1991 to avoid a cadre shortage among machinists and livestock workers. The farm director reassured anxious readers that the collective had not taken on new members lightly: "Selection is strict and careful. We study beforehand what attracted one person or another to our area, how serious his intentions are, and whether he's the sort of person who

[41] V. Chebodaev, "Problema! 'Zolotye' iabloki," *TT* 31 October 1991, 1.

[42] A. Khokhlov, "Akh, sad, ty moi sad! ... " *TT* 15 October 1991, 1.

[43] A. Konstantinov, "Uchimsia khoziaistvovat'. Budet li 'rabotat' koldogovor?" *TT* 6 June 1991, 2.

[44] "Razgovor s chitatelem. Den'gi pod nogami," *TT* 17 October 1991, 1.

is continually changing jobs, who is accustomed to flitting from one end of the country to the other."[45] Seasonal workers also often shouldered the blame for problems caused by input shortages. In January 1991, a state farm director and a party committee chairman in Kharkiv felt compelled to write to the district paper to explain that previously published criticism of seasonal workers – "*shabashniki*," a derogatory term deriving from the verb "*shabashit'*," to quit working – who had rebuilt a livestock facility had been unfounded: the visitors had worked conscientiously, but the project had gone slowly because of a shortage of building materials.[46]

Temporary agricultural workers took up residence on Black Earth collectives each summer and drew primarily on two distinct labor pools: workers, students, and schoolchildren from nearby cities, and migrant Hutsul communities from western Ukraine.[47] Agricultural collectives required seasonal labor earlier in the growing season for the cultivation of sugar beet and at harvest time for non-grain crops. In Voronezh and Kharkiv, workers usually completed the former task by hand. The process of thinning beets is highly labor-intensive: it takes place during the blazing heat of the summer months and involves long hours bent over seedlings in fields with no shade. It is punishing work, and those who agree to it have a pressing need for the income it provides. Farm managers emphasized that migrant laborers were appropriate for the task because they were capable of working long hours in extreme heat, in temperatures that in some years hovered just over 40 degrees Centigrade (104 degrees Fahrenheit).[48]

The arrival of temporary laborers in Black Earth villages became a locus of resentment and conflict in 1991. That year, fewer local seasonal workers were available, so most temporary hires were from regions outside the Black Earth.[49] Despite the difficulty of the work, local people evinced resentment toward seasonal workers for the payment they received. During the beet-thinning season, each person could work about a hectare by hand; that year, a family of four could earn one thousand rubles and

[45] V. Golovin, "Partiinaia zhizn': grani sotsial'noi zashchity. Vozrozhdennoe selo?" *LZ* 3 July 1991, 2.

[46] "Posle kritiki. 'Kogda shabashniki otshabashat...'," *TT* 24 January 1991, 2.

[47] There was a temporary decrease in the ranks of these workers in many areas. V. Pleshkov, "I koreshki, i vershki – vse ponadobitsia," *LZ* 17 September 1991, 1.

[48] Interview, director, Sil'nyi, LV, May 2000. Interview, head engineer, Utra, LV, May 2000.

[49] Pleshkov, "I koreshki, i vershki – vse ponadobitsia," *LZ* 17 September 1991, 1.

purchase up to two hundred kilograms of sugar and wheat at reduced prices.[50] The author of a letter to the editor of a newspaper in Liski wrote:

> I shared my doubts about how expedient it is to invite Hutsuls and other "Vikings" (lit., Varangians) for the cultivation of beet plantations. Me and my compatriots [sic] have pondered more than once or twice about why working conditions we can't even dream of are being created for people from elsewhere. I mean conditions of cash payment and payment in kind (*naturoplaty*).[51]

It was a measure of the depth of crisis in the Black Earth that residents of the district were willing to take on this task.[52] Even "Vikings" (here, seasonal workers drawn from local urban labor pools) provoked a tense reaction. That year, the director of a vegetable processing plant in Liski district decided not to bring in temporary workers from nearby cities, noting that "we do not require accidental 'bosses'.... And 'Vikings' are not needed." Instead, the plant would hire its own experienced veterans and pensioners.[53]

Fighting for Every Worker

Despite the new populations in Black Earth villages, agricultural collectives suffered from a shortage of skilled labor. Small problems took on larger proportions when farms were unable to hire specialists and work in warehouses, machinery workshops, and livestock farms slowed because of the absence of qualified personnel.[54] Some farms could not make full use of their machinery because they lacked cadres to take tractors and combines out into the fields,[55] and seeding campaigns in spring were

---

[50] V. Provotorova, "Vozvrashchaias' k staroi teme....I svoikh vspomnili," *LZ* 19 June 1991, 3.

[51] Ibid.

[52] By the end of the 1990s, this trend had again reversed direction, with western Ukrainians performing much of the work of beet cultivation.

[53] V. Ivanov, "Interv'iu po povodu...A trudnosti...Kogda ikh ne bylo?" *LZ* 2 July 1991, 1. Fewer urbanites helped with the beet harvest that year than in previous summers. Pleshkov, "I koreshki, i vershki – vse ponadobitsia," *LZ* 17 September 1991, 1.

[54] A. Ziuzin, "O kormakh, kak o khlebe. Plan – s pervogo ukosa," *RV* 11 July 1991, 3; A. Il'in, "Otchety i vybory v kolkhozakh. Ne ot kolosa – ot kolesa," *RV* 12 February 1991, 3; "Ferma schitaetsia luchshei," A. Golomedov, *RV* 27 August 1991, 3; A. Kalutskii, "Bez problem ne obkhoditsia" *RV*, 12 November 1991, 1.

[55] A. Khokhlov, "Interv'iu na starte," *TT* 9 April 1991, 1–4; V. Zavarzin, "Ispol'zovat' vse rezervy," *RV* 2 February 1991, 1; A. Il'in, "Kogda pogoda – ne soiuznik," *RV* 1 August 1991, 3.

hampered when fields became flooded and not enough hands were available to help.[56] Meanwhile, machinery repairs were impossible on many rural enterprises because specialists were busy with other tasks.[57] Journalists at the Khava newspaper complained that on sunny mornings, machinists on the Pravda collective farm could be found preparing livestock feed instead of working in the fields.[58]

The problem was particularly acute in livestock husbandry, where the work was dirty, difficult, and physically punishing: "You can't even chase young people to the hog farm."[59] Milk production, a major source of cash income, suffered most.[60] Declines in milk yields could be catastrophic for farms, so even collectives with an insufficient number of tractor and combine operators sometimes directed machinists to work in livestock husbandry.[61] In Khava, where some collectives had begun to delegate the task of raising animals to female pensioners, one of two sisters caring for the collective farm's calves at home described the beginning of her day:

Every morning I get up at four o'clock and I'm on my feet until late in the evening. And even then I don't always get everything done. The day isn't long enough. You feed your own livestock, milk them, and after five a.m. you get to the dairy farm. I have the smallest little calves. Before, I took them from the birthing area [*rodilka*] when they were twenty days old. Now there's no birthing area. Two milkmaids used to work there. One went on maternity leave, and the second is still very young, about sixteen years old. She doesn't want to work: it's very hard. So it's necessary [for me to do it].[62]

Regarding the problem of retaining livestock workers, "[t]he reason," one journalist observed, "is plain: working conditions."[63] The retention issue, as well as the difficulty of attracting young people to livestock husbandry, stemmed in part from the outdated infrastructure and low wages on most farms.[64] Work conditions were similar to those common two decades

[56] A. Anokhin, "Na vzaimovygodnoi osnove. Dogovor dorozhe deneg," *RV* 28 May 1991, 3.
[57] A. Khokhlov, "Trevozhit tol'ko, chto zhatki chasto vykhodiat iz stroia," *TT* 27 July 1991, 1; "Poka grom ne grianet?" *RV* 25 June 1991, 1.
[58] "Moloko. Polozhenie ne uluchshaetsia," *RV*, 28 May 1991, 3.
[59] "Problemy skorospeloi otrasli. Kak vernut' byluiu slavu?" *RV* 23 May 1991, 3.
[60] A. Reshetov, "Urok ne vprok," *TT* 31 January 1991, 3; A. Il'in, "V zamknutom kruge okazalas' molochnaia otrasl' kolkhoza im. Kalinina," *RV* 16 February 1991, 3.
[61] "Nuzhny neotlozhnye mery," *RV* 26 March 1991, 1, 2.
[62] S. Bondarev, "Kak dela, zhivotnovod. Ne khvataet dnia," *RV* 23 July 1991, 3.
[63] A. Il'in, "Na kontrole – proizvodstvo moloka. Obeshchannogo tri goda zhdut?" *RV* 17 September 1991, 3; G. Ovtsenova, "Moloko: spad prodolzhaetsia," *RV* 18 July 1991, 5.
[64] A. Reshetov, "Aktual'no! Zameniat li argumenty moloko?" *TT* 14 December 1991, 1.

before, and tasks that had been mechanized elsewhere, such as feeding on hog farms, continued to be carried out by hand.[65]

Some agricultural collectives that had trouble creating "modern" working conditions on livestock farms used other incentives to attract "young brides," who constituted the bulk of the workforce in livestock husbandry.[66] The Kharkiv press recounted one story of a local woman who had left livestock work on a state farm because of living conditions, only to find that her new situation was even worse. She had a job in construction that allowed her and her family of three only a single corner of a dormitory room. Upon returning to the state farm, she received her own room in a dormitory. Housing was one benefit that could be used to attract women to villages, and it was a common solution for collectives seeking to hire not only livestock workers, but also teachers and other professionals.[67] Such attempts to retain workers were less capital-intensive than improving mechanization on livestock farms, and they did not address the difficult and unpleasant character of the work, but managers' efforts met with some success. Farm managers, the local press emphasized, were "fighting for every worker" and showing some results.[68]

Villages in Voronezh attempted to counter personnel shortages and meet consumer demands by reviving cottage industry. Economic development was only a subsidiary aim – the real goal was to resolve a demographic crisis: "Securing brides in the village is the first goal of the renewal of cottage industry in the village."[69] In Liski, agricultural collectives set up sewing shops, smokehouses, carding and combing shops, oil presses, and brick factories. Some collectives sewed polyethylene bags and others fur hats. Such projects provided alternative work for young women: "Guys can work as drivers, machinists, and lathe operators. It's worse for the girls: if they don't want to go work on the farm, they can be left without employment." Local officials projected a convoluted path by which young women eventually would work in livestock husbandry. Cottage

[65] A. Golomedov, "Problemy skorospeloi otrasli. Kak vernut' byluiu slavu?" *RV* 23 May 1991, 3.

[66] G. Ovtsenova, "Moloko: spad prodolzhaetsia," *RV* 18 July 1991, 5.

[67] V. Golovin, "Partiinaia zhizn': grani sotsial'noi zashchity. Vozrozhdennoe selo," *LZ* 3 July 1991, 2; A. Il'in, "Otchety i vybory v kolkhozakh. Ne ot kolosa – ot kolesa," *RV* 12 February 1991, 3.

[68] A. Sashin, "Nashi interv'iu. Zimovka idet normal'no," *TT* 10 December 1991, 2.

[69] M. Liskin, "V novykh usloviiakh khoziaistvovaniia. Dokhodnyi promysel," *LZ* 30 April 1991, 3.

industry would be a step to the livestock farm: "And what about opening a sewing shop? The young people will work there, they'll start families, they'll need higher salaries – and the young women will go to work on the farm."[70]

When skilled cadres were not available for livestock husbandry, collectives outsourced production to households. A reporter in Khava wrote, "Remembering that the homestead ... is a large reserve in the resolution of the food problem," the Kalinin collective farm in Khava "organized assistance" for the collective farm population, which in turn played an important part in helping the collective fulfill its plan for meat production. The collective farm began allotting young calves to villagers and supplied them with feed.[71] A few pensioners accepted as many as twenty-five pigs into their small homes and courtyards, but these arrangements were not governed by any formal contract. One private swine tender explained her participation in this crowded and demanding process: "It's necessary to help the farm."[72]

No Right to Remain Silent

The growing difficulty of securing supplies and labor was accompanied by increasing stress on agricultural land resources. In June 1991, a group of Kharkiv party leaders and state farm representatives gathered to discuss the question of how much land would be required for the operation of the Red Partisan state farm. The director of Red Partisan at the time, N. D. Sofienko, had seen 170 hectares of state farmland alienated that year for individual plots and dachas, together with an additional 40 hectares for farm employees. These were not the first land losses the farm had experienced: no fewer than 400 hectares had been alienated from it in recent years, more than 10 percent of its total area.[73] Even after Red Partisan had made those allotments, a state order required the farm to maintain its previous acreage for seeding of vegetable and feed crops. The lack of coordination between state demands for production and the alienation of land for private cultivation gave Sofienko a headache: the

---

[70] Ibid.
[71] A. Golomedov, "Nizhnebaigorskie kontrasty," *RV* 15 January 1991, 3.
[72] A. Golomedov, "Problemy skorospeloi otrasli. Kak vernut' byluiu slavu?" *RV* 23 May 1991, 3.
[73] By the end of the decade, the farm covered a total of 2,690 hectares. Interview, director, Red Partisan, 23 July 1999.

state plan that year called for seeding 100 hectares of sunflower, but Red Partisan could seed only 80 hectares because it did not have enough access to land.[74]

The move in the early 1990s away from collective agricultural production and toward household production had occurred in response to shortages of consumer goods and agricultural inputs, and it required the alienation of collectively held land for private garden plots. New land codes granted village councils and other branches of local and regional government new powers to distribute land, and massive construction of individual houses and dachas in rural areas of the Black Earth followed. At the same time, agricultural collectives allocated additional land for their members' household gardens. The ensuing changes in land tenure caused difficulties for collectives in meeting production plans and compensating members for their labor. Tension emerged out of the changing relationship between what was known as "social production" – agriculture to feed the general population – and household production, which provided for individual families. Even as agricultural collectives struggled with land loss, local officials expected them to support household production. The deputy chairman of the district planning commission in Khava took collective and state farms to task for their inadequate assistance of households: workers had not been provided with enough young animals or building materials, and insufficient pasture had been made available for workers' livestock.[75]

Land had been alienated from collective and state farms in previous years, but this newest shift deeply affected the productive capacity of agricultural enterprises. In Kharkiv district, the total seeding acreage for spring crops shrunk by over 5 percent between 1990 and 1991,[76] primarily because of land allotment for kitchen gardens.[77] Five state farms in the district lost at least 120 hectares each to garden plots that year, and some lost considerably more: Pesochinsky State Farm, for example, alienated 274 hectares and the Red Army state farm alienated 239 hectares. Most

---

[74] A. Khokhlov, "Mnogo li cheloveku zemli nuzhno?" *TT* 11 June 1991, 2.

[75] In 1990, 12 percent of the milk sold in Khava and 16 percent of the meat came from homesteads. V. Venevtsev, "Ekonomika raiona: itogi i prognozy," *RV*, 28 February 1991, 2–3.

[76] This loss amounted to 1,829 hectares out of a total of 34,318 hectares. "Polgoda na puti k rynku. Itogi vypolneniia gosudarstvennogo plana ekonomicheskogo i sotsial'nogo razvitiia raiona za 6 mesiatsev 1991 goda," *TT* 20 August 1991, 3.

[77] "Pestraia kartina. Itogi vypolneniia gosudarstvennogo plana ekonomicheskogo i sotsial'nogo razvitiia raiona za 9 mesiatsev 1991 goda," *TT* 9 November 1991, 2.

state farms in the district encompassed between 1,500 and 4,000 hectares of land, and such losses were sufficient in some cases to cause significant disruption of crop rotation and cultivation plans.[78] Land transfers also contributed to cadre shortages. When Bezliudovsky state farm in Kharkiv lost 200 hectares of land to a neighboring enterprise, the press observed that, "many workers started to leave, believing that their state farm had wound up among those considered to be unpromising."[79]

Land alienation from agricultural collectives had a particularly negative effect on livestock husbandry and, in turn, on crops that required organic fertilizer.[80] The widespread scarcity of animal feed in 1991 stemmed in part from shortages of skilled cadres and the vicissitudes of weather, but some enterprises simply lacked the land they needed to grow feed crops in volumes adequate for supporting their own cattle.[81] In Kharkiv district, the local press reported in September that the volume of winter wheat planted that year would be sufficient to feed the human population, but that the district would produce only about a third of the amount of livestock feed required.[82] A reporter blamed a state farm head veterinarian for the feed crisis on one collective: the technician, the reporter argued, had no right "to remain silent while practically all of the ravines were distributed to dacha owners" and, in the case of part of the land used by the collective, to "some organization," which left livestock without grazing land.[83]

---

[78] "Polgoda na puti k rynku. Itogi vypolneniia gosudarstvennogo plana ekonomicheskogo i sotsial'nogo razvitiia raiona za 6 mesiatsev 1991 goda," *TT* 20 August 1991, 3.

[79] A. Reshetov, "Kommunist. Rukovoditel'. Direktorskie zadumki," *TT* 20 August 1991, 2. The recent history of farms labeled "unpromising" by the Soviet state had resulted in closures and population relocations. For a local discussion of this phenomenon, and the small market in skilled labor it created, see V. D'iachenko, "Kto est' kto? Khleb predrika," *LZ* 26 January 1991, 1–2.

[80] Less livestock meant, naturally, less manure. This problem, which was of great concern to farm managers in Kharkiv, is recorded in dozens of articles. For example, L. Kushnir, "'Po shchuch'emu veleniiu' zemlia ne rodit," *TT* 26 January 1991, 3; L. Ivanov, "Prodolzhaetsia vyvozka navoza," *TT* 13 April 1991, 1.

[81] In contrast, most enterprises did not produce their own feed for their pigs. A. Kochukov, "Svinovodstvo: opyt, problemy, poisk. Slovami delu ne pomoch'," *LZ* 27 March 1991, 3.

[82] "Mestnye Sovety: radius deistviia. Reshat' kollegial'no," *TT* 5 September 1991, 2. There was substantial variation among enterprises in feed supplies. As of September in Kharkiv district, Bezliudovsky state farm had 78 percent of the feed it required for the winter, whereas Liptsy and Red Partisan state farms had only 22 percent.

[83] A. Reshetov, "Zhivotnovodstvo: slagaemye produktivnosti. Nuzhny konkretnye deistviia," *TT* 18 July 1991, 2.

In response to the feed crisis, some heads of collectives culled their herds, "unloading livestock on meat processing plants and households, while laying an economic foundation for that action and hiding behind the will of labor collectives." Enterprises in Khava lost a total of 2,600 head of cattle in the spring of 1991 for this reason.[84] Reduction in livestock holdings solved immediate feed shortages, but it suppressed milk production, which in turn affected consumers and reduced farm revenue potential. Households that had come to rely upon the pasture of agricultural collectives were likewise left without a reliable source of feed for their livestock.

Our Daily Bread

At first, state demands on collective and state farms did not reflect the changed circumstances. Late winter of 1991 was difficult for Black Earth regions: a drought in a number of large grain-producing areas in the southern Urals, western Siberia, and along the Volga River had affected state supplies of grain. The situation in Russia was further complicated by the fact that Ukraine and Kazakhstan had refused grain deliveries to the Russian republic.[85] This placed greater pressure on local producers in Kharkiv and Voronezh, intensifying for state buyers the perennial problem of extracting harvested goods from agricultural collectives.[86]

Partially in response to this situation, the Russian republican government introduced a new set of obligations in 1991, adding to the state order an in-kind tax (*prodnalog*) to be paid by agricultural collectives on the land that they used.[87] In Voronezh, requirements for the food tax and state order comprised approximately one-third of projected grain production and 80 percent of projected sugar beet production.[88] The Council of

---

[84] "Nuzhny neotlozhnye mery," *RV* 26 March 1991, 1–2. The Russia collective farm decreased livestock holdings by 687 head, Kirova by 437, and Red Star by 300.

[85] G. Panevin, "Khleb nash nasushchnyi," *RV* 3 August 1991, 1–2.

[86] For perspectives on this problem in the 1930s, see Lynne Viola, *Peasant Rebels Under Stalin: Collectivization and the Culture of Peasant Resistance.* Oxford: Oxford University Press, 1996; and Sheila Fitzpatrick, *Stalin's Peasants: Resistance and Survival in a Russian Village After Collectivization.* Oxford: Oxford University Press, 1994.

[87] Prikaz Minsel'khozproda RSFSR 7 February 1991. The name of this tax is somewhat misleading when placed in an historical context. Under NEP, the *prodnalog* had been applied as a replacement for state requisitions (*prodrazverstka*). The 1991 reintroduction of the *prodnalog* placed an additional burden on agricultural enterprises, as the state order (*goszakaz*) was not rescinded.

[88] Calculated from figures given in V. Venevtsev, "Ekonomika raiona: itogi i prognozy," *RV* 28 February 1991, 2–3.

Ministers demanded close adherence to the new rule, specifying that payment of the food tax for deliveries of grain was "strictly obligatory."[89] Fines for neglecting contractual agreements could reach five or six times the value of undelivered goods, and payment of fines would not relieve the producers of their responsibility to pay the tax. As a result of these conditions, and despite substantially lower purchase prices for goods redeemed for the food tax,[90] enterprises paid the production tax first even as they increasingly shied away from fulfilling state plans.[91]

However, by the dawn of the new decade, state subsidies and other supporting infrastructure had begun to wane, and the social contract that supported those relationships had begun to dissolve. If violence had sustained state-farm relationships in the early years of collectivized agriculture, agricultural collectives' compliance with state demands by the time of *perestroika* depended on a quid pro quo: "The state order is the same entirely ordinary production, but realizing it stipulates an exchange, providing farms with material resources, let's say, with equipment or construction materials."[92] By 1991 central planning had stopped holding up its end of the bargain, and many collectives stopped delivering on theirs.

Agricultural enterprises responded to economic pressure by complying only partially with state demands, and state institutions gradually adjusted their requirements as well as their incentives structure to try to attract the business of agricultural collectives. Meanwhile, collective and state farms sold their production on world markets.[93] Where collectives continued to sell to state buyers, they did so not because they were coerced into sales

---

[89] By order of the Chairman of the Council of Ministers of the RSFSR, "O dopolnitel'nykh merakh po formirovaniiu gosudarstvennykh khlebnykh i drugikh resursov v 1991 godu."

[90] There was a significant difference in purchase prices for the production tax and the state order. A metric ton of milk sold in Liski to fulfill the production tax would bring 620 rubles; the same amount would bring 680 rubles if sold to fulfill the state order. V. Pleshkov, "Sdelat' bol'she nam predstoit," *LZ* 16 April 1991, 3.

[91] There was some indication that enterprises feared actual fines, which were not an empty threat. G. Ivanova, "Moloko. I letom spad," *RV* No. 97, August 1991, 3. Enterprises generally fulfilled the food tax before the state order, even though this was less profitable for enterprises. For example, "Miaso. Khotia i vypolnili plany," *RV* 16 April 1991, 3; "Moloko. Po-prezhnemu minusuem," *RV* 16 April 1991, 3.

[92] V. Pleshkov, "Sdelat' bol'she nam predstoit," *LZ* 16 April 1991, 3.

[93] "Budem zarabatyvat' valiutu?" Budet ne po-khoziaiski, esli ustupim takuiu vozmozhnost'," *LZ* 27 July 1991, 1.

but because they lacked storage space for the harvest and could not afford to wait for higher prices.[94]

Collective and state farms rebelled against the demands of state buyers and, even before the Soviet collapse and introduction of major economic reforms, responded to market pressures. In Voronezh, the Khava newspaper reported in August of 1991 that local collective farms planned to keep most of their grain for "our daily bread": for seed, feed, sale to farm members, and "so-called barter transactions."[95] A similar ethos governed the sale of sugar beet in the district: seven agricultural collectives in Khava sold between 20 percent and 45 percent of planned levels, despite having produced 63 percent of the state plan.[96] Other enterprises reportedly chose the profitable path of selling meat "freely" rather than selling to state buyers.[97] The local press in Liski registered "serious concern" that a number of collective farms were "forgetting about their own plans and tasks [and] conducting a generous sale of piglets to the population": the Voskhod collective farm had sold 304 piglets to local villagers but did not fulfill the state plan, which had specified that 126 piglets be sent to a local farm which fattened and slaughtered animals.[98]

Meanwhile in the Ukrainian SSR, Kharkiv agricultural collectives preemptively announced in February of 1991 that they would not be able to fulfill state orders for that year's harvest.[99] At harvest time, the Kharkiv district newspaper reported that farms were not selling their share of wheat to state buyers.[100] By November, only four collectives had fulfilled their grain obligations to the state, and the chief state inspector for the purchase of agricultural production in the district noted that "the rest, we have to assume, have become confused. They don't know to which god to pray, which state to serve."[101] A number of dairy farms

94 A. Konstantinov, "Urozhai-91. A v sovkhoze tom vse spokoinen'ko," *TT* 8 June 1991, 2. Also see L. Barkanov, "Grani arendnogo podriada. Nagrada – urozhai," *TT* 21 May 1991, 2.

95 G. Panevin, "Khleb nash nasushchnyi," *RV* 3 August 1991, 1, 2.

96 Calculated from V. Venevtsev, "Ekonomika raiona: itogi i prognozy," *RV* 28 February 1991, 2–3.

97 "Itogi raboty zhivotnovodov za 11 mesiatsev. Kogda nastupit perelom?" *RV* 14 December 1991, 2. A. Il'in, "Aktual'naia tema. Kak vpisat'sia v rynok?" *RV* 26 December 1991, 3.

98 A. Kochukov, "Svinovodstvo: opyt, problemy, poisk. Slovami delu ne pomoch'," *LZ* 27 March 1991, 3.

99 S. Lobas, "Ekonomicheskoe obozrenie. Kuda zhe my idem?..." *TT* 9 November 1991, 1.

100 "Mestnye Sovety: radius deistviia. Reshat' kollegial'no," *TT* 5 September 1991, 2.

101 L. Pomaza, "V zerkale tsifr. Podschitali – proslezilis'," *TT* 16 November 1991, 1–2.

began "systematically ignoring" requests to furnish information about daily milk yields,[102] and fifteen of the collectives in Kharkiv district were reported as delinquent in their milk sales to the state.[103]

Near the end of 1991, the chairman of the local state oversight organization for livestock husbandry complained of massive, "groundless" decreases in milk production district wide, leading him to wonder whether managers were "unused to working without the district committees' prodding stick."[104] Inspections by the Ukrainian Ministry of Finance showed significant underpayment of tax obligations and hiding of income by agricultural collectives in Kharkiv region.[105] By the end of the growing season, the sale of greenhouse vegetables to the state had declined by 16 percent despite a bumper harvest.[106] State farm managers in Kharkiv marketed vegetables in urban areas, where purchase prices were higher than in village stores.[107] In turn, the state agency *gostorg* judged the asking prices of state farms in the district to be too high and contracted with suppliers in a neighboring district.[108]

Many farms did experience genuine declines in production as the Soviet empire drew its last breaths, but records of sales to state buyers provide an incomplete picture of the health of those enterprises.[109] Previous decades had seen the development of informal distribution networks that eroded official production levels at the margins, as employees engaged in petty trade of sausage and other goods. The situation in 1991, however, went far beyond pan-toting. A reporter in Kharkiv made reference to

---

[102] F. Klepitsa, "O nabolevshem – otkrovenno. Sovresh' – ne pomresh'...?" *TT* 2 July 1991, 1.

[103] T. Butsykina, "Zhivotnovodstvo v zerkale tsifr," *TT* 29 October 1991, 1.

[104] V. Surmilo, "Otrasl' v upadke. Pochemu?" *TT* 14 November 1991, 2.

[105] This was reported in the Khava district paper by a TASS correspondent. V. Fomenko, "Urok dlia sebia i drugikh. Prishlos' raskoshelit'sia," *RV* 11 July 1991, 3.

[106] "Polgoda na puti k rynku. Itogi vypolneniia gosudarstvennogo plana ekonomicheskogo i sotsial'nogo razvitiia raiona za 6 mesiatsev 1991 goda," *TT* 20 August 1991, 3.

[107] A. Timofeev, "Pochemu ovoshchi – ostryi defitsit v 'ovoshchnom' prigorode?" *TT* 15 August 1991, 2.

[108] Danilenko, "Razve tol'ko tseny kusaiutsia?" *TT* 17 August 1991, 2.

[109] See "Pestraia kartina," *TT* 9 November 1991, 2. An additional way in which those numbers distort actual production figures is that they did not take into account spoilage, which afflicted vegetable crops in general and potatoes in particular. See L. Pomaza, "Den'gi pod nogami. Gde-to teriaem, gde-to nakhodim," *TT* 30 May 1991, 3; A. Reshetov, "Ostryi signal. Nu, kartoshka! . ." *TT* 23 May 1991, 2; and E. Klochko, "Konfliktnaia situatsiia. Spasibo za printsipial'nost'," *TT* 1 March 1991, 3. Genuine difficulties with infrastructure, feed, weather, and, in the case of livestock husbandry, artificial insemination also plagued Black Earth farms and were covered in hundreds of local press articles.

the mysterious disappearance of unprecedented volumes of agricultural goods: "It's impossible, let's say, to understand how given a state order of 1080 tons, Ukrainka sold only 270. There's meat there, but where it goes – is also unknown."[110] The answer to this question was an open secret: agricultural collectives in the Black Earth were outsourcing production to households and selling their goods on an emerging market to the highest bidder.

Amidst widespread shortage, selling to state buyers at low prices seemed irrational to producers. Some farms pursued strategies to force higher prices, leading a reporter in Liski to ask the head of the district division of livestock husbandry, "Do urbanites have reason to suspect that farms deliberately are holding back milk?"[111] A high-ranking official in Khava observed that the fulfillment of milk production and sale plans had "fallen through,"[112] and in the dairy sector, the high cost of producing milk meant that "sale brings nothing other than losses." State purchasing prices for milk almost doubled in that year, but salaries for livestock workers had risen and some machinery costs had likewise doubled.[113]

Meanwhile, the supply of inputs through state channels had further deteriorated. The chairman of a livestock fattening enterprise in Kharkiv complained at the time that he was able to obtain only 30 percent of enterprise inputs – in this case, livestock feed – from state sources, even as the state order for meat remained relatively stable. The increase in feed prices prompted a greater need for self-reliance, leading him to break away from state coordination and seek out reliable business partners. This particular chairman, who would later become one of the district's best-known "reformers," saw the solution to input shortages in the breaking of "traditions." Otherwise, he argued, Kharkiv collectives would "no sooner see the market than our own ears."[114]

The refusal of some agricultural collectives to participate in command structures compelled a reaction from the state. Acknowledging that state prices for agricultural goods were low relative to the cost of production,

[110] S. Lobas, "Ekonomicheskoe obozrenie. Kuda zhe my idem? ... " *TT* 9 November 1991, 1.

[111] V. Ivanov, "Chrezvychainye obstoiatel'stva. Ekh, liudi, liudi...I vy eshche khotite 'bol'shogo moloka'... " *LZ* 14 November 1991, 1.

[112] V. Venevtsev, "Ekonomika raiona: itogi i prognozy," *RV*, 28 February 1991, 2–3.

[113] "Kachestvo – kategoriia ekonomicheskaia. Gde teriaem," *RV* 22 October 1991, 3. The cost of a Don-1500 more than doubled that year. A. Il'in, "Aktual'naia tema. Kak vpisat'sia v rynok?" *RV* 26 December 1991, 3.

[114] A. Reshetov, "Rynochnaia ekonomika: nakanune. Uverennost' pridaet sily," *TT* 16 April 1991, 2.

and that enterprises were free to sell surplus production to non-state entities,[115] state buyers tried to induce collectives to sell produce to the state
rather than on the open market. In Liski, state agencies raised prices on
produce, whereas in Khava, the district press reported that up to 50 percent of grain sold to state buyers beyond the food tax would be paid for
at world prices.[116] Other tactics included offering agricultural enterprises
the opportunity to exchange grain for prepared feed – but only after they
had fulfilled their contractual obligations to state buyers.[117]

The republican governments, facing widespread food shortages,
offered agricultural collectives additional material incentives for participating in central planning programs. In Khava, the local press advertised a national program of premiums to stimulate sale of agricultural
goods to state buyers. The Russian republic allotted a nationwide total of
100,000 light vehicles, 200,000 refrigerators, 150,000 washing machines,
and 200,000 televisions to enterprises that continued to supply agricultural goods to the state. In Russia, promises of technical assistance and
the subsidized sale of agricultural machinery and other material-technical
resources accompanied the imposition of the new food tax.[118] That state
buyers made such concessions suggested two things: that the state had lost
its control over collective and state farms, and that an informal commodities market had begun to develop. The state was no longer the only game
in town, and officials needed to work hard to gain the cooperation of agricultural collectives. The invisible hand of market coordination had begun
to work, even without a new institutional framework to support it.

Care for People

With the dissolution of Soviet power, the command structures that had
governed distribution at every level lost their grip on the countryside. At
the national level, the political forces of the day were centrifugal, spinning
fragments of the Soviet periphery away from Moscow into their own

---

[115] See, for example, A. Reshetov, "Urozhai-91. Khlebnyi krizis," *TT* 3 October 1991, 3.
[116] For example, state prices on squash in Liski in August 1991 were raised from seventeen
to thirty kopeks per kilogram. The state did not absorb the increased cost but passed it
on to consumers. Petrenko, "Rabotat' na sklad? Eto sovsem plokho?..." *LZ* 6 August
1991, 1.
[117] G. Panevin, "Khleb nash nasushchnyi," *RV* 3 August 1991, 1, 2. The terms of the
exchange were one ton of grain for one ton of kombikorm, or .7 tons mixed fodder for
one ton of rye.
[118] G. Panevin, "Khleb nash nasushchnyi," *RV* 3 August 1991, 1, 2.

orbits, and allowing rural locales greater autonomy. Meanwhile, weakened administrative chains of command granted new *de facto* discretion to local government institutions. After the Soviet collapse, transportation infrastructure deteriorated and fuel prices rose, and people on agricultural collectives traveled less to towns and cities. In the countryside, centripetal forces generated by this new isolation allowed local farm elites to gather strength and fill the vacuum created by the center's abandonment of its rural mandate.

Left to their own devices, directors of agricultural collectives and local state officials first focused on local development. Prior to the introduction of structural adjustment policies in Russia in 1992, heads of agricultural collectives on both sides of the border expanded assistance to workers and invested in social infrastructure. Chairmen of collective farms, who were elected by collective farm members, had a political incentive to do so. In Liski, one collective had invested more than 1 million rubles in infrastructural improvement in 1990, laying gas lines and asphalt, and constructing homes. The chairman expected that farm members would take notice and re-elect him.[119] In local state offices, officials responded similarly, outlining plans for economic development that mirrored platforms of candidates for the regional legislature and calling for "concrete assistance to the village" in the form of gas lines to village homes, health care improvement, and school construction (Illustration 1).[120]

Directors of state farms, who in contrast to chairmen of collective farms were not subject to electoral accountability, undertook many of the same social improvements. In 1991, the director of one state farm in Kharkiv reported spending 20 percent of the farm's profits on social programs, including laying new sidewalks and repairing the kindergarten building.[121] The farm offered workers meals for twenty kopeks in the company cafeteria and provided meat and honey at farm-subsidized prices.

---

[119] N. Pribytkov, "Otchety i vybory v kolkhozakh. Razgovor po bol'shomu schetu," *LZ* 13 February 1991, 1.

[120] O. Stoliarov, "'Nuzhen budu – vyberut. Liudi razberuts'ia...' schitaet Viktor Vladimirovich Shevtsov, glava mestnoi administratsii," *LZ* 19 November 1991, 2 and A. Levchenko, "Tvoia predvybornaia platforma, kandidat! 'Ia – za konkretnuiu pomoshch' selu...'" *LZ* 9 July 1991, 1.

[121] While this was a typical choice for well-off enterprises, it should be noted that many other enterprises did not have the resources to conduct repairs, let alone maintenance work on buildings. This problem is described in detail in A. Timofeev, "Deistvovat' obstoiatel'no, nastoichivo. Zametki s zasedaniia ispolkoma raionnogo Soveta narodnykh deputatov," *TT* 1 August 1991, 2.

ILLUSTRATION 1. A pensioner's kitchen in the village adjoining Chayanovskoe former collective farm, Voronezh, 1998. This household benefited from infrastructural improvements in the late Soviet period: note the gas burner on the lower right.

In the midst of developing market conditions, the director emphasized, the main thing was to improve the "everyday living conditions of our workers, provide necessary help with foodstuffs, and even to see how our people can more rationally use their salaries."[122]

Other state farms displayed their "care for people" by providing monthly subsidized food packages to their workers and pensioners, offering seasonal laborers the opportunity to purchase grain at reduced prices, building new housing for employees and new storage facilities, and providing transportation to urban areas.[123] Above all, agricultural collectives attempted to improve conditions through vertical consolidation of

[122] A. Reshetov, "Uverennost' pridaet sily," *TT* 16 April 1991, 2.
[123] For example, V. Lemishchenko, "S zabotoi o liudiakh. U rabochikh – svoia ferma," *TT*, 1 January 1991, 3; Lemishchenko, "I kartofel' sozrel..." *TT* 28 May 1991, 3; A. Sashin, "Sel'skie gorizonty: vremia, zemlia, liudi. Kakoi vklad, takaia i otdacha," *TT* 23 July 1991, 2; M. Gal', "Otchet direktora," *TT* 5 March 1991, 1; A. Reshetov, "Kommunist. Rukovoditel'. Direktorskie zadumki," *TT* 20 August 1991, 2; Reshetov, "Nazyvali zakholust'em," *TT* 10 September 1991, 2; G. Aleksandrov, "Na novykh nachalakh," *TT* 27 April 1991, 3.

production, adding processing facilities where possible.[124] All of these efforts were of particular importance in the changing fiscal environment of the Black Earth, where local state budgetary allocations for social spending receded even before the formal dissolution of Soviet power.[125]

State farm directors and officials who did not support local development answered to the press. When the deputy director of the Kharkiv district *gostorg* contracted with a neighboring district for vegetables because local state farms charged higher prices, the local newspaper criticized him for doing so.[126] Meanwhile, journalists enjoined local stores to sell greater volumes of goods produced in their district.[127] Local development was a matter of compelling professional interest even for Black Earth leaders who may not have held strong normative commitments to social welfare. Amidst a countryside already "on the verge of financial panic,"[128] they would no longer be protected by Moscow if they failed to respond to a rising sea of calamity.

The importance of agricultural collectives extended beyond the grain silos and tractor depots of Black Earth villages, as collective and state farms played newly crucial roles for nearby urban populations. At the urging of local executive and legislative bodies,[129] some collectives created "a union of hammer and sickle," repairing broken supply chains through reciprocal arrangements with local factories, and providing land and young animals for factory workers' household production in exchange for machinery, labor, and infrastructural repairs for farms.[130] Others traded thousands of kilos of meat, oil, milk, and vegetables for home appliances produced by nearby factories.[131]

Black Earth villagers continued to work on agricultural collectives despite the emerging importance of household production as a source

[124] A. Semin, "Zasedanie soveta APO," *TT* 26 October 1991, 1. These strategies would be characteristic of successful agricultural enterprises in the region a decade later.

[125] A. Khokhlov, "Zametki o zasedanii raiispolkoma. Bez alternativy," *TT* 23 November 1991, 1.

[126] For example, Danilenko, "Razve tol'ko tseny kusaiutsia?" *TT* 17 August 1991, 2.

[127] A. Timofeev, "Mestnye Sovety: radius deistviia. A tovarov bol'she ili men'she?" *TT* 21 December 1991, 2.

[128] "Chto bylo na nedele? Opiat' den'gi 'zhgut karmany'," *LZ* 17 September 1991, 1.

[129] "Nuzhny neotlozhnye mery," *RV* 26 March 1991, 1, 2.

[130] A. Golomedov, "Soiuz serpa i molota. Dogovor o vzaimopomoshchi zakliuchili truzheniki Uglianskogo zavoda pressovykh uzlov i kolkhoza imeni Sverdlova," *RV* 6 April 1991, 1. Other agreements are outlined in "Aktual'no. Na vzaimovygodnoi osnove," *RV* 30 March 1991, 1 and A. Anokhin, "Na vzaimovygodnoi osnove. Dogovor dorozhe deneg," *RV* 28 May 1991, 3.

[131] O. Reshetov, "Poshuky kontrakty," *TT* 4 April 1991, 2.

of food for both rural and urban populations.[132] Household production required capital; the absence of strong rural labor markets, together with limited mobility due to continuing registration regimes, led rural people to stay on the farm. Furthermore, state and collective farms offered an important set of social entitlements: housing and a residence permit; education for children; health care and transportation to a hospital in emergencies; payment for weddings, funerals, and other community expenses; and discounted prices for garden inputs.

Amidst widespread economic crisis and political uncertainty, agricultural collectives fulfilled a critical social function – ensuring the survival and stability of rural communities. Just as the rhetoric of national politics in Russia and Ukraine began to focus on open trade, export-driven economies, and individual responsibility in the workplace, collectives came to resemble small social welfare states deeply embedded in district-level networks. A time of deep social, political, and economic transformation had arrived in Black Earth villages, and collective and state farms were the only lifeboats passing by.

---

[132] Similar rural–urban linkages have been observed elsewhere, including Turkey. Paul Kaldjian, "The Small-Holder in Turkish Agriculture: Obstacle or Opportunity?" in Kurt E. Engelmann and Vjeran Pavlakovic, eds. *Rural Development in Eurasia and the Middle East: Land Reform, Demographic Change, and Environmental Constraints.* Seattle: University of Washington Press, 2001.

2

Keeping the Collectives

Amidst the economic crises that plagued Black Earth villages in the months following the Soviet collapse, the news that collective and state farms were to be privatized and, perhaps, disbanded was met with consternation in the countryside. In the early and mid-1990s, when land privatization first took place, political instability added to the burden that local elites faced in reforming major rural institutions. Just as collective farms had begun to adapt to emerging market conditions and had started to withdraw from the web of state control and incentives that characterized late Soviet life, reorganization policy brought the state back into the village.

Those charged with overseeing privatization were local officials, including heads of district administrations, state agricultural management officers, land tenure specialists, and members of land committees and village councils. Members of each of these categories had their own, distinct views on privatization, but their strategies in implementing reform usually converged under the leadership of district heads. Chairmen of collective farms and directors of state farms, hereafter referred to as farm directors, took part in the task at the enterprise level. However, they represented their own interests as businessmen during the process and were no longer employed by the state after the first, early round of enterprise reorganization.

Unsure of their political fortunes in an environment of uncertainty, and struggling to make decisions that would satisfy the current regime but forestall possible retribution by future leaders, local elites responded to initiatives from Moscow and Kyiv with dissimulation. Black Earth officials fulfilled the letter of the law, all the while encouraging and supporting farm directors' strategies to maintain collectives and prevent

worker-shareholders from leaving and taking their land and assets with
them. These actions were not always discernible in the written record
of reform, but they were observable at the local level – on farms and in
meetings between district level officials and farm directors.

In both Kharkiv and Voronezh, farm directors and local officials' efforts
to preserve collectives were not expressions of resistance to economic
liberalization as such, for their behavior did not stem from ideological
opposition to markets. Rather, they objected to individuation of property
insofar as it would both break apart local economies of scale, leaving the
countryside more vulnerable to crisis, and weaken the foundations of both
their power and the prevailing social order. Their choices were consistent
with market adaptation: farm directors were unwilling to allow workers
access to new rights at the expense of their own careers or the fortunes
of the farms they managed, and district administrators strove to retain
collectives as engines, however flawed, of rural development.

Each Will Know He Is an Owner

Land privatization began earlier in Russia than in Ukraine, but initial
efforts in both countries were flawed, leading national executives to call
for successive attempts to extricate agricultural collectives from state control and transfer farm assets to their members. The process was prolonged,
lasting over a decade in each case. On both sides of the border, land privatization centered on two policy initiatives: the reorganization of collective
and state farms as private enterprises in which workers and pensioners
would hold shares, and the creation of private family farms.[1] Amidst
battles over land reform in the national legislatures, presidential decrees
became the impetus for many of the changes that reformers in Moscow
and Kyiv envisioned for the countryside.

The rhetoric surrounding reform suggested private ownership would be
a panacea, with dramatic benefit to the economy, the state, and rural populations. Many proponents of privatization envisioned sweeping changes
that would transform the countryside. In their view, farm reorganization
would do away with collective agriculture as Russia and Ukraine knew
it, improving the lives of the entire rural population. As Sergei Nikol'skii

---

[1] Land codes in both countries provided for the private ownership of agricultural land and
private farming (Land Code of Ukraine (1991) S2/Ch7/A55 and Land Code of RSFSR
(1991) S3/Ch10/A58), followed by subsequent legislation affirming and clarifying those
rights.

has noted, the timing of the official introduction of reorganization policy in Russia, on 27 December, 1991, recalled Stalin's inauguration of collectivization on the same day in 1929, and Russian government officials likely chose the anniversary to mark the end of sixty-two years of collectivized agriculture.[2] The character of claims in Ukraine was equally revolutionary. The national newspaper *Den'* bragged at a late stage in the reorganization process that it "will affect the 22 million man army of land certificate holders."[3] After a December 1999 presidential decree on land reform, then Ukrainian Minister of Agrarian Politics Ivan Kyrylenko declared that by the time spring fieldwork had begun in the southern and central regions that year, "all collective agricultural enterprises should disappear from the social-economic map of Ukraine."[4]

Private ownership, in the view of its proponents, would make rural people more efficient producers. Mainstream policy makers held that formalizing new property relations would foster a strong sense of personal ownership and agency, as titling " ... will show peasants that they are creating their own, non-state, private enterprise."[5] Reformers also expected that reorganization would lead to a sense of individual control and responsibility. In Pavlovsk district of Voronezh, the local press proclaimed that, " ... each will know that he is an owner, he'll approach everything more thriftily (*po-khoziaiski*), he won't tolerate scofflaws, no-shows, loafers."[6] According to this logic, if workers held shares in agricultural enterprises they would be more motivated to work, as farm profits would be divided among shareholders. The head of the Kharkiv regional state administration captured these tropes in declaring his support for reform at his last press conference of 1999: measures passed by the regional council for implementation of land reform would, in his view, "provide the opportunity to make the villager an owner, a real master (*hospodar*), and in

---

[2] S. A. Nikol'skii, "Kollektivizatsiia i dekollektivizatsiia: sravnitel'nyi analiz protsessov, posledstvii i perspektiv," in V. P. Danilov and T. Shanin, eds. *Krest'ianovedenie 1997: teoriia, istoriia, sovremennost'.* Moscow: Aspekt Press, 1997.

[3] E. Kanevskiy, "Kuchma obeshchaet vvesti chastnuiu sobstvennost' na zemliu i rasformirovat' kolkhozy," *Den'*, December 3, 1999.

[4] N. Perstneva, "Vesna prishla! Chinovnik torzhestvuet... " *ZN* 25 March 2000. See also Yu. Kryklyvyi, "Liudyna kriz' pryzmu reform" *SK* 27 January 2000, 1–2.

[5] V. Uzun, ed. *Sotsial'no-ekonomicheskie posledstviia privatizatsii zemli i reorganizatsii sel'skokhoziaistvennykh predpriiatii 1994–96.* Moscow: Entsiklopediia rossiiskikh dereven', 1997, 37. The idea that titling will lead to development is a staple of economic analysis in the West. See, for example, Hernando de Soto, *The Mystery of Capital: Why Capitalism Triumphs in the West and Fails Everywhere Else.* New York: Basic Books, 2000.

[6] L. Dolgashova, "Gotovimsia k peremenam," *MP* 21 January 1992, 3.

the final analysis make a breakthrough in the agrarian sector of the economy."[7]

Reform had an explicitly normative purpose as well, in which privatization would be an instrument of independence for rural people.[8] The local press in Voronezh voiced this perception, albeit with slight irony, asking, "Will privatization allow the villager to feel like the master of the land on which he is fated to live and work? Probably it will. It will force the peasant to become his own master more quickly, for it will bring with it the incomparable joy of free labor."[9] In this view, the parceling of land plots and non-land assets of collective and state farms would provide agricultural workers the opportunity to transform their state of subjugation into a state of self-reliance.

Land privatization also targeted broad social transformation, shifting the meaning and purpose of economic activity from the locally oriented equilibrium of the early 1990s to a profit-oriented set of values and corresponding property rights and incentives. Through this process, it was thought, ownership would compel market behavior and introduce personal virtue into the life of the countryside. In a social scientific version of an old biological canard, personal evolution was expected to parallel the economic development of nations.[10] The peasant who owned the means of production would no longer be "free from ownership, and from responsibility."[11] Like colonial-era projects of "improvement" directed at indigenous populations, land privatization was a project to transform not only property rights, but also people.[12]

Reformers further imagined that privatization would serve a subsidiary political function. In conscious imitation of the Stolypin-era, "wager on the strong" policies of the early twentieth century that consolidated and parceled the land of communes, Russian reformers in the 1990s sought

---

[7] M. Khablak, "Oleh D'omin: ia viriu v uspikh reform," *SK* 31 December 1999, 1.

[8] Hillary Appel, *A New Capitalist Order: Privatization and Ideology in Russia and Eastern Europe*. Pittsburgh: University of Pittsburgh Press, 2004.

[9] "Kolkhozy: ne speshite davat' nam poslednee slovo," *LI* 10 October 1991, 5.

[10] The canard is that ontogeny, or the development of an individual organism, recapitulates phylogeny, or the evolution of a group of organisms. Stephen J. Gould, *Ontogeny and Phylogeny*. Cambridge: Belknap Press, 1977.

[11] A. Nikonov, "Sotsial'no-ekonomicheskie problemy agrarnoi reformy v Rossiiskoi Federatsii," *APK: ekonomika, upravlienie* (10) 1993, 15.

[12] The logic of development in Eastern Europe echoes ideas long applied to the global south. Frederick Cooper and Randall Packard, eds. *International Development and the Social Sciences: Essays on the History and Politics of Knowledge*. Berkeley: University of California Press, 1997.

to spur the development of a rural middle class that would act as a buffer between countryside and sovereign.[13] The beneficiaries of land privatization would support their liberal benefactors, so a rural property-holding class would serve the government as well as agricultural workers. As one representative of the Russian state land committee put it, "[a] broad stratum of owners is the foundation of stability for the entire state."[14]

The key stated aims of reorganization – improved production efficiency and the creation of an independent rural class of property owners – were linked to one another and to a pair of assumptions on the part of reformers: first, that individual ownership was key to an efficient use of resources; and second, that the system of collectivized agriculture could be successfully transformed by reforming individual enterprises. By dividing title to collective farm resources among their members, enterprises would fulfill two of the aims of reorganization at once. Workers would become owners, and with the financial incentives believed necessary for hard work in place, reorganized enterprises would function more effectively. The first of these aims met organized opposition from local state officials and farm directors throughout the process. The second, as Chapter 5 shows, foundered on the shoals of pricing, marketing, and trade regimes.

One Revolution Is Enough

Despite statements of support for reform when they spoke before television cameras and to journalists from the national capitals, state officials in the Black Earth responded to privatization policy with a distinct lack of enthusiasm. Confronted with local audiences, officials articulated deep concern about the possible effects of land distribution.[15] In Ukraine, opposition was widespread and prolonged: speaking of loan conditions the IMF had imposed on Ukraine in 1999, the deputy director of the state property fund remarked of land reform, "Most of official Ukraine doesn't

---

[13] See David Kerans, *Mind and Labor on the Farm in Black-Earth Russia, 1861–1914*. Budapest and New York: Central European University Press, 2001, 313; David A. J. Macey, "Reforming Agriculture in Russia: The 'Cursed' Question from Stolypin to Yeltsin," in Michael Kraus and Ronald D. Liebowitz, eds. *Russia and Eastern Europe After Communism: The Search for New Political, Economic, and Security Systems*. Boulder: Westview Press, 1996. 103–121; Teodor Shanin, *Russia, 1905–07: Revolution as a Moment of Truth*. New Haven: Yale University Press, 1986.

[14] *Trud*, 15 February 1996, 2.

[15] See Jessica Allina-Pisano, "Sub Rosa Resistance and the Politics of Economic Reform: Land Redistribution in Post-Soviet Ukraine," *World Politics* 56 (July 2004) for a discussion of the "public transcript" of reform in Ukraine.

want privatization to proceed in the manner outlined in the 2000 privatization program, but the need to raise money for the budget is forcing their hands."[16] In Russia, district officials likewise paid public lip service to the aims of privatization but worried about its effects. The deputy state administration head in Liski warned in 1992 that "One revolution in the village is enough for us. Russia won't survive a second.... I'm convinced that private farming has a big future. But today it's the collective farms nonetheless that feed us."[17]

Ambivalent positioning toward privatization began at the top, with legislation that called for the individuation and distribution of land shares, but allowed preservation of collectives. In this respect, Russian and Ukrainian reform policy recalls the mixed signals and reversals articulated by governments in Romania, Bulgaria, and elsewhere.[18] The regional deputy head of Kharkiv state administration suggested that politicians in Kyiv might have intended for local officials to resist, noting that reform legislation "doesn't provide for the destruction of the collective agricultural enterprise at all, it's even the opposite."[19]

Even in Ukraine, where most state officials answered to Kyiv rather than to the local constituencies that voted to elect some of their counterparts in Russia, officials executed the formal requirements of privatization while defying key elements of reform policy – despite threats from the presidential administration to fire functionaries who did not carry out its demands.[20] Hidden insubordination was not unusual in post-socialist Europe: in Transylvania, Verdery describes the notion that local officials would comply with national policy as "a laughable image."[21] It should be noted, however, that uncertainty shaped the covert character of state officials' resistance. In the event of a regime change – in particular, a communist resurgence – officials could claim to have avoided the "selling

---

[16] A. Berdnick, "New leader to face up to IMF targets," *KP* 11 November 1999.

[17] V. Pleshkov, "Chtob zemliu krest'ianam v Rossii otdat' ne obiazatel'no v odnochas'e kolkhozy uprazdniat'," *LI* 9 January 1992, 2.

[18] David Kideckel, "Once Again, the Land: Decollectivization and Social Conflict in Rural Romania," in Hermine DeSoto and David Anderson, eds. *The Curtain Rises: Rethinking Culture, Ideology, and the State in Eastern Europe.* Atlantic Highlands, NJ: Humanities Press, 1993; Gerald Creed, "The Politics of Agriculture: Identity and Socialist Sentiment in Bulgaria," *Slavic Review* 54:4 (Winter 1995) 843–868.

[19] Yu. Kryklyvyi, "Zemel'na reforma ne lyshe dlia sela, a i dlia vs'oho narodu," *SK* 21 December 1999, 2.

[20] OT (Oral Testimony), Kharkiv regional farmers' association conference, 18 January 2000.

[21] K. Verdery, "Seeing Like a Mayor, Or, How Local Officials Obstructed Romanian Land Restitution," *Ethnography* 3:1 (2002) 27.

off" [*razbazarivanie*] of land – an action, they believed, that could bring punishment in the future.

Despite their powers of discretion in implementing reform, officials at the district and village level had little say in its formulation. Privatization policy originated in national capitals; notwithstanding the revolutionary character of reformers' claims, land privatization policies mandated far less support or active participation from the center than previous attempts at redistribution. Unlike in other major land reform efforts earlier in the century, Moscow and Kyiv did not dispatch cadres to the countryside to oversee and secure the implementation of reorganization.[22] Officials charged with implementing post-Soviet land privatization were rural insiders with broad legislated and *de facto* power in implementing reform policy. The enactment of enterprise reorganization and land privatization depended to an almost unprecedented degree on their cooperation – cooperation that, as Verdery likewise found in Transylvania, was not forthcoming.[23]

The reasons local officials gave for their opposition to land privatization included a mix of pragmatism and normative commitments rooted in Soviet-era culture. In contrast to land reform in post-socialist Bulgaria, where Creed has shown that major party structures and distinct ideological persuasions were central to land battles, political ideology did not play a central role in shaping Black Earth officials' response to reform.[24] Participation in strategies to preserve collectives crossed ideological lines and included supporters of state parties, members of the communist and nationalist oppositions, and officials who identified themselves as apolitical. Foot-dragging and other covert attempts to forestall large-scale transformation occurred at all levels of local bureaucracy: among leaders of district administrations; in the offices of state economists, land tenure specialists, and land committee members; and within village councils.

[handwritten margin note: Bureaucratic weapons of the weak.]

---

[22] For an account of the use of supervisory cadres during the attempts at land reform implemented under Russian Prime Minister Petr Stolypin (1906–1911), see George Yaney, *The Urge to Mobilize: Agrarian Reform in Russia, 1861–1930*. Urbana: University of Illinois, 1982. For Soviet era campaigns, see Lynne Viola's study of the *dvadtsatipiatitysiachniki* (25,000ers), the shock troops of the rural mobilization campaigns of the first Five-Year Plan. Viola, *The Best Sons of the Fatherland: Workers in the Vanguard of Soviet Collectivization*. Oxford: Oxford University Press, 1987.

[23] K. Verdery, "Seeing Like a Mayor, Or, How Local Officials Obstructed Romanian Land Restitution," *Ethnography* 3:1 (2002) 5–33.

[24] Gerald W. Creed, "The Politics of Agriculture: Identity and Socialist Sentiment in Bulgaria," *Slavic Review* 54:4 (Winter 1995) 843–868.

Many local officials were career agricultural professionals who regarded the privatization and individuation of collectively held land as potentially disastrous.[25] All hoped to avoid the catastrophic disruption in production that radical, large-scale land repartition would inevitably bring. Agricultural collectives were not only the main producers of food and a crucial source of inputs for household gardens, but also social linchpins: institutions that provided a set of social goods and services to rural populations and helped maintain social order and stability. In Kharkiv, a district representative of city administration warned that the division of collective farm land into shares would mean "the collapse of agricultural production, and therefore for the entire economy,"[26] and the chairman of the Khava agro-industrial association argued, "In the end it's not the organizational forms of the agrarian sector that are so important for us, but rather . . . whether or not we can quickly solve the food problem. . . . "[27]

Given the absence of viable alternatives to collective farms at the time, some local officials expressed head-shaking amazement at the proposals emanating from Kyiv and Moscow. In Voronezh, a district agricultural official articulated a common sentiment when he marveled in 1992, "But now, when private farms have started to appear, they're simply physically incapable of feeding the people. And at the same time to liquidate the collective farms. . . . "[28] Such responses persisted over time. In Kharkiv, the head of the regional council noted in 2000 that "we have to live within the laws of economics, and not in conflict with them." A reporter commented on the bitter tone of the these last remarks, comparing them to "the intonation I felt from 'Afghans' [Soviet veterans of the war in

---

[25] K. Verdery discusses the professionalism of Romanian state farm directors, as well as unflattering stereotypes about them, in *The Vanishing Hectare: Property and Value in Postsocialist Transylvania.* Ithaca: Cornell University Press, 2003, 283–4. The professional quality of post-Soviet rural cadres was thrown into relief in the wake of Ukraine's "Orange Revolution," as political appointees with no experience in agriculture came to populate Kharkiv government offices, bringing much work to a standstill. As one young lawyer put it, "I stood on Maidan [the square in Kyiv that drew hundreds of thousands of protesters in 2004], so the President thanked me by giving me this post" as a deputy district head. Another newly appointed district agricultural official, until recently the director of a brewery, noted that he didn't plan to stay in his new position unless it allowed him to make business deals. OT, Kharkiv region, July 2006.

[26] M. Mel'nyk, "Chy rai zemel'nyi pai?" *SK* 7 October 1995, 2.

[27] A. Bykhanov, "Zavtra – Den' rabotnikov sel'skogo khoziaistva i pererabatyvaiushchei promyshlennosti. Nesmotria na trudnosti." *RV* 16 November 1991, 1.

[28] V. Biriuchinskii, "I vse-taki reorganizatsiia neizbezhna," *MP* 26 January 1992, 3.

Afghanistan] who spoke about the unjust character of the war where they spilled their blood."[29]

Some of those who oversaw privatization emphasized Soviet ideas of social responsibility in explaining their positions.[30] In Voronezh, the regional legislature made explicit this idea by offering debt relief for enterprises of "social significance."[31] As one Ukrainian reform working group member emphasized, "The thing is that *kolkhozy* or collective agricultural enterprises are not only a collective method of production, but a collective method of life."[32] Rural people regarded agriculture not as a profit-generating mechanism but as a means of feeding the population,[33] and farm directors were willing to run at a slight loss to produce "goods of social significance."[34] As the head of a Kharkiv district emphasized in 1999, "Production is for people, and not the reverse."[35] Provincial officials either shared this approach or, as the aforementioned statement may suggest, believed that they needed to be seen as sharing it.

State officials did not frame their choices exclusively in terms of Soviet norms. Some used the idiom of the market to explain their actions. When a district head in Kharkiv spoke at a closed meeting to discuss implementation of land privatization policy, he defended his decision to protect

[29] Yu. Kryklyvyi, "Liudyna kriz' pryzmu reform," *SK* 27 January 2000, 1–2.

[30] Irina Koznova, "Sovremennaia agrarnaia reforma i istoricheskaia pamiat' russkikh krest'ian," in *Uspekh reform – v osoznanii ikh neobkhodimosti. Opyt provedeniia agrarnykh preobrazovanii v Orlovskoi oblasti.* Orel: Turgenevskii berezhok, 1995, 370. References to these ideas with respect to agriculture are far too numerous to discuss here; evidence of the belief that land should not be commodified may be found in the Russian and Ukrainian parliaments' more than decade-long debate about legalizing the purchase and sale of agricultural land.

[31] Prilozhenie k postanovleniiu glavy administratsii oblasti, 18 April 1997, No. 406.

[32] Yu. Kryklyvyi, "Zupynka na pivdorozi. Rivnoznachna vidstupovi," *SK* 6 January 2000, 2.

[33] For this and other reasons, commodification of land was not supported by much of the rural population. A random sample survey ($n = 925$) conducted in 1998 by the national land committee in Kharkiv and Volyn regions found that only 12.5 percent of those surveyed reported a positive attitude toward the purchase and sale of land held by agricultural enterprises; 27.1 percent agreed that "the purchase and sale of land must be regulated by the state"; and 57 percent said they were against the commodification of agricultural land. "Informatsiinyi biuleten' shchodo reformuvannia zemel'nykh vidnosyn v Ukraini," Kyiv: Derzhkomzem, 1998.

[34] Interview, director, Chayanovskoe, 21 August 1998.

[35] M. Mel'nyk, "'Vyrobnytstvo – dlia liudei, a ne navpaky': interv'iu z holovoiu derzhadministratsii Kharkivs'koho raionu V. I. Pugachovym," *SK* 13 May 1999, 2. This sentiment is echoed in hundreds if not thousands of press materials from the late Soviet period and post-Soviet decade in the region.

collectives from dissolution and their leadership from change using the language of long-term economic viability: "How will Western investors see this? The Western investor will see that it's possible to work with a single person for ten years."[36] Such statements, however, were less frequent than references to social responsibility. In Kharkiv, the prevailing atmosphere among the local agricultural elite was not favorable initially to changes associated with capitalist modes of production. A sign of this atmosphere was evident in a speech by one successful and reform-minded enterprise director who said "excuse me" every time he introduced market terminology, as in " ... excuse me, profits."[37]

This set of apparently conflicting narratives may suggest that ideas served mainly as rhetorical justification for actions driven mainly by more practical concerns. It is worth noting, however, that one set of ideas consistent with local economic incentives structures and common to both Soviet agricultural practices and contemporary agribusiness may have motivated local state officials who resisted the partition of land. This objection was not rooted in opposition to private property as such but to proposed radical shifts in the scale of production.

State officials maintained an allegiance to ideas developed under Soviet rule, but observers who impute obstruction to communist ideology wrongly identify *which* Soviet-era beliefs drove their behavior. As they did in other socialist contexts, rural officials in Russia and Ukraine shared a belief in the centrality of agriculture to national life.[38] In the Black Earth, this included a commitment to modernization – scientific, mechanized, large-scale agricultural production – that was a more important ideational component of their opposition to privatization than belief in collective ownership as such. In the Black Earth, one reason for resisting partition was painfully obvious to anyone who passed through fields of successfully partitioned former collectives in late autumn at the end of the twentieth century: without access to appropriate technology for small-scale production, dissolution of large-scale enterprises sometimes meant that men driving massive machinery literally were replaced by men

---

[36] OT, L'viv district, 8 January 2000.

[37] OT, L'viv district administration, 13 January 2000. The same director is quoted in Chapter 1, 47.

[38] Gerald W. Creed, "The Politics of Agriculture: Identity and Socialist Sentiment in Bulgaria," *Slavic Review* 54:4 (winter 1995) 843–868, and Arvid Nelson, *Cold War Ecology: Forest, Farms and People in the East German Landscape.* New Haven: Yale University Press, 2005.

pulling wooden plows.[39] Local officials, as well as people who worked the land, frequently bemoaned such a "return to the nineteenth century," and as workers grew tired of back-breaking labor for little profit, such a condition would not last for long.

An additional, unspoken reason also likely motivated officials' behavior. Although state officials had more to gain personally by pushing privatization and collecting rents on land distribution than by undermining it, resistance also brought them some benefit. Some local officials, as Hellman has suggested, may have reason to obstruct *market entry* in order to maintain access to monopoly rents, but Black Earth state officials acted to prevent the individuation of land ownership on enterprises that were themselves already participating in markets.[40] Therefore, as Verdery suggests was the case in Transylvania, local officials had an incentive to withhold titling of a finite good that, once distributed, would no longer serve as a basis for patronage.[41] Furthermore, resistance to privatization offered state officials an opportunity to recapture power they had lost following the Soviet collapse. As at-will marketization by agricultural collectives drained coercive power from the state, local state officials saw their control over economic life wane. Those officials must have understood that if they were to regain the control they had wielded under the command system, it would be necessary to preserve collective forms of production. Such enterprises would be far more "legible" and easier to regulate than the small-scale farms that reformers envisioned.[42]

With Only My Stamp in My Hand

For different reasons, farm directors also responded with apprehension to the radical promises of privatization policy. Their concerns were known early in the process, so much so that the chairman of the Liski agro-industrial association felt compelled to offer reassurances that reform would improve, not destroy, agricultural enterprises: "The talk is not

---

[39] Because of the cost of feeding draft animals, "even a horse is a luxury," in the words of one local cliché.

[40] Joel S. Hellman, "Winners Take All: The Politics of Partial Reform in Postcommunist Transitions," *World Politics* 50 (January 1998), 205.

[41] Katherine Verdery "Seeing Like a Mayor, Or, How Local Officials Obstructed Romanian Land Restitution," *Ethnography* 3:1 (2002) 18.

[42] James C. Scott, *Seeing Like a State: How Certain Schemes to Improve the Human Condition Have Failed*. New Haven: Yale University Press, 1998.

about disbandment, but about privatization."[43] Directors had multiple reasons to oppose the individuation of property rights, and while some directors' statements about privatization had normative undertones, as in a Pavlovsk chairman's observation of "a troubling tendency of land transfer to private hands,"[44] directors' opposition to the individuation of property derived mainly from their professional milieu and personal ambition.

Agricultural collectives already had embarked upon market-oriented transformation without prodding from Moscow and Kyiv, and the practical challenges that consumed directors' workdays revolved around problems that would not be addressed by property rights reform: broken supply and distribution networks, shortages of skilled labor, incursions of urban populations, and the provision of social services in the context of ever tightening budgets. The decisions of national politicians seemed, in the view of one Liski farm chairman, to be at best "all words":

Their actions are more like the opposite. They undertake everything so that collective and state farms don't get firmly on their feet, with their price game on agricultural machinery, vehicles, fertilizer, various types of services. They've set as their goal bankrupting the collective and state farms. Supposedly only private farmers can feed the country. That's all nonsense! Ask any one of our 800 collective farm members whether they're for the dissolution of the collective farm. I'm sure that not one of them will give a positive answer.[45]

Whether or not all rural people would have shared that assessment, Black Earth villagers had "already tasted Pavlovian experiments"[46] and, like the directors of agricultural collectives, faced more pressing concerns than enterprise reorganization.[47]

---

[43] V. Pleshkov, "Chtoby zemliu krest'ianam v Rossii otdat' ne obiazatel'no v odnochas'e *kolkhozy* uprazdniat'," *LI* 9 January 1992, 2.

[44] V. Kolodiazhnyi, "Otchety i vybory v kolkhozakh. Kholoden li veter peremen?" *MP* 14 Feburary 1998, 3.

[45] V. Golovin, "Partiinaia zhizn': grani sotsial'noi zashchity. Vozrozhdennoe selo," *LZ* 3 July 1991, 2.

[46] "Chto bylo na nedele? Opiat' den'gi 'zhgut karmany,'" *LZ* 17 September 1991, 1.

[47] See Jessica Allina-Pisano, "Reorganization and Its Discontents: A Case Study in Voronezh oblast'" in David O'Brien and Stephen Wegren, eds. *Rural Reform in Post-Soviet Russia.* Washington and Baltimore: Woodrow Wilson Center Press and Johns Hopkins University Press, 2002; Liesl Gambold Miller and Patrick Heady, "Cooperation, Power and Community: Economy and Ideology in the Russian Countryside," in Chris Hann, ed. *The Postsocialist Agrarian Question: Property Relations and the Rural Condition,* Vol.1. Halle Studies in the Anthropology of Eurasia. Münster: Lit Verlag, 2003.

ILLUSTRATION 2. Collectively cultivated field, with private allotment in center, Kharkiv, 2006.

The privatization and allotment of land parcels threatened to create a patchwork of collective fields. Should it succeed, farm personnel faced the prospect of navigating tractors and combines through vast fields of industrial crops interrupted by scattered private plots – allotments that, most likely, would be planted with crops appropriate for manual cultivation rather than the grain, sugar beet, and other industrial crops common in the late twentieth-century Black Earth. In order to reach those plots, private owners would trample the seedlings cultivated by the reorganized collective (Illustration 2). For farms already struggling to survive or compete in a hostile economic environment, such a future was unthinkable. The allotment of land seemed to some directors a road to serfdom: as one Kharkiv director put it, echoing villagers in Bulgaria who described decollectivization as an "old song in a new voice,"[48] "Where are we hurrying to?... Let's not once again end up hungry on a harvest of sorrow, as after... collectivization in the beginning of the 1930s."[49]

---

[48] Gerald W. Creed, "The Politics of Agriculture: Identity and Socialist Sentiment in Bulgaria," *Slavic Review* 54:4 (Winter 1995) 859.
[49] M. Mel'nyk, "Chy rai zemel'nyi pai?" *SK* 7 October 1995, 2.

Directors also worried about their own fortunes. The acting minister of agriculture in Ukraine warned in 1999 that "the government will have to overcome strong opposition... by collective farm directors, who have previously blocked all attempts to reform the sector, fearing that they will lose their lucrative positions."[50] In Kharkiv, a director of a large agricultural enterprise who also headed a private farm observed, "If I were the director [of a collective that shareholders were leaving], I'd run away... I'd be left with only my stamp in my hand."[51] Directors had a direct personal incentive to prevent allotment of land to workers, for as a farmer in Zolochiv put it, "Disinterest in these reforms lies first of all with chairmen of the collectives, that's first of all. Because it's out from under their easy chairs... Who wants to concede [power]...? Therefore, he'll hang on by any means to collective ownership."[52]

In the face of multiple, overlapping incentives to preserve large-scale agriculture, and as the state withdrew from the provision of social services and agricultural subsidy regimes, farm directors had little to gain by complying with all of the demands emanating from Moscow and Kyiv. As farm directors learned to negotiate markets, they sacrificed the rights of members of collectives to short-term profit and consolidation of their own power. Meanwhile, they avoided possible retribution for opposition to reform by hiding their strategies to preserve collectives behind a facade of compliance with the law.

You Can't Invite Everyone

On 2 March 1992, members of Chayanovskoe, a collective farm in a central district of Voronezh, gathered to vote on the reorganization of their enterprise. The collective farm commission charged with overseeing the reform process had proposed to reorganize the collective as a limited liability partnership. According to farm records, and in keeping with a long tradition of relegating dissent to the margins of political life on the collective farm, the membership voted unanimously to do so. The same records testify that in 1992, members of the collective unanimously passed every motion related to privatization. Minutes of the 2 March meeting show that of 357 members, 238 attended the meeting – precisely 66.7 percent of the *kolkhoz* population, the same proportion needed to approve changes

[50] K. Gorchinskaya, "President issues land reform decree," *KP* 9 December 1999.
[51] Interview, director, Modern, XK, 14 January 2000.
[52] Interview, farmer Chernets'kyi, ZK, 3 January 2000.

in the legal status of the farm. According to attendance records, the same number purportedly attended every meeting in 1992 that required a vote on some aspect of the reform process, though it is unclear how many members actually attended.[53] As the farm chairman pointed out six years later during a subsequent round of reorganization, he tried to select a meeting time convenient for all members of the collective. However, "you can't invite everyone"[54] to the general assembly.

The scene on Chayanovskoe was typical, and over 80 percent of the collective and state farms in its district were also reorganized as limited liability partnerships.[55] In Liski, directors of collectives described reorganization as having been conducted "from above," according to the usual procedure: the general assembly would vote "unanimously" after the chairman had spoken, and "whatever was proposed, they chose."[56] In Semiluki, the head economist of the Il'ich collective noted that "the general assembly voted unanimously . . . no one rebelled," adding that the farm retained its name because "our uncle [Lenin] didn't do anything wrong."[57] Across the border in Kharkiv, similar social hierarchies governed voting procedures and behavior on collectives. Directors determined the outcomes of ostensibly collective decisions and faced the administrative challenge of enumerating numbers of shareholders and locating halls where hundreds of people could assemble to participate in the liturgy of privatization. In a southern district of Kharkiv, one agricultural official justified a less than democratic procedure in precisely the terms used by the chairman of Chayanovskoe: "In our district we don't have a space for 250 people."[58]

Reorganization involved two basic steps: the formal constitution of collective and state farms as non-state enterprises, and the transfer of ownership rights from the state to the individuals who lived and worked on the farms in question. Unlike the industrial privatization that occurred parallel to rural reforms in Russia and Ukraine, collectively held assets were transferred directly to workers and pensioners rather than privatized at

---

[53] Minutes of the general assembly of Chayanovskoe, 1992.

[54] Interview, chairman, Chayanovskoe, 10 September 1998.

[55] This form of collective organization had since been declared invalid. In 1998, Chayanovskoe and other collectives in the district reregistered for the third time in seven years, that time simply as a commercial organization.

[56] Interview, head economist of Fatherland, LV, May 2000; interview, director of the Chapaev cooperative. Humphrey observes a similar procedure in *Marx Went Away But Karl Stayed Behind*. Ann Arbor: University of Michigan Press, 2001.

[57] Interview, Il'ich kolkhoz, SV, May 2000.

[58] OT, district administration, BK, 30 March 2000.

auction. Under land privatization policy, worker-shareholders and some pensioners were entitled to shares in the land and non-land assets of former state and collective farms. As the holders of new rights, they were free to use or lease their land shares, and to collect rents on their shares. They could not, for the first decade of the reform period, sell their land or use it as collateral.

Not all members of agricultural collectives were included in the process. Long-retired pensioners, as well as education, health care, and other social service workers, did not initially receive shares, "as if all that time they lived and worked not in the village but on another planet."[59] This procedural rule struck many villagers as unfair and arbitrary, and because most social sphere workers were women, it introduced a dimension of gender inequity into the privatization process. Humphrey quotes a Siberian schoolteacher arguing on this account that "I have worked my entire life educating your children, and now you deny me enough hay-land to feed my two cows."[60]

In contrast to the procedure in other countries in Eastern Europe, where state and collective farms began the post-socialist period as very different kinds of enterprises and followed distinct privatization trajectories, the procedure for reform was nearly identical for collective and state farms in Ukraine and Russia. There, the two farm types retained different payment and governance principles but otherwise had converged as organizational forms during the late Soviet period. Furthermore, increasing localization and the disintegration of party structures in the countryside allowed collective farm chairmen and the directors of state farms similar degrees of *de facto* control over the reorganization process.

Directors of collective and state farms chose from a variety of organizational options: joint-stock companies, agricultural cooperatives, private enterprises, limited liability companies, and others.[61] Some forms offered distinct advantages. For example, managers of heavily indebted collectives could individuate risk and debt by declaring the collective bankrupt and reregistering it as an agricultural cooperative in which individual members would share legal liability.[62] Most collective and state farms

---

[59] Mikhail Nikonov, "V partiiakh i dvizheniiakh. SPS – na pul'se krest'ianskogo interesa," *KO* 21 August 2003.

[60] Caroline Humphrey, *Marx Went Away But Karl Stayed Behind*. Ann Arbor: University of Michigan Press, 2001, 453.

[61] For an exposition of the mechanics of reorganization in Russia, see Wegren, *Agriculture and the State in Soviet and Post-Soviet Russia*. Pittsburgh: University of Pittsburgh Press, 1998, Ch. 3.

[62] In Voronezh, see Annick Grandmange, "Ni immobilisme ni chaos: les mutations de la propriété et de l'usage des terres à Verkhni Ikorets (Russie), *Mappemonde* 67 (2002.3) 2.

in Russia either became limited liability companies or retained their former form of organization.[63] In early iterations of enterprise reorganization in Ukraine, the majority of collective and state farms became collective agricultural enterprises, and later, private enterprises and limited liability companies.[64] However, because of the organizational autonomy granted all reorganized enterprises, meaningful variation in most formal attributes of the new forms was, as Humphrey suggests, "something of an illusion."[65]

Directors who retained previous organizational forms did so strategically. On Chapaev collective farm in Liski, as on many former collectives, an agricultural workers' cooperative was chosen because it "corresponded to the previous form": "It was a collective farm before, and it remains a collective farm."[66] The managers of another Liski collective likewise chose a workers' cooperative because it was "closest to a collective farm," rather than a joint stock company, which was "too expensive."[67] In Kharkiv, private enterprises and limited liability companies were "most popular" because "to a certain degree, a [limited liability] company can be considered a collective."[68] Finally, closed forms of ownership allowed directors to avoid potential outside interference.[69]

The State Farm Kept All the Certificates for Itself

Farm directors in Voronezh and Kharkiv used a number of strategies to retain control over worker-shareholders' labor, land, and assets.[70] Some

---

[63] *Sel'skoe khoziaistvo Rossii*. Moscow: Goskomstat, 1995, 49.

[64] Mykola Pugachov with Don Van Atta, "Reorganization of Agricultural Enterprises in Ukraine in 2000: A Research Note," *Post-Soviet Geography and Economics* 41 (October–November 2000).

[65] Caroline Humphrey, *Marx Went Away But Karl Stayed Behind*. Ann Arbor: University of Michigan Press, 2001, 448.

[66] Interview, director, Chapaev, LV, 8 May 2000.

[67] Interview, head economist of Fatherland, LV, May 2000. Also see Humphrey, *Marx Went Away But Karl Stayed Behind*. Ann Arbor: University of Michigan Press, 2001, 449.

[68] Interview, district administration, CK, 21 July 2006.

[69] See Simon Johnson and Zanny Minton-Beddoes, "The Acquisition of Private Property Rights in Ukrainian Agriculture," in John McMillan and Barry Noughton, eds. *Reforming Asian Socialism: The Growth of Market Institutions*. Ann Arbor: University of Michigan Press, 1996, 254.

[70] Others have observed this tendency, including Verdery, *The Vanishing Hectare: Property and Value in Postsocialist Transylvania*. Ithaca: Cornell University Press, 2003, and Wegren, who interprets such strategies as ordinary, self-interested managerial behavior but assigns a positive normative value to it, noting that "obtaining the best through privatization was often condemned by Western analysts," *The Moral Economy Reconsidered: Russia's Search for Agrarian Capitalism*. New York: Palgrave, 2005, 78.

manipulated lists of shareholders, and people with a right to land shares were "dropped off the lists."[71] Conversely, as Kideckel has observed in Romania, people with no claim to land sometimes were included on those lists.[72] Some directors withheld land share certificates, preventing worker-shareholders from gaining access to their land. On reorganized farms in both Russia and Ukraine, villagers at first received a certificate entitling them to an amount of land on the territory of the farm where they worked. The location of the plot would not be identified, and the land would not be allotted, until and unless the shareholder wished either to lease the land to an entity other than the reorganized collective, or to use the land personally. Worker-shareholders who allotted land received a new document, a state act. However, they could lease land shares to the reorganized collective using their certificates, without identifying a concrete plot of land. Because allotment required that shareholders have their land certificates in hand, directors who withheld access to the certificates helped prevent worker-shareholders from exiting the collective and ensured the collective continuing use of their land.

Reports from the two sides of the border announced a single story with dull regularity. In Voronezh, "land is leased to the chairman. Nominally, to the cooperative or joint-stock company but in essence to the chairman . . . [73] and in Kharkiv "the chairman [of each farm] leased the land and non-land assets . . . He feels that to some degree it's his."[74] In 1999, on the heels of a presidential land-reform decree, the deputy head of the Kharkiv regional administration thus complained that, "Here and there the conditions concerning the lease of land and non-land shares are being ignored . . . preventing the exit of villagers from collective agricultural enterprises."[75] Ordinarily, there was no managerial turnover upon

---

[71] Interview, farmer, L'viv district, 12 April 2000.

[72] Kideckel, "Once Again, the Land: Decollectivization and Social Conflict in Rural Romania," in Hermine DeSoto and David Anderson, eds. *The Curtain Rises: Rethinking Culture, Ideology, and the State in Eastern Europe.* Atlantic Highlands, NJ: Humanities Press, 1993.

[73] Y. Chernichenko, "Burov mgloiu nebo kroet. Kak novyi predsedatel' kolkhoza Burov dovel starikov do ubiistva korovy," *NG* 25 April 2005.

[74] Interview, deputy head, L'viv district, 19 July 2006. This sentiment had a parallel in Soviet industry, where " . . . the directors [of factories] consider them to be theirs." Aleksandr Vysokovskii, "Will Domesticity Return?" in William Craft Brumfield and Blair A. Ruble, eds. *Russian Housing in the Modern Age: Design and Social History.* Washington, DC, and Cambridge: Woodrow Wilson Center Press and Cambridge University Press, 1993. 271–308.

[75] Kryklyvyi, "Zemel'na reforma ne lyshe dlia sela a i dlia vs'oho narodu," *SK* 21 December 1999, 2.

reorganization, so most directors controlled the process from start to finish. Privatized farms were "the same enterprises, the same chairmen,"[76] and worker-shareholders had few options for using their property at the start of the process. As a milkmaid in Nizhegorodskaia region of Russia described leasing to ethnographer Irina Koznova, "They told me, where you work is where you'll turn in [your share].'"[77]

Black Earth directors of reorganized farms kept records showing that they had distributed land share certificates to individual shareholders. However, many kept those certificates out of the reach of shareholders – in their office safes.[78] For this and other reasons, as the chairman of a Russian parliamentary committee put it in 2006, villagers who wanted to allot their land had to "walk through the fires of hell...several times."[79] This was true of both relatively successful and foundering enterprises: the director of one of the strongest collectives in Kharkiv was famous for keeping shareholders' certificates in the company safe. During large public gatherings in his district, audience members occasionally heckled him on this account.[80] This strategy was widespread, though not omnipresent, in the Black Earth. A survey conducted by the Ukrainian state land committee in Kharkiv in 1998 showed that in initial rounds of land share certificate distribution, 26 percent of respondents had not received a certificate at all, and 14 percent reported that their certificate was being kept by the enterprise for safekeeping.[81]

The practice of withholding access to certificates was widely acknowledged among shareholders on both sides of the national border, but it did not often appear in the documentary record. Where it did, negative confirmations could be most telling. One Kharkiv journalist implicitly acknowledged the generalized character of the practice by pointing to its absence in a particular instance: "The managers of the farms hid nothing; they

[76] Interview, department of agricultural management, ZK, 19 July 2006.

[77] Koznova, "Traditsii i novatsii v povedenii sovremennykh krest'ian," in *Identichnost' i konflikt v postsovetskikh gosudarstvakh, sbornik statei.* Moscow, 1997, 363.

[78] L. Lohvynenko, "Zemlia ne za 'simoma zamkamy,'" *SK* 11 January 2000, 2; A. Andreevna, "Sertifikatu doveriai, no proveriai," *Sovetskaia Chuvashaia* 17 May 2003; Miroslava Dem'ianchuk, "Zemel'nyi marafon na vyzhivanie," *Krasnoiarskii rabochii* 4 June 2002.

[79] "Predsedatel' komiteta Gosdumy po agrarnym voprosam Gennadii Kulik: 'Chtoby oformit' sebe uchastok zemli, nado ne prosto proiti muki ada, a sdelat' eto neskol'ko raz'" *Izvestiia* 1 August 2006.

[80] OT, district administration, XK, 13 January 2000.

[81] "Report on responses to land reform in Kharkiv and Volyn regions." Kyiv: Derzhkomzem, 1998.

even opened the safes to demonstrate the absence of land certificates."[82] Likewise, a private farmer in the region acknowledged the practice and legitimated it as a signifier of the rule of law as he defended a man who was "squatting" by cultivating on his own land: "He's not a criminal. His certificate is in the director's safe."[83]

Other directors found additional ways of controlling access to the new land documents. Among private farmers, stories of directors trading bottles of alcohol for land certificates abounded during the late 1990s. It is unlikely that alcohol served as payment in such cases; rather, it was a symbol that provided a veneer of social legitimatization for a coerced exchange, an offer that shareholders were not in a position to refuse. More commonly, shareholders spoke of directors who simply insisted they sign a document stating that they had received their certificates.[84] In the 1998 study, 82 percent of respondents in Kharkiv reported that they did not have contracts for the use of their land share, despite the fact that their home enterprises were using their shares.[85] One Kharkiv village council member summed up the situation most simply, noting the "the state farm kept all the certificates for itself."[86]

Do Not Allow Dissolution

Directors had active assistance from local officials in maintaining status quo production relations.[87] Local officials counseled farm directors behind closed doors to "preserve the integrity of the property complexes of farms."[88] In Kharkiv, when the deputy head of agricultural management, the second most powerful figure in the regional agricultural bureaucracy, was asked in 1999 about the proper "degree of partition" for collectives, he replied that it was necessary to "preserve a single non-land asset

---

[82] Yu. Kryklyvyi, "Ponedilok pochynaiet'sia v subotu," *SK*, 15 January 2000, 2.

[83] OT, Kharkiv regional farmers' association conference, 18 January 2000.

[84] Ibid. Private farmers were more likely than shareholders to point out illegal behavior among directors of collectives. But see H. Pronina, "Reformuvannia ahrarnoho sektora: pershi 'huli': Iz zasidannia kolehii oblprokuratury. *ZH* 13 January 2001, 2.

[85] "Report on responses to land reform." Kyiv: Derzhkomzem, 1998. The survey question was, "Chy ukladavsia dohovir orendy na svii zemel'nyi pai z hospodarstvom, iake nym korystuiet'sia?"

[86] OT, Vidmovka village council, L'viv district, 12 April 2000.

[87] Humphrey observes similar practices, *Marx Went Away But Karl Stayed Behind*. Ann Arbor: University of Michigan Press, 2001, 449.

[88] At the time, this strategy was observed throughout the country. For example, M. Saenko, "Reforma pod kolesami ochkovtiratel'stva," *DP* 4 April 2000.

complex" – a requirement, he emphasized, that was not actually in the legislation in question but could be found in the commentary on it. The main thing, he continued, was "not to allow the farms to be broken apart."[89]

On a separate occasion, the rector of a Kharkiv regional agricultural university announced that while "our future is tied to private property," those implementing land privatization "must do everything so that the enterprises do not break up into pieces."[90] And in a speech at a meeting closed to the press, the head of L'viv district state administration urged directors of collective farms in his district "to maintain the collectives in their entirety, do not allow dissolution." He continued, "You must be of one mind, retain the enterprises, just in another form – a private form."[91]

Some state officials helped directors in this task by manipulating the order of operations for implementing privatization.[92] As the head of L'viv district saw it, "To ensure the preservation of the land mass it is necessary to conclude [leasing] contracts."[93] Farms reregistered in a new form based on private ownership of land and assets, signed leasing contracts with shareholders, and then, once it was too late for those who wished to exit, turned their attention to the partition of land plots.[94] As the deputy head of agricultural management in a southern district of Kharkiv put it, "The tendency is at first to do the reforming, and then allot the land shares."[95]

An instance of this practice in Ukraine illustrates the implications of such a reversal. After President Leonid Kuchma's December 1999 land reform decree, the Kharkiv regional state administration gave farms until 1 March to identify the physical location of individual plots. In both Russia and Ukraine, some district state administrations required establishment of leasing relations much earlier.[96] During the first week of January, the head of L'viv district gave directors of collectives a deadline: "By 14 January, decide on the form of organization... By 15 January confiscate all the certificates and shares."[97] Other districts set deadlines for

---

[89] OT, Kharkiv regional farmers' association conference, 14 December 1999.

[90] OT, L'viv district administration, 13 January 2000.

[91] OT, L'viv district administration, 8 January 2000.

[92] "Visti iz Zachepylivshchyny. Zemliu – selianam," *SK*, 29 January 2000, 1.

[93] OT, L'viv district administration, 8 January 2000.

[94] M. Mel'nyk, "Shans dlia fermera," *SK*, 21 December 1999, 1.

[95] OT, district administration, LK, 30 March 2000.

[96] "Na zdiisnennia ahrarnoi reformy" *SK*, 5 January 2000, 1; V. Pleshkov, "...Pokoi nam tol'ko snitsia," *LI*, 13 February 1992, 6.

[97] OT, district administration, L'viv district, 8 January 2000. The deadline was issued in the form of a directive, not a suggestion: the district head used the stronger infinitive form of the verb, rather than the imperative, to articulate his command.

the middle of February.[98] Once certificates had been collected and leasing agreements with the collective signed, shareholders lost control over the disposition of their shares and could no longer request partition of their land. On 16 January – one day after members of collectives were to have lost the ability to use their land shares outside the collective – the district state administration ordered directors of enterprises to have maps of land shares drawn up.[99]

Shareholders relinquished control over their land shares for the duration of contracts with collectives, so the head of L'viv district advised directors of collectives to sign ten-year leasing contracts. Many leasing contracts were renewed automatically, and Kharkiv shareholders who signed away their land during the first weeks of the decree's implementation lost control over the use of their land for an indeterminate period. Furthermore, rents on land were not adjusted for inflation, so rents for long-term leases were likely to lose value each year.

The reversal of the prescribed process for allocating land shares and contracting for land leasing eliminated many of the possible benefits of reform for worker-shareholders. Although the land share certificates were sufficient to establish leasing relationships, without identifying the location of concrete land shares it was impossible to lease land to any entity but the original collective: legally, shareholders could lease their land to private farmers using only certificates, but knowledge of the location of the land was necessary for most private farmers to be willing to enter into such agreements. Those private farmers who risked leasing without initial surveying encountered a lack of clarity in the allocation of land rights in the fields. As one private farmer who later took over an entire collective described it, "It's the certificates that are partitioned, not the land."[100] More than four months later, a regional state official in the Kharkiv division of private farms described the dilemma of a farmer who had attempted to lease land shares in a neighboring collective: "He doesn't know where his land is. It's like that for the majority."[101]

The outcomes of the 1999 decree in Kharkiv illustrate the extent of the problem. Prior to the decree, 721 land-share leasing contracts had been signed in the region. By 11 January, long before most enterprises had

[98] "Visti iz Zachepylivshchyny. Zemliu – selianam," *SK* 29 January 2000, 1.
[99] OT, dispatcher's office, division of planned economy, L'viv district, 16 January 2000.
[100] OT, Kharkiv regional farmers' association conference, 14 December 1999.
[101] OT, Kharkiv regional division of private farms, 4 April 2000.

identified concrete land shares, 21,709 such contracts had been signed.[102] It is worth noting the time of year during which this vast increase in leasing contracts occurred: ordinarily, little formal business gets done between late December and mid-January. The preparation for and celebration of a multitude of holidays – the New Year, Orthodox Christmas, the New Year by the Julian calendar, and the celebration of Christ's christening – stretch across those weeks, consuming time and resources, closing state offices, and making serious attempts to complete paperwork impossible. That such an increase in leasing arrangements occurred at that time suggests that the impetus for making the agreements and conducting the time-consuming business of obtaining the necessary signatures, notarizing, and delivering the necessary documentation most likely originated with those who had an interest in prompt creation of leasing contracts: local officials and directors of collectives, not individual shareholders.

We're All Among Friends Here

Enterprise and wage debt provided another powerful instrument for directors who wished to maintain control of worker-shareholders' assets. Most Black Earth collectives were deep in debt at the time of reform, and directors' effective parrying of debt into access to land and labor was a central tool in their repertoires.[103] As the head of the Kharkiv regional council put it, "The majority [of farms], as you see, will remain whole, and debts won't play an insignificant role."[104] Debts-for-shares strategies were accompanied by attempts to frighten shareholders, as a farmer from Zolochiv complained: "They scare people – particularly grandmothers and pensioners – with debts...They put the brakes on at the local level [*na mestnosti*]."[105] Local officials sometimes participated in such tactics. Across the border in Pavlovsk, a local journalist complained that the chairman of a village council was "frightening" villagers with public statements

---

[102] M. Khablak, "Zatsikavlenist' u reformuvanni velychezna," *SK*, 11 January 2000, 1. Figures from the Ministry of Agriculture show that nationwide, almost 1,000 enterprises had concluded leasing contracts between the end of December and the end of February, before there likely had been time to allot land shares in kind.

[103] N. Semena, "Vragi reformy obnaruzhili sebia....X s"ezd fermerov Ukrainy, kotoryi sostoitsia na budushchei nedele v Kieve, potrebuet ot prezidenta...vypolneniia ego ukaza," *ZN* 12 February 2000.

[104] Kryklyvyi, "Liudyna kriz' pryzmu reformy," *SK* 27 January 2000, 1, 2.

[105] OT, Kharkiv regional farmers' association conference, 18 January 2000.

such as, "I see by your faces that the cold winds of change have blown on you. It smells like a nobleman soon will rule upon the land, and not we."[106]

Some farm directors complied with creditors' demands that reorganized collectives use shares to extinguish commodity credit debt.[107] In Khava, one new agricultural cooperative was "founded on shares" from a bankrupted farm: "In reality it's a completely stolen *kolkhoz*."[108] On a Kharkiv farm saddled with nearly 3 million UAH (Ukrainian national currency – the hryvnya) in debt at the end of the millennium, "they took the cars" and "they divided the property... seventy percent for debts, thirty percent for shares."[109] Directors who chose this strategy did so within the law and at the urging of local and national state officials.[110] In 1999, Pavlo Haiduts'kyi, then first deputy head of presidential administration in Ukraine, noted that many of the least profitable farms "possibly will be led to relinquish their land shares, so as to extinguish their debts at least partially."[111] Some private farmers and shareholders viewed such demands as an affront. If criminal or irresponsible behavior on the part of directors had produced the debt, why, they reasoned, should pensioners wishing to leave a collective be held responsible for a director's theft or negligence?[112]

Other directors apportioned a share of enterprise debt to each worker-shareholder. Should worker-shareholders wish to strike out on their own, this amount would be subtracted from the value of non-land asset shares.[113] Such fees were a substantial disincentive for shareholders contemplating exit. In Kharkiv, private farmers attempting to lease land

[106] V. Kolodiazhnyi, "Otchety i vybory v kolkhozakh. Kholoden li veter peremen?" *MP* 14 Feburary 1998, 3.

[107] Interview, debt collector for foreign pesticides and fertilizer company, Kharkiv, 3 April 2000.

[108] OT, former economist of district branch of agricultural bank, VV, 13 May 2000.

[109] OT, farm director, L'viv district, 13 January 2000.

[110] Russian Civil Code 3/1022. See also E. Polynkova "Poshla zemlia na rynok, a iski – v sudy," *Lipetskaia gazeta* 4 August 2006, "Kak pravil'no oformit' zemel'nyi pai," *Kubanskie novosti* 3 December 2004, N. Gritchin, "Chernaia dyra. Stavropol'skie predsedateli otniali u krest'ian zemliu," *Izvestiia* 5 March 2002.

[111] Novyny APK, UAPP Agriweek 1U 2000.

[112] OT, district administration, L'viv district, 8 January 2000 and OT, Kharkiv regional farmers' association, 14 December 1999.

[113] For accounts of various debt-land arrangements in Ukraine, see Kliakhin, "V obraztsovo-pokazatel'nom KSP dazhe 'vykhod iz kolkhoza' pokazatel'nyi," *Den'* 30 June 1999 and Rybalka, "Rab na svoei zemle? Reforma na sele," *DU* 3 February 1999, 3.

shares from members of collectives reported fees of up to 4,000 UAH, or 800 US$, for each hectare of a land share.[114] Such sums were impossibly high in a region where the mean monthly salary for all professions at the time rarely exceeded 30 US$. Such payments often exceeded the assessed value of the land, and the mere mention of them would have been sufficient to dissuade most worker-shareholders from attempting to leave the collective. A Kharkiv journalist commented on the resemblance of this strategy to the "Stalinist Constitution, where each republic had the right to leave the Union, but just try to use [that right]... General debts block the initiative of those who want to work independently."[115]

In addition to having commercial debt, most collectives undergoing reform also owed their workers several months back wages. This was a particular problem in Kharkiv, where state farms predominated: in contrast to collective farms, which paid members according to the residue principle, state farms paid salaries to their workers.[116] In some districts, local officials advised directors to solve this problem by paying off wage arrears through liquidation of enterprise assets. Worker-shareholders were supposed to receive non-land farm assets in shares, but allocation of non-land asset shares to shareholders happened only rarely in any case: most enterprises could not afford the cost of reassessing the value of assets with every major currency and price fluctuation.[117] When the question of receiving non-land asset shares came up at a meeting of the Kharkiv regional farmers' association, the response was unanimous: "That's not realistic."[118]

Some shareholders brought their cases to court, but as the regional representative of a cadastral company in Kharkiv observed, "Those who have brought their case to court are in a good situation because they are the first. Nothing will be left to the last ones [who sue]." At a closed meeting, the head of the L'viv district administration answered a question about wage debt: "The best thing to do is to let those who want to take [their wages] in the form of assets."[119] Worker-shareholders were owed both back wages and shares in collective assets. By paying out wage debt through liquidation of enterprise assets, directors avoided paying

[114] OT, Kharkiv regional farmers' association conference, 18 January 2000.
[115] Kryklyvyi, "Zemel'na reforma ne lyshe dlia sela a i dlia vs'oho narodu," *SK* 21 December 1999, 2.
[116] In Voronezh, collective farms predominated.
[117] OT, division of agricultural management, LK, 30 March 2000.
[118] OT, Kharkiv regional farmers' association council meeting, 25 May 2000.
[119] OT, district administration, L'viv district, 8 January 2000.

members their non-land asset shares. Where this procedure was followed, no non-land assets remained for division into shares.

Directors and state officials defended their actions by arguing that if asset shares were allotted first, nothing would be left to pay off wages, and the enterprise could be sued for wage debt. The L'viv district administrator was careful to mention that only wage laborers had the right to sue for wages: in a collective agricultural enterprise, everyone else received shares of the profits. In such cases, only the first to sue would reap any benefit: "The pioneer gets something, but the rest, the masses, won't get anything." However, in the end, not all farm directors thought it necessary to solve the problem of wage debt at all. One director in L'viv district asked the local head of administration, "We're all among friends here. Should the collective try to pay off wage debts or just freeze them?"[120]

Whoever Doesn't Have a Shovel, Go and Buy One

Amidst farm directors' attempts to retain control over land and labor, and state officials' efforts to retain large-scale agriculture, worker-shareholders also faced economic constraints that prevented them from demanding their land. The economic context in which rural populations lived and worked overdetermined their quiescence in the face of elite-driven resistance to the individuation of property rights. The simultaneous implementation of privatization and other elements of structural adjustment policies created a hostile environment for farms and rural populations: during the early years of farm reorganization, IMF conditionality required the Russian and Ukrainian governments to resolve balance of payments problems by reducing budgetary expenditures rather than by raising tax revenue. Expenditures so targeted included the very infrastructure and social services that former collectives had provided, so no reliable public sphere awaited shareholders who dared step beyond the "*kolkhoz* archipelago."[121]

Members of collectives thus had good reason to worry about the consequences if collectives foundered or were dissolved. In remote areas, collective and state farms were often the sole employer. People received their housing, health care, and education through the infrastructure attached

---

[120] Ibid.
[121] See Peter Lindner, *Das Kolchoz-Archipel im Privatisierungsprozess: Wege und Umwege der russischen Landwirtschaft in die globale Marktgesellschaft*. Bielefeld: transcript Verlag, forthcoming; Grigory Ioffe, "The Downsizing of Russian Agriculture," *Europe-Asia Studies* 57:2 (March 2005) 179–208.

to collective agricultural production.[122] When and if those enterprises were disbanded, there would be no institutions to support rural society or to sustain economic activity beyond the household production – itself directly dependent on collective production.[123] In 1997, Koznova noted that in Russia, "Right now people fear the destruction of collective farms the way that people feared collectivization in their day."[124] Such a prospect led members of collectives to close ranks against those who wished to leave: as long as allotment required the approval of the collective's general assembly, a rule that governed allotments during the first years of reform, villagers faced social pressure to keep their land in collective use. In 1992, at a meeting of livestock workers in Liski, it was proposed that the collective be dissolved, "and you know what people said? 'If you want, Ivanych, leave the *kolkhoz*, but we're staying. And actually, we won't let you go.'"[125]

Under conditions prevailing at the time, it would have been irrational for most worker-shareholders to leave collectives.[126] Some farm directors had only to emphasize what awaited worker-shareholders if they left the collective: "The chairman goes to people and says, 'have you heard about the decree? So, whoever doesn't have a shovel, go and buy one. We'll give you three and a half hectares each, and you do what you want. If not, go back to the collective.'"[127] Without appropriate machinery or access to credit on reasonable terms, on land that was likely to be several kilometers away from their homes over fields rather than roads, and in a pricing environment in which agricultural goods cost more to produce than they brought on the market, most worker-shareholders faced formidable

---

[122] In a formal sense, this changed in the mid-1990s in Russia, when district administrations were charged with subsidizing these and other services. The budgets of most district administrations were inadequate for this new mandate; in practice, former collectives remained the chief providers of social services.

[123] See Chapter 6, pp. 174–177.

[124] Koznova, "Traditsii i novatsii v povedenii sovremennykh krest'ian," in *Identichnost' i konflikt v postsovetskikh gosudarstvakh, sbornik statei*. Moscow, 1997, 368–9.

[125] V. Ivanov, "Segodnia desiatok let... igraet vsemi kraskami 'Rassvet'," *LI* 30 April 1992, 4.

[126] Carol Scott Leonard, "Rational Resistance to Land Privatization: The Response of Rural Producers to Agrarian Reforms in Pre- and Post-Soviet Russia," *Post-Soviet Geography and Economics* 41:8 (2000); Maria Amelina, "Why Russian Peasants Remain in Collective Farms: A Household Perspective on Restructuring," *Eurasian Geography and Economics* 41:7 (October-November 2000).

[127] E. Kanevskiy, "Ukaz Kuchmy ob agrarnoi reforme: fermery i mestnye rukovoditeli gotoviatsia k boiu," *Den'*, 6 December 1999.

obstacles to extracting value from their land rights.[128] As Meurs has shown in post-socialist Bulgaria, local incentives structures led rural people to remain on collectives as a hedge against risk.[129]

An additional obstacle to exit lay in the cost of land allotment. Farms used their own resources to pay for cadastral services, but in most cases, those costs were passed on to shareholders: it was impractical, illogical, and unaffordable for the vast majority of collectives to conduct extensive surveying, only to lose surveyed land. In practice, shareholders who wished to allot their land paid for surveying. For several years, in some places, a single company provided those services. In Kharkiv, where "you can't get by without Ronco's help," shareholders faced "a line, you can't even get in" at the office of Ronco, a principle contractor with USAID that issued land titles in Ukraine.[130]

Those who chose to pursue allotment of their land shares faced additional practical challenges linked to low status, infrastructural decay, and poverty. Aside from the considerable expense involved, bureaucratic procedures for land allotment took place in district and regional government offices, not in the fields of reorganized collectives. Even in villages relatively accessible to urban areas, worker-shareholders would often have to travel several kilometers on foot in order to board a bus at the nearest town served by public transportation (Illustration 3). Such walks often took place in sub-freezing temperatures, since most households could not afford to lose a pair of hands during the labor-intensive spring, summer, and fall months. From more remote former collectives, the trip could take hours. Having made the trip and their excuses for missing work that day, and having indebted themselves to neighbors or family members for care of children or household livestock while they were away, shareholders faced the likelihood that the bureaucrats they had come to see would be busy or otherwise unavailable, and that they would be told to come back a different day.

Once inside the building of the district state administration, shareholders risked running into the director of their collective, who would be

---

[128] See Louise Perrotta, "Coping with the Market in Rural Ukraine," in Ruth Mandel and Caroline Humphrey, eds., *Markets and Moralities: Ethnographies of Post-Socialism.* Oxford: Berg, 2002.

[129] Mieke Meurs, *The Evolution of Agrarian Institutions: A Comparative Study of Post-Socialist Hungary and Bulgaria.* Ann Arbor: University of Michigan Press, 2001. Also see Johnson and Minton-Beddoes, "The Acquisition of Private Property Rights," (See n69, p. 69).

[130] OT, local representative of Ronco and director of a collective farm, L'viv district, 13 January 2000.

ILLUSTRATION 3. View from a main street in the village adjoining Chayanovs-koe former collective farm, Voronezh, 1998. Many Black Earth village streets are unpaved and turn to mud in spring, impeding travel.

curious at best to know why they were there: such buildings generally are small, with one main entrance and waiting areas in the hallways, and most directors were summoned to district offices on a weekly basis, if not more often.[131] Appeals to regional authorities were even more intimidating, expensive, and risky, requiring even longer travel as well as additional preparatory labor on personal appearance, as those from rural areas with no running water or indoor washing facilities went to great lengths to put their best foot forward in the city (Illustration 4).

For most rural residents, the prospect of land privatization offered little comfort amidst great upheavals, and at times anxiety manifested itself in protest. At a seminar held in Liski for agricultural professionals, discussion of the time it would take to allot land to private farmers caused an uproar: "And once again, a commotion in the auditorium: we're on the verge of sowing – why talk about farmers, let's think about the collective farms."[132] In Kharkiv, as a public meeting to discuss land distribution commenced in darkness and without a working microphone, an audience

---

[131] See Chapter 4, p. 116.
[132] V. Pleshkov, "...Pokoi nam tol'ko snitsia," *LI* 13 February 1992, 6.

ILLUSTRATION 4. A courtyard in the village adjoining Chayanovskoe former collective farm, Voronezh, 1998. The tub leaning against the building is used for washing.

member loudly complained, "There's no electricity. And you're busy with privatization."[133] Some members of rural society had believed at the start of the 1990s in privatization's promise of efficiency and independence. However, the record of both industrial and agricultural privatization by mid-decade had left little hope that land privatization would result in the resolution of the practical problems that made life in the countryside such a challenge.

The Land Is Quietly Being Taken from Us

Amidst economic constraints on worker–shareholders' demands for land share allotment, strategies to forestall the individuation and distribution of land were successful in districts where district administrations had retained or regained a high degree of capacity. Resistance to privatization required coordination and effort on the part of local officials: in the absence of coordination, it is likely that ambitious farm directors would have intervened even more directly in the process, but it is also possible

---

[133] OT, district administration, L'viv district, 13 January 2000.

that villagers would have received their shares relatively unimpeded. Collectives do not persist out of inertia, but require energy to maintain themselves. The preservation of collective forms of production is not itself an indication that state officials failed adequately to attempt privatization; instead, there is evidence of desire and action to impede its march – all the while fulfilling the letter of the law.

Farm directors' and local state officials' interests and norms were different, but aligned as they sought to preserve collectives. Local officials were not simply relenting to pressure from a societal group: farm and state elites cultivated close professional relationships, but the primary economic levers lay in the hands of state personnel. Regional and district-level officials allocated commodity and other credits, provided information about markets, regulated crop rotation, exacted contributions to regional grain funds, and exercised a variety of other controls over agricultural production. The compliance of agricultural elites with these controls was linked to the benefits – subsidies, lower-priced fuel, and loans – that a relationship with state officials could provide.[134]

Directors, in responding to personal ambition and incentives inherent to industrialized agriculture, used privatization to strengthen their own hand.[135] By limiting villagers' access to land shares in the early stages of privatization, directors gained control over land and labor. Farm reorganization thus had the effect of concentrating power in the hands of farm managers and undermining worker-shareholders' agency in the disposition of their rights. Privatization was meant to catalyze a shift from collective to individual responsibility, but the individual responsibility of members of the rural elite was in practice greatly exceeded by their newfound power and discretion.

During the critical early years of post-socialist capital accumulation, worker-shareholders thus were not free in practice to enter into contracts: "We had no rights before, and that's how we've remained."[136] This greatly complicated their prospects for future gain and diminished the likelihood that subsequent iterations of land exchange would be efficient or competitive. Rather than fostering independence for most villagers, land

---

[134] Farm directors could deliver votes for incumbents. However, the timing of reform efforts relative to elections suggest this was not of major importance in opposition to land distribution.

[135] Pugachov and Van Atta, "Reorganization of Agricultural Enterprises in Ukraine in 2000: A Research Note," *Post-Soviet Geography and Economics* 41 (October–Novenber 2000).

[136] Interview, worker–shareholder, L'viv district, 12 April 2000.

privatization became a mechanism of dispossession. As one member of a Kharkiv collective farm complained, "The land is quietly being taken from us. They're doing everything they can so that no one ever leaves the head of the *kolkhoz*."[137]

[137] OT, Kharkiv regional farmers' association conference, 18 January 2000. The man's words express an interesting relationship between farm management and ideas about how collective enterprise identity is constituted: exit from the collective, it is implied, constitutes a personal betrayal, a rejection of one's patron.

3

The Social Origins of Private Farmers

Even as local state officials and farm directors sought to "maintain the collectives, just in a different form," reformers continued to envision the realization of a Jeffersonian dream in Eurasia. For advocates of land privatization, one path to modernization lay through the creation of yeoman farms. These farms would be similar to the family farms that, until the last decades of the twentieth century, had come to typify the North American landscape: small commercial agricultural companies managed by a single owner or group of owners.

Private farming, instituted as a successor policy to the leasing brigades of the late 1980s and modeled in part on the Stolypin-era reforms of the early twentieth century, emerged prior to the fall of the Soviet Union and continued, parallel with the reorganization of collective and state farms, in independent Ukraine and Russia. The modest scale and success of the private farming movement did not equal the attention it initially received from both policy makers in Moscow and Kyiv and foreign observers.[1] In the countryside, local state officials did not appear to share the dream they were charged with bringing to fruition, and the new class of market-minded, efficient peasant producers that would provide food for the cities did not emerge the way reformers hoped it would.

---

[1] Among many works on the subject are Don Van Atta, ed. *The Farmer Threat: The Political Economy of Agrarian Reform in Post-Soviet Russia.* Boulder: Westview Press, 1993; Myriam Hivon, "The Bullied Farmer: Social Pressure as a Survival Strategy?" in Sue Bridger and Frances Pine, eds. *Surviving Post-Socialism: Local Strategies and Regional Responses in Eastern Europe and the Former Soviet Union.* London: Routledge, 1998; Stephen Wegren, "The Politics of Private Farming in Russia," *The Journal of Peasant Studies* 23:4 (July 1996) 106–40.

During the 1990s, the Russian and Ukrainian governments issued multiple decrees and legislative acts to support the creation of private farms. In both countries, agricultural land could be allocated to any qualified person who wished to start his or her own enterprise in two ways: from publicly administered lands through an allotment from a district land redistribution fund, or by using or leasing land shares in a former collective or state farm. Private farmers turned to the latter method with increasing frequency later in the reform process, but early on, obtaining land from reorganized former collective and state farms was fraught with political risk and bureaucratic difficulty. As a result, only a small proportion of the rural population benefited from the creation of private farms.

The Chairman Was Against It

Just as farm directors resisted apportioning collective farm land to shareholders, they also obstructed allotments for private farms. People who wished to establish their own farms faced resistance from directors who opposed allotments for private farming on the practical grounds that land redistribution disrupted the cultivation cycle and negatively affected land-labor ratios.[2] In some cases, directors articulated their admittedly self-serving position through critiques of Soviet-era economic practices. As one collective farm chairman suggested, "Don't interpret my . . . views as a refusal to accept private farming in general. . . . But under no circumstances should private farming be 'developed' by force, according to a command procedure."[3]

Farm directors in both countries were sometimes open in their dislike of distribution policies, noting that they "wouldn't like to hand over land."[4] Because they were not legally responsible for allotting land for private farms, such directors intervened through back room deals with local state officials to prevent allotment of land for private farming or, more directly, denied farmers physical access to land that had already been allotted to them. Private farmers who encountered difficulty in obtaining land thus often found that "the [collective farm] chairman was against it."[5]

---

[2] Andrew Barnes, *Property and Power: The Struggle for Assets in the Remaking of Russia.* Ithaca: Cornell University Press, 2006.

[3] V. Roshchupkin, "Stavka – na arendu," *LZ* 4 February 1991, 3.

[4] Interview, director, Voroshilov *kolkhoz*, LV, May 2000.

[5] Interview, farmer, LV, July 1998. Interview conducted by Mikhail Savin.

This was true whether the private farmer in question sought to have land allotted through a local redistribution fund or wished to lease land from shareholders. Private farmers nearly always described "leasing land from the *kolkhoz*" rather than from the individual people who, in a legal sense, owned the land. In Semiluki, a farmer who leased land from a former collective described facing "envy" for the first five years of his operation, leaving him unable to take on any workers. In his case, this meant that all land and labor arrangements in the area had to go through the local director of the former collective.[6] In Semiluki, as elsewhere, this was standard practice. As an officer of the Semiluki district farmers' association explained, "If someone makes an arrangement with people and cultivates land shares . . . the worst land is allotted."[7]

Serious Slips Were Allowed

Officials in district state administrations shared farm directors' concerns and were often reluctant to allot land to individual producers. The "many among us who wish to establish our own businesses"[8] in Liski found themselves at odds with state bureaucrats overseeing land distribution, and the small number of private farmers in the district at that time belied the larger number of Liski residents who hoped to start their own enterprises.[9] After spending years working on an ice trawler in Nakhodka, the daughter of a dekulakized peasant who had been exiled to Siberia returned to Liski, hoping to start a private farm. When she inquired about obtaining land, a member of the district executive committee reportedly "rolled her eyes," explaining, "Look, dear, don't you know that the *kolkhoz* was granted that land by the government for permanent use?"[10] Later, local land management officials insisted that the public had been uninterested in private ventures, arguing that "no one announced a desire [to create] private farms," and "people don't want to establish private farms. It's not realistic."[11]

Across the border in Kharkiv, district officials responded to similar local economic conditions with similar tactics. In some districts, often

---

6 Interview, farmer Ivanov, SV, May 2000.
7 Interview, district farmers' association, SV, May 2000.
8 V. Pleshkov, "Teper' ia sam sebe khoziain," *LZ* 10 September 1991, 3.
9 V. Pleshkov, "Nas malo, no my . . . v 'tel'niashkakh'. Tak mogli by skazat' Liskinskie fermery," *LI* 3 December 1991, 2.
10 V. Ivanov, "Posle moria, na prostore, u Mocharki v chistom pole . . . 60 let spustia obrela ona dedovskuiu zemliu," *LI* 5 November 1991, 3.
11 Interview, department of agricultural management, LV, 8 May 2000.

those with strong collective farms, local officials refused to allot land to some applicants for private farms. In Chuhuiv, home to a thriving agriculture and food-processing businesses but fewer than thirty private farms throughout the post-Soviet period, one would-be farmer who had struggled for years to obtain land complained that local officials were "interested in not having any farmers...I know so many people who would like to take [land], but just try it – it's a nightmare."[12] Several years later, the head of the district described obstruction as having been a deliberate strategy that made it "possible to preserve a great deal" without the "dangerous tendency toward incorrect reform."[13]

Even in districts where local officials initially were positively inclined toward land distribution for private farms, or, as one member of the Kharkiv regional agro-industrial council put it, where "leaders displayed a clear interest in a variety of forms of farm management,"[14] practical considerations led bureaucrats to limit allotments. Anna district was one of the leaders in land distribution for private farms in Voronezh,[15] and during the early 1990s, the district administration had allowed more extensive development of private farming than in nearby Liski, which had similar acreage under collective cultivation but fewer private farmers per hectare than most other districts in the region (Table 3.1).[16]

For several years, the local economic climate in Anna was relatively favorable for private commercial agriculture, where "people have free money...they're working, receive a salary...they can invest it."[17] However, the relative ease of acquiring land in districts such as Anna did not last. By the end of the decade, Anna officials grew reluctant to allot land for private farming. The head of the district land resources and land tenure committee noted in 1999 that "we remember the time when there was much talk about how farmers will feed the country. During that time

---

[12] Interview, farmer Mrinyk, CK, 24 February 2000.
[13] Interview, district administration, CK, 21 July 2006.
[14] "'Fermery – narod serioznyi,' – hovoryt' pro vlasnykiv selians'kykh hospodarstv providnyi spetsialist oblahropromrady M. T. Velykorodnyi," *SK* 30 April 1991, 2.
[15] Interview, farmer Valentinovich, AV, 11 May 2000.
[16] If land distribution for private farms were determined by land supply, then we might expect somewhat more private farmers in Anna than in Liski. However, outcomes in other districts of Voronezh region do not lead us to expect such a disparity: some districts with less land than Liski have many more private farms. *Goroda i raiony Voronezhskoi oblasti*, Part 3, *Raiony*. Voronezh: Voronezh regional committee of state statistics, 1997, 102.
[17] Interview, former bank collector known locally as "Ivan 2%," AV, 11 May 2000.

TABLE 3.1. *Land by enterprise type in Liski and Anna districts, Voronezh 1997*[a]

	Liski	Anna
Hectares agricultural land	148,000	174,000
Hectares used by collectives[b]	161,800	158,000
Number of agricultural collectives	29	35
Number of private farms	14	221
Hectares used by private farms[c]	653	6,884

[a] *Goroda i raiony Voronezhskoi oblasti*, Parts 3, 3–8, and 106–113.

[b] Eksplikatsiia zemel' sel'skokhoziaistvennykh predpriiatii Voronezh-skoi oblasti po sostoianiiu na 1 ianvaria 1997 goda, g. Voronezh 1997. 4–6, 34–35.

[c] Ibid.

serious slips (*upushcheniia*) were allowed by the former staff of the land committee, who allotted land to anyone who wanted it – although many didn't even have machinery and other implements for the cultivation of land."[18] At the same time, state officials saw fewer applications for private farms: by the end of the decade, state support for loans had all but evaporated, and hyperinflation had receded, making loan repayment more difficult.

Land distribution intensified over time in areas where rural elites discovered opportunities for imitating the rent-seeking behavior that had characterized industrial privatization. During the first two years of post-Soviet land reform, individuals who applied for land in Bohodukhiv district of Kharkiv generally were told that none was available. However, when the son-in-law of the head of the Bohodukhiv state district administration decided to establish a private farm, and received land for that purpose, the district experienced an apparently sudden surge in interest in private farming. Once members of the district elite had received large tracts of land, local officials could no longer plausibly claim that there was a shortage of land.[19] By 1994, there were 120 registered private farmers in the district and Bohodukhiv had become a regional leader in private farming.[20]

---

[18] A. S. Sannikov, "Zemlia – istochnik zhizni," *AV* 6 April 1999, 2.

[19] Interview, district farmers' association, BK, 27 May 2000.

[20] Statistics obtained from Kharkiv regional division of private farming. According to the register of the Bohodukhiv district farmers' association, the number of private farmers in the district had fallen to 114 by 2000.

Other Than a Shovel and a Pitchfork, I Have Nothing

As farm directors and local officials limited the supply of land to the population, economic constraints limited rural peoples' demand for it. Private farmers in post-Soviet Russia and Ukraine faced a host of problems that complicated the always precarious enterprise of living off the land: price scissors; the need to rely on inefficient commodity credits because of a lack of appropriate cash credits[21]; high fuel prices at harvest time; expensive agricultural machinery and a lack of appropriate technology; underdeveloped market infrastructure; and ostracization and exclusion from village networks of exchange.

Few saw any sense in farming small plots amidst such conditions. "Regarding fragmentation [of land]," one district agricultural management official in Kharkiv argued, the Ukrainian President "did not understand the conditions in which people work. For [small scale cultivation] you need to create the right conditions. There was no launching pad." He owned a share that he could have farmed, but even in his position, "other than a shovel and a pitchfork, I have nothing."[22]

Private farming thus entailed a level of risk that most rural people were unwilling to accept. This was not a function of simple cultural conservatism, but of economic incentives specific to the time.[23] In a situation similar to that in Bulgaria and Hungary, the preservation of agricultural collectives reduced significant transaction costs for rural producers.[24] Given the risks and costs involved, individuals' ability or desire to work outside of collective cultivation was not the limiting factor in suppressing demand for land for private farms. Instead, as one pensioner explained, "fuel prevents me, machinery prevents me" from starting a private farm.[25]

Despite the manifest institutional, material, and social reasons why the great majority of rural people did not choose to leave agricultural collectives to strike out on their own, policy makers nonetheless placed the onus

---

[21] Maria Amelina, "Why Russian Peasants Remain in Collective Farms: A Household Perspective on Restructuring," *Eurasian Geography and Economics* 41:7 (October–November 2000).

[22] Interview, district administration, NK, 21 July 2006.

[23] James C. Scott, *The Moral Economy of the Peasant: Rebellion and Subsistence in Southeast Asia*. New Haven: Yale University Press, 1976.

[24] Mieke Meurs, *The Evolution of Agrarian Institutions: A Comparative Study of Post-Socialist Hungary and Bulgaria*. Ann Arbor: University of Michigan Press, 2001.

[25] Interview, pensioner, VK, 18 July 2006.

for the apparent failure of reform policy on worker-shareholders. When commentators on land reform observed successful instances of land distribution, they often mistook social standing and social ties established under Soviet rule for entrepreneurial personality characteristics – noting, for example, that "at the present stage exit from former collective structures and transition to independent private farming appear to be an option only for the bravest."[26]

Impossible to Obtain Land through Normal Channels

Social capital and informal networks that provided access to bureaucrats and production factors largely determined who would demand and obtain land to become an agricultural entrepreneur in the Black Earth. Though the vast majority of rural people had little access to the benefits of privatization, a small proportion of the rural population did, and those individuals were of a particular social origin. Paradoxically, an ordinary level of access to social and state informal networks was least likely to result in the receipt of land or even an attempt to obtain land for private farming. Rather, people who had either a relatively high degree or a very low degree of access to informal networks succeeded in breaking through bureaucratic obstruction to receive land allotments.

The mechanisms that governed allocation of land for private farms produced two distinct categories of private farmers. The first category was composed of rural state and farm elites, who were usually male.[27] The second category included people on the margins of rural society: ethnic minorities and immigrants from other former Soviet republics; transplanted urbanites; single, middle-aged women; and people in low-status positions on former collectives. Both of these groups were positioned to take on the risks of social and economic alienation and strike out on their own to form private farms. Elites with access to state or enterprise resources occupied commanding positions in networks of social and economic interdependence, and people on the margins had little to lose

---

[26] *Ukraine: Review of Farm Restructuring Experiences.* Washington, DC: The World Bank, 1998, ix.

[27] For household plots, Wegren has found an association between expansion of land holdings and gender, income, and educational level. "Why Rural Russians Participate in the Land Market: Socio-Economic Factors," *Post-Communist Economies* 15:4 (December 2003) 483–501.

because their low or "outsider" social status already excluded them from local economic networks.

Although certain years in the first post-Soviet decade were characterized by relatively more or less fluidity in land transfers, the socially bifurcated character of distributional patterns persisted throughout the decade. People excluded from ordinary networks of social and economic interdependence turned to small, private farm holdings for survival; rural elites who saw an opportunity for viable commercial production aspired to create private farms, and sought to acquire land.

Distribution of land to the well-connected was not a new or unique phenomenon, but rather an extension of mechanisms of distribution that had governed Soviet society. The unwritten rules that governed allocation and receipt of scarce goods in Soviet society also helped determine who could obtain land for farming.[28] Because of the constraints on land distribution, many would-be farmers turned to *blat* (personal and professional connections) – most of which had been established during the Soviet period – in their efforts to obtain land. The following statement of a farmer in Kharkiv illustrates one way this process worked. She and her husband applied for land twice in two different districts: once to start their farm, and once to expand their holdings:

First I went to a member of the regional council, who said "we'll help you once you tell me where you've been refused land." My husband and I tried all the district offices, but of course we were refused everywhere. I went back to see that member of the regional council, but he was on vacation. His deputy was there, and an interesting conversation ensued: he took me for a friend of the council member, you understand? He called the village council and solved the problem. But then the village council expected to receive a bribe from us. You know how it is....

We had an acquaintance, a journalist, who had a dacha near ours. She was the one who had pushed us to consider private farming. That was in 1993. She said she would help us. She had a very good relationship with the head of the regional administration. She called the head of the regional council, the head of the regional council called the district land tenure office, and the land tenure person immediately came to find us. He solved the problem on the spot. Just like that. Otherwise that would have been practically impossible....

---

[28] Alena Ledeneva, *Russia's Economy of Favors: Blat, Networking and Informal Exchange.* Cambridge: Cambridge University Press, 1998; Ledeneva, *How Russia Really Works.* Ithaca: Cornell University Press, 2006; Elena Osokina, *Our Daily Bread: Socialist Distribution and the Art of Survival in Stalin's Russia, 1927–1941.* Trans. Kate Transchel and Greta Bucher. London: Sharpe, 2001.

If you spend time with private farmers, you'll find that it's practically impossible to obtain land through normal channels. Many people ask me how I did it without paying a cent. I didn't pay off anyone. The first time it happened by chance that the vice-deputy thought we were a friend of his boss and called the village council for us. The second time, our high-level acquaintance gave the order from above.[29]

Such an exercise of power does not suggest land was allotted through illegal or extraordinary means. In most instances, officials followed policy provisions, but the considerable discretion granted to village councils and district state administrations meant that they could apply the letter of the law selectively: local officials chose for whom to push paper and whom to turn away or direct to the office of another bureaucrat. Furthermore, members of local land committees or land tenure offices always could find legitimate reasons to refuse a request: land scarcity; a lack of knowledge, seriousness, or capital on the part of the farmer; or paperwork that was somehow not in order.[30]

State officials' posture with respect to land distribution led to a sometimes unpredictable, if technically legal, process. Officials helped maintain status quo production and ownership relations while distributing enough land to make credible claims that they had implemented reform in good faith. In the end, only those applicants who could muster sufficient power to mobilize local bureaucracies in their favor, or those who were sufficiently unthreatening, were able to participate successfully in the process.

In contrast to rural elites, people on the margins of rural society were able to obtain land because they posed no threat of competition to local large-scale enterprises. The irritating frequency with which some such applicants appeared in government offices, combined with the low cost of allotting a small amount of land, led some state officials to accede to their requests. Some rural people even saw distribution to low-status villagers as a provocation intended to thwart further land reform. In Krasnograd district of Kharkiv, one farmer described this view: "They say that in many cases the local administration sooner gives land to a weak farmer than to a strong one, and afterwards sanctimoniously throw up their hands: 'Well, you see [private] farming hasn't worked here.'"[31]

---

[29] Interview, farmer, DK, 7 February 2000.

[30] While some instances of bureaucratic refusal can be ascribed to deficiencies on the part of applicants, the vast tracts of unused and poorly managed collective farm land in the two regions suggest a double standard at work.

[31] L. Barkanov, "Za kem budushchee? Zametki s otchetno-vybornoi konferentsii fermerov oblasti," *TT* 23 March 1995, 2.

Familiar Last Names

It is difficult to say precisely how many farmers received land through connections or social status established during the Soviet era, or to know with any certainty whether the use of social capital and informal networks to obtain land was a more widespread phenomenon on one side of the Russia-Ukraine border than on the other. Such precision would require knowledge of the personal networks of thousands of people. However, it is possible to identify the incentives that structured local officials' responses and to point to the causal mechanisms that did lead to land distribution in specific instances. Furthermore, acknowledgment of the scale of such a phenomenon by state officials, private farmers, and members of collective agricultural enterprises provides additional evidence for such a phenomenon. Finally, some indication of farmers' social status appears in official records. In 1999, for example, 87 of the 119 farmers in Kharkiv district had received a higher education.[32] What should be emphasized here is not the fact that elites received land, but how and why they managed to navigate the land allotment process successfully. In certain instances, access to local networks influenced distribution in a way that was directly observable at the time.

It should be noted that the use of connections was largely a hidden phenomenon: the formal documentation that accompanied the process of distributing land to private farmers does not always directly reveal the social origins of those farmers. The district-level farm registration record is among the most comprehensive types of documentation of land transfers. Such records include the names of the individuals to whom land has been allotted, their ages, gender, education, and basic information about the use of the land: how much was allotted and the acreage of each crop planned.

Even these documents, however, do not show the names of many of the rural elite who became private farmers. It was a common practice for directors of collectives and state officials to have their wives, who usually held less prestigious professional positions, register as owners of private farms.[33] When the wife of a former head of the division of agricultural management (the highest-ranking bureaucratic position in the agricultural sector) for a large grain-producing region in eastern Ukraine registered as a private farmer in Kharkiv district,[34] the Kharkiv

---

[32] Data obtained from district land tenure office, XK, November 1999.

[33] Interview, farmers, BK, May 2000.

[34] Interview, farmer Poltavenko, XK, 3 November 1999, and data obtained from district land tenure office, XK.

district newspaper, publishing the names of people to whom land had been allotted for this purpose, reported her identity simply as "a female worker on Chapaev state farm."[35] That she had received fifty hectares, the largest allowable tract of agricultural land, suggested to local readers that she was no ordinary applicant for land, but the newspaper otherwise provided no indication of her husband's elevated status. Likewise, in an equally common permutation, some couples divided their labor between private farming and collectivized agriculture, as husbands became private farmers and their wives worked as chief accountants in neighboring collective farms. These and similar arrangements, as in the case of the chairman of a *kolkhoz* in Semiluki who owned a private farm on its territory and thus "has machinery,"[36] offered significant opportunities for private farmers to acquire or borrow agricultural inputs, but official records alone offered no indication as to their existence.

Prominent business and high-ranking state elites' use of connections to obtain land was sufficiently widespread that it was an open secret in provincial communities. An excerpt from a newspaper editor's interview with the chief economist of a district division of agricultural management in Kharkiv in 1994 offers implicit acknowledgment of the *modus operandi* for allotting land for private farms:

Editor: A delicate question for you, Volodymyr Hryhorovych. Among our farmers one glimpses last names renowned in our district: Abramenko, Kravtsov, Fedotova...

VH: Yes. Familiar last names. Kravtsov is the former director of the Kalinin state farm, and Tetiana Abramenko and Hanna Fedotova are the wives of current directors of state farms. But this is a normal phenomenon. Ukrainian legislation does not prohibit anyone from becoming a farmer.[37]

As this district official acknowledged, the transfer of land to the relatives of powerful people was not unusual; what was uncommon was the open admission by a state official that insiders were the beneficiaries of land distribution.

Apply Pressure Where Necessary

Members of the rural elite who became private farmers tended to include men who belonged to one of four professional categories: (1) managerial

---

[35] "Maizhe dvadtsiat' pytan': pro biudzhet i ne til'ky..." *TT* 8 September 1992, 2–3.
[36] Interview, district farmers' association, SV, May 2000.
[37] V. Lemishchenko, "Selo na shliakhu do rynku: aktual'ne interv'iu. Fermer dopomozhe derzhavi, iakshcho derzhava dopomozhe fermeru," *TT*, 17 September 1994, 6.

ILLUSTRATION 5. Bohodukhiv private farmers with author in tractor yard, Kharkiv, 2000. The farmers are former collective farm machinists, a former head engineer on a collective farm, and a prominent academic who became a private farmer.

cadres of agricultural collectives, including directors, head agronomists, head engineers, and head veterinarians; (2) people who held specialized or prestigious positions within collectives, such as machinists; (3) government officials at the village council, district, or regional level; and (4) retired army and security services officers, often with peasant origins. These individuals were well-positioned to take advantage of reform policy; the executive director of the Kharkiv regional farmers' association described them as "those who were closer to the apparatus that oversaw distribution."[38]

In the face of formidable constraints to obtaining land, such individuals wielded the influence necessary to secure allotments and had access to the material resources crucial for financial success. Members of this category possessed resources they could devote to private farming: financial capital to invest in machinery and labor, and social capital to guide business transactions (Illustration 5). Some such farmers received tracts of scores of hectares from district land redistribution funds, occasionally in gross

[38] Interview, Kharkiv regional farmers' association, 6 December 1999.

violation of national or district limits on the size of allotments, while others took *de facto* possession of entire former collectives. In 2000, the two largest holdings in Semiluki belonged to former directors of collective farms, and both allotments encompassed more than 1,200 hectares each – well above the district norm for land distribution to private farmers.[39] Meanwhile, across the border in Bohodukhiv district, enterprise directors "made three collective agricultural enterprises into private farms . . . They seized all of the land shares."[40]

Farmers whose social identity included roles in both state and business – for example, high-ranking former members of collectives who also participated in local government – had special access to land allotments. One of the most successful private farmers in Kharkiv exemplified such a category. In contrast to many others in his situation, this farmer was willing to discuss openly the connection between his social status and his success in obtaining land. He was a leader in his community and had held high-ranking positions in local collective farms. In addition to his own high status, he had the support of close family members who were lawyers, and his wife, who was an accountant.

Despite his position, the process of acquiring land was onerous. When this farmer first started his enterprise in 1991, his land was allotted in seven or eight different plots, all in different locations and spanning several village council jurisdictions. His initial attempts to obtain the land were thwarted by changes in the leadership of the collective farm on whose territory the allotments were located.[41] When he took over the land shares of two collectives at the end of the decade, local officials did not wish to approve his request: according to a regional state official, "They gave him their word, but processing of the documents was impeded at the local level." The head of the district administration, however, stood by this farmer and promised to "apply pressure where necessary." As a result, he received the allotment.[42]

This farmer's difficulties were resolved through his status and access to bureaucratic channels at the local and district levels. He commanded formidable administrative knowledge and influence, mustering government support to bring an asphalt road to his farm as well as to construct

---

[39] Interview, district land tenure office, SV, May 2000. The head of the district farmers' association provided somewhat different information, asserting that these two enterprises covered more than 1,800 hectares each.

[40] Interview, district farmers' association, BK, 27 May 2000.

[41] Interview, farmer Chernets'kyi, ZK, 3 January 2000.

[42] OT, Kharkiv regional division of private farmers, 4 April 2000.

houses with electricity for himself and those of his family who were also engaged in private farming. As a member of a local governing body in charge of allocating land, he addressed some of the problems associated with land allotments himself: "I assigned 200 hectares of land to the reserve – already, so to speak, for myself. Therefore, in contrast to other farmers, I find myself in an advantageous position in that I did that for myself.... if I were, for example, a simple worker, then it would be impossible."[43]

His assessment is suggestive of the obstacles that less powerful people faced in attempting to acquire land: "I'm not exactly the lowest man on the totem pole in the village or in the district, and even I can't [obtain land]. So a rank-and-file person, a regular person who has the desire and even an idea [of how this all works] will never break through."[44] It is possible, of course, to imagine a scenario in which it was precisely this individual's existing power that moved local officials to curb his business venture; however, as the next section shows, resistance to the distribution of land to private farmers affected people of all social backgrounds. Status and personal connections acted not as hindrances but as capital that could be traded for bureaucrats' willing assistance in the privatization of land.

Local officials' and farm directors' resistance to land distribution challenged even those farmers who had preserved state connections they established during the Soviet period. One prominent Kharkiv farmer was a KGB lieutenant colonel who, before joining the security services, worked as a specialist in agricultural machinery in Cuba. Other farmers regarded him as an insider par excellence, for "a farmer is [by definition] a dissident, but that one is KGB."[45] He requested land that had been cultivated by his grandparents before the collectivization drives of the 1920s and 1930s. He had been born on his grandparents' parcel, and he wished to live out his retirement on it. In an unusual instance of successful *de facto* restitution, early in the 1990s he applied for and received fifty hectares on that spot.[46]

The parcel was at the juncture of three collectives farms, and allotting land for a private farm at the edge of any one of the collectives should not have posed any practical problems for the farm in question. Nevertheless,

---

[43] Interview, farmer Chernets'kyi, ZK, 3 January 2000.
[44] Ibid.
[45] Interview, farmers, BK, 27 May 2000. This understanding of private farming as a political act can be found in other contexts. Gerald Creed, "The Politics of Agriculture: Identity and Socialist Sentiment in Bulgaria," *Slavic Review* 54:4 (Winter 1995) 843 – 868.
[46] Interview, farmer Razvedchikov, XK, 31 August 1999.

the director of one of the collectives found ways to resist, at first demanding 200 head of cattle from the district administration in exchange for the alienation of collective land. Then the director requested that the allotment be further delayed because of the collective's financial instability. In the end, the district administration compelled the director of the collective to allow the land allotment.

This farmer was a close acquaintance of one of the members of the district land committee, and his reputation in the district made the other members of the committee amenable to his requests as well. His son, at the time a prominent veterinarian for the district, also linked him to district-level officials. The combination of the farmer's elevated status, specialized knowledge, and deep family roots in the area helped him to overcome a variety of obstacles to obtaining land. If the administration had not played an active role, pressuring the director of the collective to step into line with the law, it is unlikely that the land would ever have been allotted for a private farm.[47]

Other individuals who established private farms were not themselves exceptionally powerful, but they gained the assistance of well-placed individuals in order to obtain land. Another farmer in Kharkiv district provides an illustration of this point. This farmer had worked as an agronomist on collective and state farms in various regions of the Soviet Union for twenty years before starting his own agricultural enterprise. When he left his collective in 1993 to begin farming independently, he had been the collective's deputy director. He held a high-ranking position, but he had neither deep roots in the area nor the attendant personal connections that would have smoothed the process of obtaining land.

This farmer's greatest obstacle was obtaining the various signatures necessary to complete the process of farm registration. Individuals seeking to establish a private commercial agricultural enterprise were required to gather signatures from no fewer than ten different offices (the fire commissioner, the land tenure office, the local council, the health and sanitation department, and so on). Often, these offices were far apart and required extensive travel. This farmer frequently would travel as many as fifty kilometers to find that the person whose signature was required was not in the office. He was met with absence and "more important concerns" on the part of officials, not outright refusal: "they – the conservatives – just sat there, they didn't sign anything."[48] What saved this farmer from permanent delays and entanglement in red tape was his membership in

---

[47] Ibid.
[48] Interview, farmer Zelenyi, XK, 17 December 1999.

the Green Party of Ukraine. After two years of making the rounds to state offices, he received land after a Green Party deputy of the Ukrainian parliament stepped in and assisted him by making a few telephone calls to the regional state administration.[49]

Elite status could mean access not only to land but also to the infrastructure necessary to run a commercial farm. For example, the head of an association of private farmers in a southern district of Kharkiv – hours south of the provincial capital and close to the coal basin cities of Donetsk and Dnipropetrovsk – was the son of a former *kolkhoz* director. He received land on the territory of the farm that his father managed. While his father was head of the collective farm, he had a good asphalt road, which the son now uses, built around the entire *kolkhoz*. The private farm is three kilometers from a stop on the suburban train, and at harvest time as many as 140 people come to work.[50] An auspicious location and transportation infrastructure ease both crop production and marketing, distinguishing his situation from that of most other private farmers in the region.

Not all elites, however, enjoyed the same privileged access to inputs or infrastructure. The degree of individual farmers' access to local state and social networks was decisive. The local son of a Soviet hero of labor and Central Committee representative obtained land for a private farm in Kharkiv, but the chairman of a neighboring *kolkhoz*, who had reregistered the collective as a private farm, "was given fuel and seeding material in addition," because when it came to "real" private farmers, "they don't give us anything."[51] Business elites of the late Soviet era, with their close ties to local officials, had relatively freer access to state resources – access that could mean the difference between farm success and failure.

The local press sometimes advertised the Soviet-era credentials of farmers who had gained the support of local authorities. A successful farmer in Liski district of Voronezh who grew and processed buckwheat and keeps bees (which pollinate the buckwheat and produce honey from it)[52]

---

[49] This interview took place in a Kharkiv district land tenure office. The farmer was unwilling to disclose this information in the presence of a land tenure office representative, but instead waited until the representative had left the room. I never heard the entire story because the representative returned before he finished telling it. For a discussion of the related phenomenon of "telefonnoe pravo," see Alena Ledeneva "Behind the Facade: 'Telephone Justice' in Putin's Russia" in Mary McAuley, Alena Ledeneva and Hugh Barnes, *Dictatorship or Reform? The Rule of Law in Russia*. London: The Foreign Policy Centre, June 2006.

[50] Interview, district farmers' association, LK, 30 March 2000.

[51] Interview, farmer Didenko, BK, 27 May 2000.

[52] Interview, farmer Kuz'mich, LV, 8 May 2000. Also "'Fermer': vyrastil, obrabotal, prodal," *LI*, 5 December 1996, 5.

was the subject of a pair of articles in the local paper in 1996. Some of farmer Kuz'mich's success emanated from a diversified but unified business model, in which a combination of production and processing allowed him special subsidies at the local level. But Soviet-era legacies played an important role as well. One reporter emphasized his industry and recognition by the earlier regime by noting that Kuz'mich "is the pride of his family. Khrushchev himself came to see him [when he worked at] the poultry plant. V. K. has been to various sorts of conferences and has medals." Kuz'mich had strong party ties – his father became a party member and activist after his grandfather was dekulakized. The reporter continued, "And it's understandable. He had nine children to raise. That means you have to live peaceably with the government, with the regime, with the party. Otherwise – calamity. So he tried hard and was active."[53] His background, know-how, and sensible production model meant a comparatively friendly relationship with the district state administration; when I visited him in 2000, he continued to receive financial subsidies and other limited assistance from state institutions – a benefit unimaginable at the time for most private farmers.[54]

Elite farmers, especially members of village councils and other organs of local government, sometimes commanded the power of the local press to support their endeavors. Failing that, they could at least act to prevent the press from undermining them. Press outlets complimented these farmers not for their independence or marketizing activity, but rather for their ability to function efficiently within a Soviet framework for agricultural production. In 1992, when the deputy head of the executive committee of a peri-urban settlement in Kharkiv obtained fifty hectares from Chapaev State Farm,[55] he was lauded in the district press as one of the few farmers in the district who did "not badly execute state orders for the sale of grain."[56] When he ran for public office in 1994, the district press described him as the "chairman" of a private farm.[57] Ordinarily, "heads" led private farms, whereas collective farms had chairmen.

Village elites who received farmland were not only rural professionals and officials, they also included the lieges of much smaller kingdoms. In

53 V. Kolodezhanskii, "Liskinskii sobstvennik, ne isporchennyi kollektivom," *LI* 30 March 1996, 2.
54 Interview, farmer Kuz'mich, LV, 8 May 2000.
55 "Maizhe dvadtsiat' pytan': pro biudzhet i ne til'ky... " *TT* 8 September 1992, 2–3.
56 V. Lemishchenko, "Selo na shliakhu do rynku: aktual'ne interv'iu. Fermer dopomozhe derzhavi, iakshcho derzhava dopomozhe fermeru," *TT*, 17 September 1994, 6.
57 V. Lemishchenko, "Vybory-94: kak golosovat'? Stavka – bol'she, chem zhizn'," *TT*, 19 March 1994, 1.

1991, a reporter visiting the home of one of the first private farmers in Liski encountered an older woman's description of her son and daughter-in-law. The couple had begun a private farm two years earlier as part of a leasing brigade: "Viktor wasn't the last worker in the collective farm, and no one would say a bad word about Galia – she worked in a store."[58] At first glance, such a statement may seem an innocuous, and not very meaningful, compliment offered by a mother about her son of whom she is proud. But the statement is telling of the couple's position in the community. To work in a store at the end of the 1980s meant not only status within village society, but also substantial power at the local level. Employees of stores had control over the distribution of scarce consumer goods. No one said a bad word about Galia not because she occupied an especially high position, but because wind of an insult could deny the speaker sausage for as long as Galia saw fit to "run out" when the speaker got to the front of the line. Such minor positions of power became significant when it came to doing favors, such as expediting paperwork for a land allotment for private farming.

They're Inserting Sticks in the Wheels

A second category of people who were able to form private farms included those on the margins of rural society. If elites were granted land because they could not be refused, this second group of people generally received land for two reasons. First, facing few other economic options, they were persistent in their requests. Second, because of their marginal status they were not believed to pose a serious threat of competition to collective forms of production. Thus, state officials often did not oppose allotting small parcels of land to them. The farmers who belonged to this category of land recipients were ethnic minorities, newly arrived from other former Soviet republics; women, usually single, middle-aged, and socially marginalized; and city people who moved to the countryside seeking a way to make a living off the soil.[59]

State officials at the district level treated people on the margins of rural society differently in their attempts to obtain land than they treated rural elites. Farmers on the margins were more likely to be subject to difficult encounters, including intrusive queries about how they intended to manage their land and their finances. The state institutions charged with

---

[58] "Delo Samarinykh," *LZ*, 22 January 1991, 1, 3.
[59] See, for example, V. Lemishchenko, "Hospodari na svoii zemli," *TT* 12 August 1995, 1.

distributing land also were responsible for overseeing land use and management – in other words, for controlling its use. Local state officials took this charge seriously, or at least wished to be seen as doing so: speaking hypothetically of an older woman living in a village of Chuhuiv district, one official wondered in 2006, "Who other than the state can protect her interests?"[60] Because of their multiple mandates, state officials were protective of land when they could afford to be. Officials demanded higher standards of land management from farmers on the social margins, who were more likely to be engaged in expanded household production than in strictly commercial activities. For most people on the margins, interactions with state officials were likely to include humiliation and criticism, followed by refusals of their requests.

In 2000, a Kharkiv farmer attempted to obtain pasture for her livestock. She and her husband had received land in Kharkiv district and were seeking to trade it for ten hectares of pasture in a neighboring district adjacent to her farm. When she arrived at the district land-tenure office, a high-ranking official immediately attacked her intentions and credentials: "What do you think this is, a bazaar? Like an apartment – here you are, here are the keys, go ahead … ?" A representative of a local organization that supported private farmers argued on the farmer's behalf but was in turn rebuffed with questions such as "What is the standard amount of grazing land per head of cattle?" which were intended to expose her ignorance of agricultural practices. An official present demanded a business plan from the farmer and then used a common strategy for emptying a state office of supplicants: he suggested she return after she had filled out additional paperwork.[61]

In Voronezh, the district press made an effort early in the 1990s to portray farmers as outsiders and the private farm as an alien institution. There was a racialized aspect to these efforts.[62] Some of the first private farmers in Voronezh were from the Caucasus: Chechnya and Dagestan. These farmers were outsiders not only by virtue of their relatively recent arrival in Russian villages but also because of their ethnic background. In Liski district, the local paper did its best to emphasize this fact. Among the first farmers in the district was a family from Grozny and Rostov that leased land from a local collective farm. The local paper described them as

---

[60] Interview, district administration, CK, 21 July 2006.

[61] OT, district administration, DK, 7 February 2000.

[62] This occurred in a context generally hostile to people from southern republics and regions. In one district of Voronezh region, for example, Chechens and Dagestanis were blamed for a cholera outbreak in 1995. *AV* 19 July 1997, 2.

a "large family" of four brothers and their wives.[63] While such business arrangements among family members were not uncommon among ethnic Russians and Ukrainians, they went unremarked upon in the press. In a subsequent newspaper article about this "settler" family, the author assured readers that there were also [ethnically] Russian men interested in private farming – Kiselev, Sichkov, Grachev – who would do no worse than the settler family: "And that's reassuring, right?"[64]

Some farmers who were not members of ethnic minorities encountered resistance simply because they had not been born in the village or region in which they farmed, and some residents who had spent "only" twenty or more years of their lives in the area also confronted special obstacles in obtaining land. As with farmers from the Caucasus in Voronezh, and as Kaneff has found in Bulgaria, conflicts over land distribution became (or were at least perceived by locals as becoming) battles for the establishment of territory.[65] Suspicion of outsiders did not always manifest itself as overt prejudice, but being from somewhere else meant simply that members of the community or state officials "didn't particularly help."[66] In an environment and economy in which local ties could mean the difference between commercial success and failure, exclusion from circles of mutual assistance could itself be a form of economic discrimination.

One of the first private farmers in Voronezh was a sheep farmer originally from Makhachkala, the capital city of Dagestan, in the northern Caucasus. Kamil Makhmudov managed to obtain ten hectares of land in Voronezh only after protracted negotiations with the collective farm where he had worked. In the district press, a reporter describing Makhmudov's situation immediately called attention to the fact that Makhmudov had moved around – something most Voronezh collective farm members did not and could not do: "Having changed his place of employment several times, he convinced the chairmen of 'Donskoe' ... that he, Kamil Makhmudov, could not live without his farm." The chairman of the collective eventually relented and approved the allotment, despite reservations: "The chairman gave the go-ahead, not trusting much in the undertaking of this guy who looks so different from the local collective farm members."[67]

[63] "Stavka – na arendu," *LZ* 4 February 1991, 3.
[64] "Delo dlia nastoiashchikh muzhchin," *LZ* 6 March 1991, 3.
[65] Kaneff, "When 'Land' Becomes 'Territory': Land Privatisation and Ethnicity in Rural Bulgaria" in Sue Bridger and Frances Pine, eds. *Surviving Post-Socialism: Gender, Ethnicity and Underclass in Eastern Europe and the Former USSR*. London: Routledge, 1998.
[66] Interview, farmer Besarabov, XK, 12 April 2000.
[67] "Mechta sbyvaetsia?" *LZ* 1 January 1991, 2.

Early in the reform process, Makhmudov's farm was located on the territory of a collective farm. As such, it was subject to some collective governance. The local reporter noted that other villagers did not understand what Makhmudov was doing, and once again called attention to Makhmudov's physical appearance: "Last summer at the general meeting of the collective farm, in Makhmudov's absence, his farm was formally called into question. Proponents of the 'purity' of the collective farm ranks took Makhmudov to task, for they pale beside the farmer. At work, of course, at work."[68]

There were suggestions of racialized thinking about farming and land ownership in Kharkiv as well. In Kharkiv, the target group was Roma rather than people from the Caucasus. At a conference of private farmers in Kharkiv, a high-ranking regional official recounted how "Gypsies" in one district paid off pensioners with food in exchange for land certificates: "They found out where [the women] lived."[69] Likewise, when a farmer in a southern district of Kharkiv described the business practices of a neighbor of his, also a private farmer, who hadn't kept any accounts for five years and apparently had no regard for the authorities' opinion about his practices, he offered the following explanation: "He's a Gypsy by ethnicity."[70]

These were not isolated incidents but expressions of a generalized anxiety. The editor of a Voronezh district paper wrote of the perceived threat of outsiders taking land: "In places we're threatened by expansion through the transfer of land, including land as private property, to enterprising people from the south."[71] The anxiety voiced by ethnic Russian and Ukrainian villagers, combined with local enterprises' sometime refusal to do business with those farmers who began as outsiders, caused many farmers on the margins eventually to lose their land.[72]

Other individuals on the margins of rural society who became private farmers were single, middle-aged women. Official documentation of land distribution belies the actual gender breakdown among private farmers.

---

[68] Ibid.

[69] OT, Kharkiv regional farmers' association conference, 18 January 2000.

[70] OT, district farmers' association, LK, 30 March 2000. This remark later was followed by a story about how earlier in life the speaker had been a Soviet army officer in charge of thirteen tanks driven by soldiers from Uzbekistan. The group dissolved in laughter, wondering how it had been possible to teach Uzbeks to drive tanks.

[71] V. Pleshkov, "...Pokoi nam tol'ko snitsia," *LI* 13 February 1992, 6.

[72] Makhmudov was later among the victims of repossession by the district state administration. See "Dai! Zapiski po krest'ianskomu voprosu," *LI* 19 November 1993, 2.

For example, the Kharkiv district farm registration list in 2000 showed that 35 of the 119 private farms in the district were run by women.[73] While there were some female farmers in Kharkiv district, a number of those listed were not female-led enterprises; rather, the farms were registered in the names of the wives of prominent men.

This practice obscured the ways in which private commercial farming was a highly gendered phenomenon and created the appearance of women's participation. In reality, women faced special obstacles in attempting to obtain land. Many state officials at all levels of government approached women with skepticism and condescension, and press coverage of private farming recorded this fact without comment or irony.[74] For example, an article in the Kharkiv press took on a derisive tone in describing a "little lady" who came into the district office asking for forty to fifty hectares of land for a private farm.[75] While it might be argued that the meaning of such apparent derision was not gendered as such, but rather was rooted in objection to the manipulations of powerful men whose less prominent wives served as the nominal heads of private farms, this was not the case in the instances given here. The names of the rural elite were well known, and the women targeted for ridicule and other informal social sanction belonged to the second category of farmers identified here.

The history of a Ukrainian regional farmers' association illustrates the contrast between the experience and backgrounds of elite male and less-powerful female farmers. In particular, these two groups had vastly different relationships to the state. Through these relationships, social inequalities were replicated and deepened during the privatization process.

The Kharkiv farmers' association began as a gender-integrated organization. Over time, most of the women in the organization split off to form their own group, and by the end of the 1990s there were two independent associations. The men's association, whose members did not explicitly exclude women but rather drove them out by ignoring them at meetings, was led first by an established farmer who had begun his business

---

[73] Statistics obtained from district land tenure office, XK.

[74] I observed this repeatedly over the months during which I conducted participant-observation research in regional and district state offices. I sometimes encountered it myself: only my ties to national and regional-level officials, foreign identity and credentials, and educated speaking style insulated me from more frequent insult. The situation was far worse for local rural women who had no connections in government and, in many instances, spoke only in dialect.

[75] V. Iarmolenko, "Sovkhoz fermeru pomozhet," *TT* 19 May 1992, 3.

in the late 1980s, and then by the former head of the applied mathematics department at Kharkiv State University, who had become a farmer in 1992. The association council was composed mainly of farmers drawn from collective farm management and the upper echelons of regional and district government. During the 1990s, the men's association had offices in the building of the regional administration, a secretary on the state payroll, use of a telephone, and access to the state division of private farms, which assisted the farmers in obtaining information about markets in seed, fuel, and other inputs.

The women's association had no access to the state ties and resources enjoyed by their male counterparts. The leaders of the women's organization were widely known for their audacity and eccentricity and generally were not welcome at the office of the official association. Some were known locally as female boors, or "*khamki*" – listened to but derided and surrounded by scandal that was sometimes of their own making. Their association was composed predominantly of women who had held low-status positions in collective farms before they became private farmers. *Gosprom*, the regional state administration building that housed the official and predominantly male regional farmers' association, was not available to the women as a meeting place. Instead, these farmers gathered at various locales: at the home of the leader of the organization, in a library in the city of Kharkiv, and wherever they could find a venue.

Members of the women's association consistently articulated a sense that even if not all of them had begun private farming as marginalized, eccentric members of society, the psychological and material conflicts they constantly faced drove their leadership close to the edge. One of the prominent farmers in the women's organization described how the leader of the women's association was not "that way" when she began private farming, but that the profession had changed her: "She was a totally different person when she started."[76]

There was good reason for such a change. These women's experiences with private farming were qualitatively different than those of their powerful male counterparts. At a 1999 conference cosponsored by the women farmers' association and organizations from Dnipropetrovsk, female farmers told of violence and intimidation in their home villages. One farmer described a letter she received from the chairman of a neighboring collective farm. In the letter, he threatened to rape, kill, and burn

---

[76] Interview, farmer Buria, Kharkiv regional administration, 22 February 2000.

her and her children. She also related how her niece and others had been beaten because of conflicts over land.[77]

Some private farmers who were neither members of ethnic minorities nor women figured in public discourse in ways that we may regard as a social analogue of what Russian Formalists called *ostranenie*, or defamiliarization.[78] The poetic technique of using language to remove familiar objects and events from their usual context – or to remove them from the set of expectations and definitions with which they ordinarily are associated – appeared in press descriptions of farmers in Voronezh and Kharkiv. The parallel is not perfect: the words used to portray private farmers are the words of everyday life and not of art, but a discernible process of deliberate other-making and marginalization was present in the ways newspapers presented farmers to the public. Private farmers, journalists often implied, were in some way alien, whether because of their national origin, their transgression of late Soviet gender-labor norms, or some other feature that removed them from the sphere of the known social world. Reports about private farmers created a social gap between readers and farmers, making this new form of ownership and production seem strange, suspicious, and even, at times, worthy of ridicule.[79]

District newspapers were for most rural people the only source of print news available during the 1990s, and their reporters sometimes made private farmers into eccentric outsiders, or *chudaki*.[80] The story of a farmer-leaser on a collective in Liski is a case in point. This farmer had become dissatisfied with the enterprise leadership and charged that it had not fulfilled its financial obligations to him.[81] Representatives of regional and district divisions of agricultural management judged his claims to be "nothing more than absurd," and the chief economist of the collective charged that the farmer owed the collective 140,000 rubles. In an effort

---

[77] Presentation by V. Ivaniukovych. Conference "Legal protection of farmers and the fight with corruption in the implementation of land reform," 2 – 3 August 1999. Ukrainian Academy of State Administration, Kharkiv.

[78] Victor Shklovsky, "Iskusstvo kak priem," in *Poetika: Sborniki po teorii poeticheskogo iazyka*. Petrograd, 1919.

[79] The treatment of private farmers in local press finds some parallel in the practices of revelation and admonishment described by Oleg Kharkhordin in *The Collective and the Individual in Russia: A Study of Practices*. Berkeley: University of California Press, 1999.

[80] At the same time, the Liski press complained about a surfeit of positive coverage of private farming in the media: "We've seen enough television programs, read enough cheerful stories." V. Chernyshov, "Budushchie fermery," *LZ* 19 February 1991, 1.

[81] This was not an uncommon situation – some chairmen of collectives ensured that leasing arrangements were sealed with a handshake rather than a signed contract. What was unusual was the fact that the farmer in question made a public claim against the collective.

to recover money owed him by the collective farm, this private farmer staged a hunger strike in the building of the regional state administration. The local paper reported that the farmer had then threatened to travel to Red Square in Moscow and publicly immolate himself in protest. His former colleagues at the collective were quoted as wryly telling him to "dress warmly" so as to survive the flames.[82]

By all appearances, the Liski district press either reflected existing societal disapproval of private farming, as in the case of farmer who noted in 1992 that in his home village, "some people consider me a big *chudak* – for my healthy lifestyle, and now for my desire to become a private farmer,"[83] or, to the extent that the local press acted as a mouthpiece for local state institutions, was attempting to turn public opinion against private farmers. A typical report about one farmer expressed some skepticism about his commitment to agricultural activities: "It's unlikely that Vladimir Baranov will plow his 127 hectares this spring." Identified in the paper as a "former daredevil," this farmer "rides around in his ZIL-133 [an automobile], buys up potatoes and trades in shoes."[84]

The local press selectively applied similar treatment to well-connected urban elites who became farmers. One former head of a major automobile manufacturing plant in Voronezh turned to private hog farming in his retirement. In 1999, he found himself featured in a full-page article whose headline, right above his picture, read, "Pigs made me feel like a real person!" This farmer had attempted to obtain land in Khokhol district of Voronezh and had been refused. In Semiluki, where he eventually received land, he had the support of a collective farm chairman and the deputy head of district administration. The Semiluki press made hay of this story of a powerful urbanite drawn to a humbler line of work through high-level connections: "Authority, connections, a car, and apartment – he had everything.... But, as happens with city people, he was pulled from the asphalt to the soil."[85]

Amidst a social environment unfavorable to private farming, both local state officials and managers of former collectives saw reasons to impede the process of land distribution, and both of these groups used varying tactics to accomplish their goals. For some, there was the appearance of

[82] M. Ponomarev, "On nichto ne proshchal, szhech' sebia obeshchal..." *LI* 2 February 1993, 1.

[83] "Edva uspev rodit'sia... Obrechen uzh razorit'sia," *LI* 30 April 1992, 3.

[84] G. Aleksandrov, "Fermerskii 'lokotok'," *LI* 7 April 1994, 2.

[85] S. Eliseev, "Fermer Aleksandr Riazhskikh: 'So svin'iami ia pochuvstvoval sebia chelovekom'," *SZ*, 15 July 1999, 3.

free distribution of land; in other cases, rural people prevailed against substantial obstacles to obtain farmland. As a farmer leasing land from the Kharkiv collective "Kommunar" noted early in the reform process, even as people were willing and able to work and manage the land, "every possible agricultural bureaucrat doesn't trust us, it's obvious, it's quiet in the forest. In order not to be suspected of conservatism, they're inserting sticks in the wheels."[86]

Conclusion

Land rights alone did not predict the nature of farmers' participation in the rural economy. The social origins of private farmers in Voronezh and Kharkiv foretold the bifurcation of the private farmers' movement into commercial enterprises, on the one hand, and primarily subsistence cultivation, on the other.[87] Elite private farmers with large landholdings and access to credit and other inputs began to evince important similarities with the production practices of former collectives; these farmers possessed an economy of scale that allowed truly commercial agricultural production. Farmers on the margins, meanwhile, cultivated small plots using begged or borrowed machinery, animal-pulled plows, or hand-held tools. This division echoed the deepening of rural economic inequalities as many rank-and-file individual shareholders fell deeper into economic crisis while power increasingly became concentrated in the hands of the rural elite.

Over time, the pattern of land distribution to the well-connected and to the marginalized led to the reproduction of Soviet forms of *de facto* property rights regimes and agricultural production. The bimodal distribution in allotment for private farms explains why new commercial agricultural enterprises tend to cleave to Soviet forms of production: elites with access to large tracts of land replicated Soviet economies of scale, while farmers on the margins essentially engaged in household production. Indeed, this duality in organizational profile was anticipated in the words for these entities used in Russian and Ukrainian legislation: *krest'ianskoe (fermerskoe) khoziaistvo* and *selians'ke (fermers'ke) hospodarstvo* – terms that

---

[86] G. Chub, "Na slovakh – chto na gusliakh," *TT* 6 August 1991, 3.
[87] Judith Pallot and Tatyana Nefedova find a similar bimodal distribution in land for household plots, with a vast middle and some market-oriented and subsistence production at either end of the distribution. "Geographical Differentiation in Household Plot Production in Rural Russia," *Eurasian Geography and Economics* 44:1 (2003) 40–64.

include both peasant homestead and commercial denotations, even as there was no legal distinction between them.

Elite farmers imitated collective farms' social structure and entitlement systems both with respect to their employees and, as far as they were able, with respect to state institutions: employees were paid in kind rather than in cash; and farmers provided the minimal social safety net that collectives offered, distributing meat and grain to pensioners at holidays and contributing to the community in many of the ways that collective farms formerly had. This meant that for many workers, there was little difference in their experience of private and collective farming. Elite private farmers' long-standing relationships with local government officials allowed them to secure preferential treatment in the form of subsidies, assistance with procuring bank loans, and special access to information about local markets.

"Farmer-outcasts" replicated the household forms of production in which the entire rural population continues to be engaged, regardless of land-holding status. These farmers did not have adequate social and financial capital to sustain commercial production in the economic climate of the 1990s. Credit on reasonable terms was virtually absent – interest rates reached several hundred percent annually, with interest payable monthly; this meant keeping a portion of loans out of the production cycle in order to make interest payments. Many of these farmers eventually turned to other forms of economic activity to support themselves, and some lost their land because of technical violations of zoning regulations – that is, for improper use or non-use of agricultural land. Some of those farmers who did not lose their land reverted to growing only enough to feed their families. In other words, for farmers on the margins of rural society, a nominally commercial form of land ownership and agricultural production came to resemble household production, as ostensibly commercial farms became glorified victory gardens.

Thus, even as business elites and officials struggled to maintain collectives, some Black Earth farmland did pass into the hands of its private citizens, and limited privatization allowed state elites to claim they had complied with the letter of the law. While most rural people could not afford or did not possess the political resources necessary to participate in privatization, the fact that a relatively small number of individuals were able to claim land suggested that state officials had fulfilled their mandate. Economic and political conditions that constrained local demand for land allowed elites to frame the failures of privatization as a consequence of villagers' lack of desire to start their own businesses. Some domestic and foreign observers accepted this strictly behavioralist story, attributing limited distribution to a lack of entrepreneurship rather than to a lack of appropriate material or social resources.

The overwhelming majority of rural residents had no part in this process. Whereas the character of land distribution to private farms in Russia and Ukraine was only a small part of the entire project of privatizing land, its effects were characteristic of post-Soviet reform in general and of liberal economic reform programs in many developing countries: those on the margins were pushed further to the edge of society; the well-connected and powerful increased their wealth and influence; and the vast middle was left out of the distribution process entirely.

4

A Return to Regulation

Land privatization did not extricate the state from rural economies, whatever the desires of reform ideologists. An important underlying purpose of enclosure, the depoliticization of economic activity, did not occur:[1] as Barnes has shown, political struggles continued long after formal privatization processes had been completed.[2] Instead, the withdrawal of national governments from some areas of agriculture left a vacuum,[3] and land privatization provided local officials the opportunity to reassert their influence. In certain areas of land use regulation, state control at the district and regional levels intensified through the process of reform, even as state assistance in ordering relations among enterprises fell away. The persistence of large-scale agricultural enterprises kept the countryside "legible,"[4] and smaller-scale agricultural entrepreneurs who had managed to acquire land found themselves subject to scrutiny and regulation of their holdings by land committees, land tenure offices, offices of economic planning, and other local state institutions. Those who did leave collectives

[1] Maxim Boycko, Andrei Schleifer, and Robert Vishny, *Privatizing Russia*. Cambridge, MA: MIT Press, 1995; Roman Frydman, Andrzej Rapaczynski, and Joel Turkowitz, "Transition to a Private Property Regime in the Czech Republic and Hungary," in Wing Thye Woo, Steven Parker, and Jeffrey D. Sachs, eds. *Economies in Transition: Comparing Asia and Europe*. Cambridge, MA: MIT Press, 1997.
[2] Andrew Barnes, *Property and Power: The Struggle for Assets in the Remaking of Russia*. Ithaca: Cornell University Press, 2006.
[3] Stephen Wegren, "State Withdrawal and the Impact of Marketization on Rural Russia," *Policy Studies Journal* 28:1 (2000).
[4] James C. Scott, *Seeing Like a State: How Certain Schemes to Improve the Human Condition Have Failed*. New Haven: Yale University Press, 1998.

risked losing the support of social networks, even as they were newly vulnerable under the watchful gaze of local officials.

Amidst unreformed relationships between local state regulatory institutions and agricultural enterprises, private ownership without political power held little practical meaning. Most private farmers owned the land they cultivated, but ownership carried with it a limited bundle of rights. State administrations deployed old models of state–economy relationships in their oversight of private farms: rather than adapting their regulatory practices to new private property rights regimes, they made demands of landholders that forced many farmers out of business, frequently leading to the repossession of privately owned farmland.

Reregulation and state retrenchment as a response to economic liberalization, as well as the protection of common pool resources from individuation, have been observed in other reform contexts.[5] Local state retrenchment in the Black Earth, however, involved more than reassertion of Soviet-era regulatory norms. Russian and Ukrainian land reform legislation focused attention on the allocation of rights but offered wide discretion to local officials who regulated those rights, and Black Earth bureaucrats used the discretion available to them to reshape the social geography of land use. Where local officials had the requisite resources and will, regulation was selective and deliberate, advancing a vision of the landscape that included uninterrupted expanses of industrial crops rather than checkerboard fields of yeoman farms. Furthermore, the norms and incentives officials faced favored maintenance of status quo property relations: amidst financial crisis and political instability, collectives offered both an economy of scale suitable for modern agriculture and social protection for the village.

The extent of state control over private property does not appear in the formal record of land privatization because land repossession did not figure in assessments of reform. The initial privatization and allotment of land in Black Earth regions was the only stage of the reform process that Russian and Ukrainian national state institutions, acting at the behest of international lending organizations, assiduously surveyed and recorded. Land tenure offices of regional state administrations gathered detailed information concerning the reorganization of every former collective or

[5] Richard Snyder, *Politics after Neoliberalism: Reregulation in Mexico.* Cambridge: Cambridge University Press, 2001; Katherine Verdery, "Fuzzy Property: Rights, Power, and Identity in Transylvania 's Decollectivization" in Michael Burawoy and Katherine Verdery, eds. *Uncertain Transition: Ethnographies of Change in the Postsocialist World.* Lanham, MD: Rowman and Littlefield, 1999, 53–82.

state farm: the new form of enterprise organization, the number of members of collectives who had received ownership papers for land shares, and a host of other measurements of the progress of reform.[6] This information served to reassure the central government as well as international donors that agricultural land was passing from state ownership into the hands of individuals. However, reformers within the Russian and Ukrainian government did not demand a direct accounting from regional and district state institutions of substantive changes in state–economy relationships after privatization.

That accounting may be found in the narratives of farm directors and private farmers who faced control, exclusion, harassment, and repossession, as well as in the narratives of bureaucrats who wielded such tools of intimidation. The evidence presented here is drawn from oral sources as well as the documentary record: local press reports, conference proceedings, regional legislation, and official documents linked to court cases.

Pressure Has Remained

After reorganization and privatization, worker-shareholders held former collective and state farms in individual or, for a time, collective shared ownership. In theory, state officials no longer could hold farm directors formally accountable for managerial decisions and behavior. Land and non-land assets belonged to individual worker-shareholders rather than "the people" of the Soviet Union or collective farm: the state was no longer a proxy owner, and the legal status of reorganized farms allowed agricultural enterprises to operate mostly autonomously, free from the dictates of Soviet state planners. On paper, agricultural collectives became islands unto themselves, subject only to market forces, the hard work of their shareholders, and the vicissitudes of nature.

No such autonomy existed in practice. Local state officials used privatization to regain control over former collective agricultural enterprises and to reassert certain elements of the command system. This was perhaps not surprising in districts with a post-socialist tradition of strong state regulation. In Chuhuiv, home to some of the most productive farms in Kharkiv, local officials kept former collectives in lockstep with the wishes of the

---

[6] For example, a document from the Kharkiv regional division of land resources management #4–616 of 27 September 1999, "Informatsiia pro vykorystannia rezervnoho fondu zemel', stvorenoho pry peredachi zemel' v kolektyvnu vlasnist' v Kharkivs'kii oblasti stanom na 1 zhovtnia 1999 roku."

district administration. So long as "we remain in a transition period," one Chuhuiv official reasoned, "the criterion for evaluating state functionaries is the economy... we're obliged to keep our finger on the pulse of the economy. I can't stand aside if I see that people can be deceived or not paid for their share. I have the right to gather people together and give my opinion."[7] Likewise, collective farms in Liski could find that "the administration won't let us cull" livestock herds even though husbandry had become unprofitable.[8]

In districts where local officials did not command the resources necessary to closely regulate former collectives, they still claimed to play an important role in coordinating economic life. As a leading agricultural management official in one such district of Kharkiv explained: "Me [sic] and my [farm] leaders meet frequently. They're private owners (*chastniki*), but I have a lot of questions. We meet on Mondays."[9] Such control did not always include a *quid pro quo* that benefited farms. In Liski, the head of one former collective provided a typical assessment: "Opportunities are limited. Pressure has remained, but there's no assistance. The head of administration gives the orders. The chairman is responsible for marketing, and we try to market produce in the district."[10] Such a reconfiguration of state control was seen as even more intrusive than the social contract of the late Soviet period: farms continued to have responsibilities to the state, even when they received no support from it beyond access to commodities markets.

Agricultural enterprises were in theory free to sell on the open market, but regional and district bureaucracies continued to oversee the details of cultivation in some districts, in places dictating what crops could be planted. Crop rotation continued to be regulated, and most contracts with state buyers included a clause invaliding the contract in case of improper rotation. Even by the late 1990s, directors of collectives did not always determine their cultivation plans: if the Kharkiv regional state administration decided that the provincial capital required tomatoes, then local state administrations, which controlled access to fuel and commodity credits, would compel some number of farms to plant tomatoes, regardless of likely profitability.[11]

---

[7] Interview, district administration, CK, 21 July 2006.

[8] Interview, head economist, Fatherland, LV, May 2000. The reason for this was that livestock herds, once depleted, require years to reestablish.

[9] Interview, department of agricultural management, NK, 21 July 2006.

[10] Interview, director, LV, 8 May 2000.

[11] Interview, Kharkiv regional farmers' association, 6 December 1999. This is one narrative of state control; multiple variations on the theme existed in other districts.

Even private contracts could involve direct state intervention. In Khava, farms producing sugar beet contracted directly with the local processing plant. In order to receive the finished sugar from the plant, however, farms required the approval of the local administration.[12] Further, the executive director of the Kharkiv regional association of private farmers, himself a bureaucrat rather than a farmer, noted that some aspects of production were still guided from the top because there could be trouble if directors of collectives were given more control. On the other hand, "if there were enough control from below, [some] collective agricultural enterprises would not have disintegrated."[13]

Representatives of local state institutions sometimes appropriated harvests or enterprise assets in order to liquidate enterprise debt, which was "collected through the district administration."[14] In Liski, "the tax police wrote off machinery for unpaid taxes" on the struggling former collective Zaria.[15] Another Voronezh administration, meanwhile, did "not allow sale in cash" to extinguish debt, and profited by marketing in kind grain payments itself: at the end of the 1990s, farms that sold grain for cash could ask 1,500 rubles per ton, but payments to this district administration were calculated at 600 rubles per ton. Furthermore, by refusing to accept full payment, the administration could keep farms in debt and hostage to the grain-for-debts arrangement.[16] The mechanism by which the administration managed to accomplish this feat remained hidden, for "no one can say, because tomorrow [the one who does] will be out of a job. It's iron-clad."[17]

The ultimate destination of payments made to state offices was not always clear. As the director of one Voronezh grain elevator found, "I have too many people wishing to receive that grain, starting with the tax police...they even impound grain."[18] Some district administrations required contributions to district grain funds, but in others, "the administration doesn't order grain for the regional fund...farmers make the rounds of the administration, a bit of sugar to one person, a bit of grain to someone else...All of that is unofficial, but they bring it." Farms sometimes responded to demands by withdrawing from compliance with state requirements, for any participation could be costly: "You have to share

[12] Interview, grain elevator, VV, 11 May 2000.
[13] Interview, Kharkiv regional farmers' association, 6 December 1999.
[14] OT, debt collector, VV, 13 May 2000.
[15] OT, small business owner, LV, 12 May 2000.
[16] OT, debt collector, VV, 13 May 2000.
[17] OT, economist, VV, 13 May 2000.
[18] Interview, grain elevator, VV, 11 May 2000.

your pennies with someone... If you pay your taxes, it doesn't mean no one will touch you.... On the contrary, when you pay taxes, they start asking for more."[19]

State officials exerted unwelcome control in some areas of agricultural production, but they also withdrew pressure from exchange relationships that previously had depended on the state for contract enforcement. In the late 1990s, the Voronezh former collective farm Chayanovskoe generated no profit, producing only inputs sufficient for the following year's growing season. Its production levels depended not only on employee households' demand for inputs, which drove the labor supply to the collective, but also on the solidity and extent of its ties with other enterprises. In the absence of a viable cash economy, barter ran the business: oil, fuel, coal, and machine parts were obtained from other enterprises in exchange for seed, animal feed, potatoes, and sugar beet. Some trading relationships developed out of ties that had existed under the command system, but many were entirely new. The chairman of Chayanovskoe spent much of his time establishing and gaining access to external distribution networks. Partnerships could be risky, and farm managers were compelled to expend a great deal of energy searching for reliable business partners.

In September of 1998, Chayanovskoe encountered a typical problem when one of its grain debtors refused to make payment.[20] Transactions between enterprises often took place on the basis of personal contacts, but the relationship in question this time was an official one left over from the Soviet-era command structure. The formal character of the relationship between Chayanovskoe and its debtor meant that there were no personal ties to guarantee fulfillment of the contract. As the district head of agricultural administration put it, the pressure that formerly had ensured compliance in such situations had given way to "pure partnership relations."[21] When planners in Moscow stopped enforcing contractual agreements, the reliability of transactions depended on the strength of personal relationships between contracting parties. The director of Chayanovskoe summed up the situation: "For us, this is not a very good time in terms of the dependability of business partners. You have to work with your own

---

[19] OT, economist and debt collector, VV, 13 May 2000. Humphrey notes the practical necessity of maintaining farm bank balances at zero, in order not to attract the attention of the authorities. *Marx Went Away, But Lenin Stayed Behind.* Ann Arbor: University of Michigan Press, 2001, 468.

[20] Daily meeting of Chayanovskoe's managers and specialists (*planerka*), 21 August 1998.

[21] Interview, head of agricultural administration in Chayanovskoe's district, 9 September 1998.

people . . . people who are tried and true. You have to do your best to avoid deception and secondly, all other kinds of unpleasantness."[22] Soviet rule had embedded enterprises in networks of interdependence, and in many cases, those ties were not strong enough to survive the collapse of the power that created them.

Enterprises in Chayanovskoe's district did receive help from the local administration in identifying possible trading partners, but the reliability of those partners had then to be evaluated through personal contacts. In that district, a member of the local administration acted as a broker, periodically contacting farm chairmen with news about prospective business transactions. The chairman of the collective recorded this information in a log that he made available to farm specialists, who established partnerships on an independent basis. Alternatively, specialists contacted the district administration directly. This system supported personnel searches as well: new arrivals in the district could contact the district agricultural department to inquire about enterprises seeking employees. Although the dismantling of the command economy was to have separated the state from commerce, local government remained actively involved in the choice and identification of business partners – if not in actual contract enforcement. As the chairman of Chayanovskoe described it, "The agricultural department of the local administration plays the role of an advertising agency."[23]

Relationships between district state administrations and agricultural collectives varied by district, depending on the attitudes of local attitudes toward reform, the economic strength of the agricultural sector in the district during the late Soviet period, and the resources available to local government institutions for carrying out oversight of economic activity in the district. In districts that were relatively isolated from urban areas, local officials were able to carve out fiefdoms without competition with or interference from higher-level bureaucrats. In these districts, local control over economic activity could be stronger than in districts like Chayanovskoe's.

If state control under late Soviet rule carried with it material support for agricultural production, the social contract formed in the 1990s involved regulation but offered fewer benefits to farms. Reorganized collectives received fewer state subsidies, benefiting primarily by access to supply chains through state offices. Collectives were increasingly able to avoid selling directly to state buyers, but some high-ranking individual

[22] Interview, director of Chayanovskoe, 21 August 1998.
[23] Ibid.

state officials, often acting on behalf of their own personal or business interests rather than representing state institutions, extracted tribute from collective farm directors.[24]

Supplicants and Justice Seekers

Local state officials who kept detailed records of the economic life of collectives often possessed little knowledge about private farmers. On each side of the border, extensive local press coverage of agriculture attended nearly exclusively to former collective and state farms, and private farmers often received little mention.[25] Bureaucratic detachment, however, was not benign. Regional and district state offices controlled access to commodity credits and fuel, and private farmers' insistence on independent private ownership was often interpreted as a desire to live outside of local, informal economic networks. Ultimately, however, agricultural producers needed local business links to survive, so state-farm relationships that began with independence nonetheless sometimes ended with state control and regulation.

People who had made the choice to start their own agricultural enterprises often regarded themselves as more independent than those who continued to labor on collective farms, and this fact complicated private farmers' relationships with state institutions. In their own view, private farmers from both elite and marginal social backgrounds did not have "Soviet" personalities. In 1991, prompting anger at a conference of farmers from five Russian Black Earth regions, the Russian minister of agriculture announced plans to make the head of the national farmers' association (AKKOR) one of his deputies. Farmers feared the end of autonomy for their organization and made dire predictions about Soviet-style central planning if the appointment occurred. Liski farmers sent a telegram to Yeltsin: "We didn't elect the head of AKKOR for ministerial games."[26] In this instance, despite a much sought-after opportunity for a place at

---

[24] None of my interlocutors was willing to go on record to describe this phenomenon; in nearly every interview and interaction, however, all mentioned the phenomenon, if obliquely.

[25] For example, in Liski during the 1990s, the district press each year contained hundreds of articles about collectives, while fewer than ten articles annually were devoted to private farmers. In Kharkiv district, the only mention of private farmers in annual district agricultural reports during the 1990s was in 1996.

[26] V. Ivanov, "Kak fermery Yel'tsinu poslanie pisali..." *LI* 7 December 1991, 1.

the state trough, private farmers rejected a closer relationship with the central government.

Private farmers in Kharkiv, meanwhile, struggled to gain a seat at the table in public policy discussions at the local level. In December 1999, a high-ranking Kharkiv official spoke at a meeting of the regional farmers' association. Before an audience of farmers, the official held up a list of invitees for meetings about reform implementation. A few private farmers had been included on the list, but district functionaries had not contacted them. Except for the appearance of this official at a farmers' association meeting, farmers in the region would not have known of the meetings or even which farmers were meant to have been included in them.[27]

Ignorance of private farmers' activities, and exclusion of them from decisions about policy implementation, was not usually due to a lack of interest – though in some places, as in a southern district of Kharkiv, where the head of agricultural management could not name a single private farmer in his district when asked – this may have been the case.[28] Local officials did not always find it easy to obtain accurate information about private farms. A member of the Semiluki district committee on land resources and land tenure described this "problem," arguing that it was difficult to take farmers' reported crop yields seriously, and that "it's impossible at times to find out what small-tenure farmers really have growing in the fields."[29] Private farmers had good reason to try to elude the gaze of the state.[30] As Pallot and Nefedova have found in other Russian regions, that gaze discouraged people from accumulating land for household production.[31] The head of the Semiluki district farmers' association illustrated his own dilemma: when he purchased a tractor for 500,000 rubles, he was required to pay 380,000 rubles in taxes on the transaction. As he put it, "With taxes, you need to lie, or to pay.... We pay our taxes so as not to be ashamed." Predatory tax practices encouraged

[27] OT, regional deputy head of agricultural management, Kharkiv regional farmers' association, 14 December 1999.

[28] OT, division of agricultural management, LK, 30 March 2000.

[29] Interview, district farmers' association, SV, May 2000.

[30] James C. Scott provides a typology of "legible" and "illegible" practices and institutions, in which small peasant farms are categorized with businesses that are relatively less available for state control and appropriation. Scott, *Seeing Like a State: How Certain Schemes to Improve the Human Condition Have Failed*. New Haven: Yale University Press, 1998, 218.

[31] Judith Pallot and Tatyana Nefedova, "Geographical Differentiation in Household Plot Production in Rural Russia," *Eurasian Geography and Economics* 44:1 (2003) 62.

underreporting of production and profits – even as some business people struggled to convince tax authorities of the existence of debt:[32] "Even if you have losses, [if] you marketed your goods, it means you have to pay five percent."[33]

Although private farmers found good reasons to avoid engagement with the state, they were not always successful in doing so. Political and economic circumstances sometimes forced private farmers into a close relationship with local officials.[34] Farmers' organizations, which often served as key links to resources, emerged early in the reform period. In 1991, the Liski press reported that "in Moscow people had only just left the barricades at the White House, and we had already established our district association. Now any farmer can count on its assistance."[35] Farmers' organizations often existed cheek by jowl with government offices. In districts of Voronezh such as Anna and Semiluki, these organizations obtained offices in state administration buildings, which in many district or village council jurisdictions offered the only available space.[36]

Farmers' organizations located in state buildings had the advantage of proximity to local officials and market information and connections, but they also were potentially subject to greater control by state officials. The broader population was sensitive to such possibilities. When the Voronezh regional farmers' association began gathering in a state building, a local press report initially expressed concern about the farmers' presence there, including the presumption that farmers would raise suspicions that they were there as "supplicants" or "justice seekers" (*pravdoiskateli*) going above the heads of local officials to find solutions to their problems.[37] Meanwhile, a prominent private farmer in Kharkiv reported having visited one district where the district head of agricultural management led a meeting of private farmers.[38]

---

[32] Kathryn Hendley, "Struggling to Survive: A Case Study of Adjustment at a Russian Enterprise," *Europe-Asia Studies* 50:1 (January 1998).

[33] Interview, district farmers' association, SV, May 2000.

[34] It is a measure of the closeness of this relationship that in July 2006, officials in three Kharkiv districts and the regional administration were able within seconds to reach specific private farmers, at my request, on their mobile phones.

[35] V. Pleshkov, "Nas malo, no my… v 'tel'niashkakh.' Tak mogli by skazat' Liskinskie fermery," *LI* 3 December 1991, 2.

[36] Some farmers' associations found other solutions. In one district of Kharkiv, the farmers' association was able to rent a room in a private building from a former schoolmate of one of the farmers. OT, district farmers' association, VK, 30 March 2000.

[37] Pleshkov, "Nas malo, no my… v 'tel'niashkakh.'"

[38] OT, Kharkiv regional farmers' association, 28 March 2000.

Honest, Solid People

Where agricultural bureaucrats supported and encouraged private farming, they prescribed economic relations on a command model, arguing that " ... private farmers exist, and therefore it's necessary to provide them with seed on an equal footing with the state farms and other enterprises, and not as though they're last in line, because all are equal before the law."[39] In Kharkiv, district administrations worked with farmers to develop crop rotation plans and instructed some farmers on what to seed on their land.[40] State officials expected private farmers to mimic agricultural collectives' marketing strategies – that is, they were to sell to state buyers. The Kharkiv district head of agricultural management expressed disapproval of private farmers who did not meet this expectation, commenting in 1992 that collectives were currently signing contracts with state buyers for the sale of their goods, "which can't be said about private farmers."[41]

In some cases, the economic interdependence of farmers and state institutions provided a strong incentive for private farmers and individual households to sell crops, meat, and milk to the state, just as collectives had done under Soviet rule. This relationship was explicit in one Liski village council's call for people to sell their milk to state buyers. In return, the village council promised, sellers would experience no difficulty obtaining animal feed the following year.[42] Additionally, private farmers sometimes engaged in sharecropping arrangements with district state administrations, with state institutions providing fuel and seed in return for a portion of the harvest. In 1993, the Kharkiv district administration sold fuel to farmers or, in the words of the chief economist of the division of agricultural management, they "helped" farmers with fuel. In 1994, when they did not, the local press interpreted the lack of assistance as the main reason why private farmers did not sell much grain to the state that year.[43]

Despite some farmers' reluctance to engage the assistance of state institutions, the advocacy of powerful patrons was often necessary to resolve local problems. Patronage relationships with state officials at the regional

---

[39] "Pytannia potrebuiut' vyrishennia," *TT* 6 April 1996, 1.

[40] V. Lemishchenko, "Kudy zh use podilosia?" *TT* 12 December 1992, 1. A. Reshetov, "Fermer Anatolii Usik: Veriu v uspekh," *TT* 19 January 1991, 1–2.

[41] L. Barkanov, "Fermeru – prostor," *TT* 22 February 1992, 2.

[42] V. Ivanov, "Lichnoe – ne lishnee," *LZ* 26 March 1991, 3.

[43] V. Lemishchenko, "Fermer dopomozhe derzhavi, iakshcho derzhava dopomozhe fermeru," *TT* 17 September 1994, 6.

and national level were crucial sources of leverage for farmers' organizations. In the case of the Kharkiv regional farmers' association, the President of Ukraine served as such a resource in return for organizational support during elections. After the Ukrainian presidential elections of 1999, farmers expressed concern about their inability to deliver on a presumed *quid pro quo* relationship between the farmers' association and members of the presidential administration. One member of the council of the association complained, "How did we help the president in his election campaign? We can't do anything serious."[44] In order to try to perform the electoral favors that would gain them support from the national government, the organization decided to broaden its social base.

The administrative tasks that engaged the attention and energy of private farmers and drew them away from the soil of the Black Earth were legion: buying, trading, and borrowing machinery; locating spare parts; visiting bureaucrats' offices; settling debts; and a host of other errands.[45] Cultivating necessary informal ties with suppliers and gaining the support of local bureaucrats required countless hours spent in the buildings of district and regional administrations, and it fell to some private farmers to spend many of their working hours walking the corridors of power.[46] Much depended on the skill of private farmers in obtaining favors and preferential treatment, or just the benefits accorded them by law, from state officials. A regional official in Kharkiv described one farmer and his wife who had "learned that if you shake a spruce tree, something will, necessarily, fall from it. He works in the field while she goes around to various offices, shaking bureaucrats."[47]

As it was for former collectives, support did not always imply concrete material assistance. A Liski farmer who was reported to "walk the corridors" of the district administration found that while there were laws to help farmers with building and other projects, assistance even to him was not always forthcoming: "They help me, but our leadership doesn't have a lot of resources."[48] Local officials were not always available to assist

---

[44] OT, Kharkiv regional farmers' association, 14 December 1999.

[45] One Kharkiv farmer expressed shock and disbelief when, during one of my visits to his fields, I mentioned that my graduate school mentor had kept a flock of sheep for many years. Maintaining a Black Earth farm while working another full-time job would have been impossible, in part because of the constant need to develop and maintain personal relationships with representatives of local state institutions. This farmer's response was telling: "Surely, your mentor is a professor of livestock?"

[46] For example, see G. Aleksandrov, "Fermerskii lokotok," *LI* 7 April 1994, 2.

[47] OT, Kharkiv regional division of private farms, 11 January 2000.

[48] V. Kolodezhanskii, "Liskinskii sobstvennik, ne isporchennyi kollektivom," *LI* 30 March 1996, 2.

private farmers in resolving the legal and other land-related issues that invariably arose. One Kharkiv private farmer described the difficulty he encountered when attempting to meet with a local deputy: "It's easier to get in to see the President."[49] Such an observation was not unusual. Private farmers frequently appealed to state officials in the relatively higher echelons of regional administration in order to force change in their districts and villages. The Liski farmer quoted earlier about the lack of official help was not engaging in mere hyperbole: members of the governing council of the Kharkiv regional farmers' association frequently traveled to Kyiv in search of the support that local bosses could not or would not provide.

State regulation of private farming persisted, however, despite farmers' relatively limited access to local officials. In the mid-1990s, some processing and technical support in the Black Earth was still either state-owned or administered by district state administrations. State officials argued that without proper monitoring of and information about farmers' activities, district services would be unable to provide farmers the material assistance they needed for their businesses to survive.[50] Officials in Voronezh had a legislative mandate to establish "partnership" relationships and "constant cooperation with state administrative organs that would govern the day-to-day activity of private farmers.[51] And at first, the Kharkiv district administration exercised, or attempted to exercise, tight control over private farms. The district newspaper urged heads of local councils, the tax inspectorate, the district division of land resources, and the district division of agricultural management to develop measures that "control the financial activity and administration of private farms, the rational use of land for its designated purpose by those farmers, and the fulfilling of contractual agreements."[52] In some places, control appeared to tighten over time: by 2006, long after Ukraine's "Orange Revolution," the office for "work with private farmers" in the Kharkiv regional state administration building had become the office for "regulation of private farmers."[53]

Local officials evaluated the work of private farmers both in terms of Soviet-era public norms and in the language of economic rationality. Some did not regard private ownership as a good in itself: private farmers'

---

[49] OT, Kharkiv regional farmers' association, 4 April 2000.
[50] Barkanov, "Fermeru – prostor," *TT* 22 February 1992, 2.
[51] "O sozdanii oblastnogo fonda prodovol'stvennogo zerna," 11 August 1995, No. 845, Voronezh regional administration.
[52] V. Lemishchenko, "Vlada ie. Vlada diie. Kudy teche rika molochna?" *TT* 28 January 1995, 1.
[53] Field notes, Kharkiv, July 2006.

utility to society, as expressed through their obedience to the state, was the proper measure of their worth. The chief economist of the Kharkiv district division of agricultural management complained in 1994 that "farmers so far are capable only of a small measure of help to the state in solving the food [supply] issue."[54] Others reasoned that private farmers ought to earn their support by outperforming former collectives. A deputy of the Kharkiv district council argued that private farmers ought to be able to show that they would exceed previous years' yields on the land allotted to them, when a state farm had worked the land.[55] In Liski, others simply asked, "Do we need these kinds of land holders? What good are they capable of doing?"[56]

Early in the process, district-level agricultural managers had approached private farming with suspicion, presuming that private land ownership would lead to disorder and poor stewardship.[57] One Kharkiv official echoed a common sentiment: "Private farming should be introduced very cautiously, so that there is no misuse, no violations and squandering (*razbazarivanie*) of land."[58] Some private farmers also came to share this concern, believing "fictive" farmers discredited the whole movement. In 1995, the head of the Kharkiv regional farmers' association advocated a thorough state inventory of private farms in order to identify those who are "acting as fronts (*pidstavni osoby*) or are straw men, do not work on allotted land, but only collect the harvest."[59] In Semiluki, directors of agricultural collectives and heads of village councils also expressed an explicit interest in "bringing order to land use among private farmers."

The new form of land tenure did not, in the minds of some state officials, seem to suggest the need for a new type of political economy. Collective agricultural production remained the standard, and private commercial cultivation would be the last resort, an option available only when members of former state and collective farms had exhausted their ability or will to produce. Even long after privatization, in response to the

[54] Lemishchenko, "Fermer dopomozhe derzhavi," *TT* 17 September 1994, 6.

[55] V. Danylenko, "Fermerstvo – tse seriozno," *TT* 8 August 1992, 1.

[56] "Inye zemlevladel'tsy tol'ko muchaiut zemliu. 8 fermerskikh khoziaistv pretenduiut na likvidatsiiu," *LI* 8 July 1993, 3.

[57] Similarly, Caroline Humphrey provides an exposition of social attitudes that tie trade to perceptions of disorder in *The Unmaking of Soviet Life: Everyday Economies After Socialism.* Ithaca: Cornell University Press, 2002, 69–98.

[58] V. Iarmolenko, "Sovkhoz fermeru pomozhet?" *TT*, 19 May 1992, 3.

[59] M. Mel'nyk, "'Nas zlamaty uzhe neprosto,' – hovoryt' holova Kharkivs'koii asotsiatsii fermeriv S. V. Tsvetkov," *SK* 2 February 1995, 2.

suggestion that farmers be given land that collectives were not able to cultivate, the head of the Kharkiv district administration responded that "...under current legislation [this] procedure is very complicated, and secondly, not all is yet lost. There exist labor collectives full of the desire to work."[60] Where possible, district agricultural management offices integrated private farmers into the social contract that bound former collectives to district administrations. In Anna, a flourishing private farming sector even participated in the district-level agricultural competitions that had provided a staple labor incentive of the socialist period.[61] Officials expressed the hope that the state would assist farmers in becoming real owners (*hospodari*), "honest, solid people."[62]

For local officials, private farming presented an opportunity not only for state oversight of economic activity but also for integrating individualists into the ranks of solid citizens. Such intentions had profound implications for the future of private farming. Reformers in the capitals hoped the creation of private land ownership would foster independence and participation in world markets, but regional and district bureaucrats rejected that idea, expecting private farms to operate according to the same principles of local utility and regulation as agricultural collectives.[63] By establishing similar guidelines for private farmers' economic behavior as for that of collectives, local officials drew private farmers into webs of state regulation, shaped the content of private property regimes, and reconfigured the face of state power in the countryside.

Their Legs Cut Out from under Them

Repossession of land by state institutions was as much a feature of the privatization process as its distribution. Farmers who did not cleave to Soviet-era state-economy relationships sometimes found themselves targets of intense challenge by local officials. In the Black Earth, private ownership was for some an interim condition, not an irrevocable right.

[60] V. Lemishchenko, "Sil's'ka ekonomika: mozhlyvosti i realii. Koly zh nareshti prokynemosia?" *TT*, 20 September 1997, 2.
[61] "Bol'she produktsii polei i ferm!" *AV*, 29 July 1999, 3.
[62] Lemishchenko, "Fermer dopomozhe derzhavi iakshcho derzhava dopomozhe fermeru," *TT* 17 September 1994, 6.
[63] The devolution of state power during *perestroika* and accompanying localization of distribution networks contributed to this phenomenon. On this topic see Humphrey, *The Unmaking of Soviet Life: Everyday Economies After Socialism*. Ithaca: Cornell University Press, 2002, 69–98.

As in the battles over privatization and subsequent renationalization of industry after the turn of the millennium, land distribution did not always end with privatization. Alienation of privately held farmland by district state administrations completed a circle of local government control over property.

In the 1990s, rural regions of Russia and Ukraine witnessed a pattern of official approval of private farmers, followed by efforts to undermine them. After initial years of funding, state support for private farming was manifest primarily in directives and public relations campaigns in the district press, not in extensive material support. Once the support of the central government had abated or been withdrawn, some local state institutions backtracked, repossessing land held by private farmers. District state officials, opposed for practical economic or normative reasons to the development of smallholder farming, pursued hidden tactics that emptied property rights of stability and practical meaning. A discussion in the Liski press in 1993 described this reaction, acknowledging that although a few private farmers quit because they did not enjoy the work, "there are not many voluntary refusers. There are more of those who could not yet get on their feet for various reasons. And, unfortunately, there are enough peasants who are having their legs cut out from under them (*kotorym po nogam b'iut*)."[64]

Local officials in the Black Earth exercised wide discretion in upholding norms of social responsibility as they regulated land ownership. Officialdom in Kharkiv and Voronezh made a concerted effort across forms of agricultural production to tie ownership rights to effective use, harassing farmers if their enterprises did not fulfill their expected social role.[65] Although district land tenure offices singled out private farmers for greater surveillance and more frequent confiscation, all forms of production – private farms, former collectives, and household plots – received scrutiny and were subject to repossession. Local officials had the support of their superiors in Moscow and Kyiv in prosecuting those who misused or were believed to misuse their land. A former Russian minister of agriculture even expressed a desire in 2001 for intensified local regulation, noting, "It's still very important to prescribe (*propisat'*) a mechanism for confiscation of land that is not being used by the owner or is being used

---

[64] "Dai! Zapiski po krest'ianskomu voprosu," *LI*, 19 November 1993, 2.
[65] For example, Resolution No. 78 of the Voronezh regional legislature, 19 October 1995, "Ob uporiadochenii sdelok s zemlei, nakhodiashcheisia v sobstvennosti, vladenii i pol'zovanii iuridicheskikh i fizicheskikh lits."

with violations of use rules. That's regulated very poorly today." The former minister illustrated his point with the example of a private farmer
who "hadn't worked his fields in five years, which are overgrown with
weeds."[66]

Local officials also had the tacit support of much of the rural population in stemming the tide of land privatization. During the first wave
of distribution to private farmers, collective farm members throughout
Voronezh and Kharkiv expressed their displeasure at the appearance of
this new form of ownership. Private farmers hailing from the margins of
rural society presented special insult, as such farmers were rarely engaged
in commercial production, yet they received land plots far larger than
their neighbors who officially were engaged in household production.[67]
In districts across the Black Earth, private farmers articulated narratives
of violence at the hands of neighbors, and stories of machinery going up
in flames or farmers found decapitated were the stuff of village gossip
and news reports alike.[68] Private farmers in a southern district of Kharkiv
gave up their business because of instances of arson. One of them had
been killed, and of the first three farmers in the district, only one was still
in business by the end of the decade.[69]

Private farmers were subject to other humiliations and forms of insti-
tutionalized harassment such as public shaming. A report in Liski in 1993
found that eight of twenty-three private farms were deemed to be using
land inefficiently: 68 of a total of 1160 hectares were not producing crops.
Most of the farms in question had been operating for less than a year at
the time of the report, but the names of the offending farmers appeared in
the district newspaper, together with commentary such as, "Savvin doesn't
want to work." The report found a number of problems with these private
businesses: one farm's books indicated that melons would be planted, but
none were; some crops were purportedly in bad condition; and one farmer
missed seeding time for corn and sunflower by more than a month.[70] The

---

[66] I. Granik, "Tendentsii. 'Narod ustal ot kommunisticheskikh strashilok,'" *Kommersant*
24 September 2001, 6.
[67] Myriam Hivon, "Local Resistance to Privatization in Russia," *Cambridge Anthropology*
18:2 (1995) 13–22.
[68] Interview with farmer, DL, 15 February 1998; V. Ivaniukovich, Conference "Legal protection of farmers and the fight with corruption in the implementation of land reform,"
2–3 August 1999. Ukrainian Academy of State Management, Kharkiv; Tat'iana Koval-
eva, "Sazhaiut, zhgut tekhniku, i chut' ne ubili," *KV* 27 July 2005.
[69] OT, district farmers' association, LK, 30 March 2000.
[70] "Inye zemlevladel'tsy tol'ko muchaiut zemliu. 8 fermerskikh khoziaistv pretenduiut na
likvidatsiiu,"*LI* 8 July 1993, 3.

possibility that some new farmers may have missed autumn plowing or spring seeding because they were not granted access to their land on time was not discussed. Rather, the relevant details were behavioral: private farmers' purported laziness and irresponsibility.

Despite the tension that initially characterized the relationship between villagers and private farmers, it was not their neighbors whom private farmers most feared, for local officials had the greatest power to ruin new agricultural entrepreneurs.[71] The former chief agronomist of a state farm in Kharkiv district who had become a private farmer noted that "There are a respectable number of ill-wishers. I don't count those who level abuse at us. Scarier are those who have power, money, and material resources in their hands and have too little accountability to society."[72] State officials could threaten exposure to tax liability and more frequent visits by the various inspectorates that acted as agents of extraction for real or imagined business violations. A Kharkiv farmer thus recounted in 2000 how village authorities threatened to have him harassed: "We'll sic the 'anti-misappropriation of socialist property' police on you, the police, the fire [inspectorate], the health department... (... *My tam tebe BKhSS, my tam militsiiu na tebia, pozharnikov, sanstantsii* ...)."[73]

District level officials, including members of land committees, land tenure offices, and offices of economic management, could exert substantial economic pressure on private agricultural entrepreneurs. Land tenure offices, which oversaw compliance with zoning and other regulations, could initiate the process of land repossession: the same state agencies charged with distributing land to private farmers were also responsible for enforcing zoning and other land use laws. Private farmers were subject to intense but selective scrutiny on the part of district state administrations, and violations of these laws could lead to fines and, in many cases, land confiscation. District authorities imposed sanctions against violators unevenly: as with the initial distribution of land, those farmers with sufficient political or social capital were sometimes exempt from sanctions, but others were not so lucky.

---

[71] OT, Kharkiv regional farmers' association, 20 March 2000.
[72] L. Barkanov, "Pionery," *TT* 24 November 1992, 2.
[73] Interview, farmer Didenko, BK, 27 May 2000. In the farmer's telling, the administrators in question used the informal form of you (*ty*) in addressing him – a further sign of assertion of hierarchy and attempted intimidation. Such threats constitute a staple of post-Soviet social regulation. Humphrey, *Unmaking of Soviet Life: Everyday Economies After Socialism*. Ithaca: Cornell University Press, 2002, 69–98.

Land Must Work for People, Not for Weeds

Selective enforcement of land-use regulations sometimes turned on the ambiguity of fallow fields. Fallow land could suggest multiple scenarios: that its owner was observing crop rotation practices, or that it had been abandoned. State officials sometimes claimed that private farmers who took care of their land, letting it rest after cultivating nitrogen-leaching crops such as sunflower, engaged in "irrational use" of land. Farmers employing traditional methods of soil conservation could be accused of irresponsibility: rather than cultivating the land that had been granted them to feed the population, they had let it sit temporarily unused.

There were ways to discern whether land was truly resting or simply ignored, but the Kharkiv district paper made much of the presence of weeds on fallow fields, and it targeted private farmers for criticism: "And another farmer, Nina Radzyns'ka, who also considers twenty-four hectares of her cultivated land (*rillia*) on the territory of Vil'khivs'ka village council to be fallow. With weeds, of course...[74] Two years later, a report in the district found that 250 of 2,000 hectares of land under private cultivation were "in bad condition, not plowed since autumn. It's necessary to reexamine who among the farmers is not cultivating [his or her] plot (*dilianok*). Land must work for people, not for weeds."[75]

Across the border, the Voronezh regional administration noted in a 1995 decree that 672 of 20,700 hectares, or about 4 percent, of the land allotted for orchards were being used for other purposes. Only 135 of those 672 hectares were used for any type of agriculture, and the rest were overgrown by weeds.[76] This was a constant concern that appeared in regional legislation the previous year and in subsequent legislation,[77] and state institutions at the district and village levels issued tax sanctions to individual households for infractions of land use regulations in the planting of gardens.[78]

It was easy for district state officials to discover infractions that could lead to land confiscation, and some seemed intent upon doing so. In 1998, amidst myriad economic challenges facing the population and despite the

---

[74] Lemishchenko, "Fermer dopomozhe derzhavi iakshcho derzhava dopomozhe fermeru," *TT* 17 September 1994, 6.

[75] "Pytannia potrebuiut' vyrishennia," *TT* 6 April 1996, 1.

[76] Resolution No. 708 of the Voronezh regional administration, 12 July 1995.

[77] Resolution No. 894 of the Voronezh regional administration, 21 July 1994; Resolution No. 176 of the Voronezh regional administration, 21 February 1995.

[78] See, for example, S. Dubova, "Malo zemliu liubit'. Ee nado pakhat'," *SZ* 21 September 1999, 2.

relatively small acreage held by private farmers, "the necessity of examining the use of land by private farms" was one of the three main priorities
of the Kharkiv district state administration other than completing the district budget and liquidating debts to pensioners and workers on the state
payroll.[79] The Voronezh regional legislature had outlined in great detail
possible reasons – or justifications – for repossession,[80] and in 1999, the
district newspaper in Anna provided one catalogue of such infractions:
"misuse of land" (*beskhoziaistvennoe ispol'zovanie*), failure to "return"
leased land on time, destruction of border designations, illegal felling
of trees, and so on. These were not empty words: in the previous two
years, forty-one private farms in the district had been "liquidated, and
800 hectares of land was confiscated."[81]

One of the first farmers in Voronezh lost his land "voluntarily" because
of weeds and a problematic relationship with a local collective farm.
Kamil Makhmudov, a Liski sheep farmer from the northern Caucasus,
supplied meat, wool, and sunflower oil to a local collective farm and factory, allowing both enterprises to fulfill their state production plans.[82]
In 1992, Makhmudov received no payment for his goods. This was not
unusual for Makhmudov, who repeatedly encountered situations in which
parties to contractual agreements reneged on their obligations – the previous year he had received only a fraction of the promised sum for a
shipment of wool to the same collective farm, but documentation of that
transaction had disappeared from the records of the collective.

In 1992, after a sunflower harvest that followed eleven consecutive
years of use of his fields, Makhmudov decided to allow fifty-two acres
of his land to lie fallow for a season. Makhmudov paid a tractor driver
from the neighboring collective farm to disc-harrow the land after the
harvest. The job was not done well, and a number of seeds remained
on the fields and took root. The agronomist on the collective offered to
remove that sunflower and prepare Makhmudov's fields for winter wheat,
and Makhmudov agreed. In the beginning of August 1993, he received

---

[79] V. Lemishchenko, "Khto ide, toi dorohu osylyt'," *TT*, 7 November 1998, 1–2.
[80] Ch 9 of the law of Voronezh region "O regulirovanii zemel'nykh otnoshenii v Voronezhskoi oblasti," 25 May 1995, with changes in November 1997.
[81] A. Sannikov, "Zemlia–istochnik zhizni," *AV* 6 April 1999, 2. In 1999, 133 inspections
covering 31,000 hectares in Anna yielded seventy-one infractions covering 354 hectares
and fines totaling 4800 rubles. These figures were low relative to other districts of Kharkiv
and Voronezh.
[82] In 1992, Makhmudov supplied 5546 kilograms of meat, 916 kilograms of wool, and
26.5 tons of sunflower oil to these two enterprises. "Dai! Zapiski po krest'ianskomu
voprosu," *LI*, 19 November 1993, 2.

a visit from the head of the district land tenure committee, who warned that Markhmudov would have to get his land in shape and clean up after the sunflower or his fields would be confiscated. From Makhmudov's perspective, his arrangement with the collective farm prevented him from doing as the land tenure committee head requested. The collective farm, meanwhile, denied having made such an arrangement. After a few weeks, rather than the legally specified three months, the committee head returned with a deed for the removal of Makhmudov's land. The chair reported that Makhmudov had relinquished his land voluntarily, and Makhmudov gave up his flock save for twenty sheep, and turned exclusively to cultivation on his remaining fields.

The same year, two collectives neighboring Makhmudov's land had not brought their corn in from the fields, but the local district administration did nothing in response. The collectives paid no fines, and no officials visited threatening confiscation of collective land. Such a double standard was entirely normal. Some private farmers, like some directors of former collective farms, did regularly violate regulations governing crop rotation and other practices that safeguarded the health of the land. However, private farmers and directors who possessed unusual political or social capital were not subject to the same rules as less influential villagers. Most commonly, private farmers were punished for unproved violations, while former collectives widely known to abandon or misuse land suffered no reproof by state authorities. Reorganized collectives thus were widely permitted mistakes and inefficiencies that would cost private farmers their land and livelihood. The language used by Voronezh state officials and the district press to report reallocation of land is telling: the transfer of land from collective farms to private farmers was "seizure" (*iz"iatie*),[83] but farmers whose land was repossessed by the district state administration were said to experience a "voluntary ceasing of operations" (*dobrovol'noe prekrashchenie deiatel'nosti*).[84]

The paths to confiscation were various and could stem from problems unrelated to farmers' business choices. Individuals seeking land for private farms frequently encountered administrative delays. In a typical timeline, a would-be farmer would apply for land in late spring, expecting to receive documents and access to his fields by fall, in time for plowing. Instead, the paperwork would go through only the following winter, after the ground

---

[83] Tereshchenko, "Kak skomkali 'pervyi blin' ili kto vinovat, chto u fermerov otobrali zemliu?"*LZ* 29 June 1991, 3.
[84] "Dai! Zapiski po krest'ianskomu voprosu,"*LI* 19 November 1993, 2.

had frozen, at which point it would be too late to plow.[85] The farmer in question would be compelled to wait until spring, when the ground is a sea of mud. When the ground is dry enough to support a tractor, it is already seeding time. He manages somehow nonetheless to plant on most of the parcel, but because of the cumulative effects of the initial delays, he misses the window for seeding a small patch of his land. The district administration then fines him or repossesses his land for "improper use."

Private farmers could face other temporary setbacks that kept them from work. At the end of the decade, one district land tenure office in Kharkiv saw a constant if straggling parade of private farmers who had been threatened with land confiscation. Some had health problems that prevented them from engaging in agricultural production during a particular year, and others had aged out of the business.[86] In such cases, as well as in instances in which multiple members of a family obtained plots but not all were in a position to cultivate all of it, district land tenure offices could repossess allotments, as one Liski land committee member put it, "for such an attitude toward land," rather than issuing fines.[87]

Some cases of land confiscation from functioning farms may have been hidden under the rubric of economic failure: in Novovodolaha district of Kharkiv, "Many of those farmers gave up land. If [the fields] are not being worked, it means the farmer gave up the land . . . we know who is in a position and who's not in a position to work normally."[88] Across the border in Anna, fallow fields were attributed to farmers who "at first . . . turned to collective and state farm machinery. But times are changing. Leaders of collective farms now minutely evaluate their financial and technical resources. Each drop of fuel, each part is accounted for. As a result, many of the private land parcels have begun to lie fallow."[89]

Some infractions that led to repossession were committed not by private farmers but by individuals who oversaw land privatization. Cases in which bureaucrats committed some minor procedural error in the allotment of land to private farmers, only to have powerful local interests prevent the actual transfer by calling attention to the mistake, were legion, though not well-documented except in court records kept secret from the public.[90] In such instances, land could be repossessed without

---

[85] One of many examples was provided by farmer Nadii, KK, 2 March 2000.

[86] Interview, department of land management, NK, 21 July 2006.

[87] N. Fedina, "Samyi nadezhnyi kapital. Interv'iu s predsedatelem komiteta po zemel'nym resursam i zemleustroistvu g. Liski A. A. Batsunovym," *LI* 27 April 1993, 2.

[88] Interview, department of agricultural management, NK, 21 July 2006.

[89] "Zemlia–istochnik zhizni," *AV* 6 April 1999, 2.

[90] See Notes on Sources and Methodology on p. xix–xx.

ever having been occupied. One would-be private farmer in Kharkiv, Ivan Mrinyk, conducted a decade-long campaign to remedy just such a problem and gain access to the land he believed to be his: "When this all started, they thought, 'We'll give out the land, let them shut their mouths.' But then, when they understood that land is bread, and bread is power, 'Let's have it back.' There's your result."[91] This former driver on a collective farm decided to create a private hog farm in the early 1990s. His district, Chuhuiv, was home to some of the most powerful agricultural enterprises in the region, and the local administration did not actively encourage private farming[92] but rather actively intervened to regulate land use: "Whoever thought that bread [wheat] grows on trees counts on paper, but doesn't work. We try to confiscate land from them.... It's a constant process of repossession from those for whom things aren't working out."[93]

Mrinyk and his business partner together had requested ninety hectares of land. A road divided the tract unevenly, so the two received slightly different allotments. Individuals who received land could incorporate their resources jointly when creating a private farm. Mrinyk was allotted fifty-seven hectares, seven hectares above the fifty allowed by law at the time. He received title to his land, but his land never was allotted in the fields. The collective farm from which the land was alienated objected to the allotment, and its director parried the seven-hectare error by the district authorities into a rationale for repossessing the land.

In this case, the district administration's solution was not to repossess the excess area but rather to declare the entire process and accompanying documentation invalid. The title to the fifty-seven hectares eventually was revoked.[94] Mrinyk's subsequent appeals were refused on the grounds that although he had been allotted the land on paper, the land had never been allotted to him in the field, and he had never used it. Therefore the collective in question was within its rights to continue to use the land and to refuse to cede it to Mrinyk.[95] Here, previous physical access to fields and *status quo ante* political authority, rather than formal ownership, determined future use rights.

[91] Interview, farmer Mrinyk, CK, 24 February 2000. Also see M. Chukhlebov, "Fermer...prosyt' zakhystu," *SK*, 3 November 1993.

[92] OT, district administration, CK, April 2000.

[93] Interview, district administration, CK, 21 July 2006.

[94] Letter No. 8/23513-95 of 6 May 1995 from the Office of the Public Prosecutor of Ukraine to the farmer.

[95] Letter No. 8/55–93 of 19 July 1995 from the Office of the Public Prosecutor of Kharkiv region.

Similar situations arose amidst conflict between people seeking to establish private farms and other, more powerful individuals who wanted to use the land for some other purpose – or simply did not want the land used by anyone else. Two of the first private farmers in Liski encountered just such a predicament. In a letter of complaint to the district paper, they described what they regarded as the confiscation of land allotted for their farm. Food scarcity and inflation had prompted the two to request land on the banks of the Don to use for fish farming. At the time, the land was on the territory of a state farm, and its director refused to enter into negotiations with the would-be farmers. Because the fields in question had not been plowed for ten years, the law allowed the district administration to make the allotment without the consent of the current holder. The two completed all the necessary paperwork and prepared to cultivate the fields. Then the director of the state farm told them to get off "his" land, and the would-be farmers were inundated by "visits" from the local police, fish inspectorate, and hunting society. People who were "clearly not local" began to approach them, warning them that high-ranking individuals who "didn't need witnesses" used the area for relaxation. A suit was soon filed against them by the district prosecutor and by the director of the state farm, who intended to sue them for ruining the land.[96] Three weeks later, the paper published a response by the assistant to the prosecutor, who (rightly) claimed that land law had been applied inappropriately to transfer what amounted to water rights.[97]

Over time, former collectives also became targets of state efforts to regulate land use. In Kharkiv, reorganized collectives began to lease land to private farmers in order to prevent the land from being overgrown with weeds and, potentially, reclaimed by the state.[98] In Liski, the district administration repossessed the land and assets of three poorly performing former collective farms "on the verge of dissolution," where "salaries hadn't been paid in years, the land is unsown, and people were in despair." The district formed municipal farms on their territory. A local official explained the decision in terms of social welfare: "We understand that this isn't the best option, but under these conditions there just wasn't another solution. We couldn't abandon people. We had to give them the chance to rise from their knees, to make their spirit come alive,

---

[96] I. Getmanov, "Zemliu dali, chtoby otniat'?" *LZ* 4 June 1991, 3.

[97] V. Tereshchenko, "Kak skomkali 'pervyi blin' ili kto vinovat, chto u fermerov otobrali zemliu?" *LZ*, 29 June 1991, 3.

[98] Interview, executive director of Kharkiv regional farmers' association, 6 December 1999.

believe in themselves, help them adapt to new conditions. I think that we succeeded."[99]

Finally, in Anna, where local officials initially supported private farming to a greater extent than other districts of the Black Earth, land alienated from private farms was offered publicly to others interested in private commercial cultivation: "The land reform and land resources committee, as a result of an inspection, found that land plots are not being used in the companies 'Sviazist,' 'Voskhod,' and 'Avtomobilist.' In accordance with the law they are being confiscated (*izymaiutsia*), and if you would like to become their owner, apply to the committee on that question."[100] Regardless of the apparently pro-private farmer stance of such statements, they indicated the same essential dynamic underlying repossession and harassment: selective assertion of state control over the use of private property, even after privatization was complete.

Conclusion

As elsewhere in post-socialist Europe, the creation of new agrarian institutions did not compel the state to retreat from the village.[101] After a decade of privatization, state regulation of economic activity was stronger than it had been in the late months of Soviet rule, when collective and state farms had pulled away from monopsony and entered markets unbidden. Reform resulted in thin rights for landholders, local state retrenchment, and the preservation, in some localities, of the economic interdependence of producers and state institutions.

As land reform progressed, opportunities for state regulation expanded. With a 2002 law legalizing land markets, the Russian government created, in the guise of forestalling the spread of privately owned latifundia, a legislative foundation for renationalization or large-scale consolidation of holdings by powerful political actors. This legislation allowed the state right of first refusal on land purchases. Those who wish to sell their land allotments must first petition regional and district authorities, which may refuse to allow the transaction and purchase the land itself

[99] N. Kardashov, "Raionnye budni. Glavnoe dlia nas–eto stabil'nost'," *KO* 22 June 2004.

[100] "V raionnoi administratsii," *AV*, 29 July 1997, 2.

[101] David Kideckel, "Once Again, the Land: Decollectivization and Social Conflict in Rural Romania," in Hermine G. DeSoto and David G. Anderson, eds. *The Curtain Rises: Rethinking Culture, Ideology, and the State in Eastern Europe*. Atlantic Highlands, NJ: Humanities Press, 1993, 62.

instead.[102] Given that Russian imperial anxieties about sovereignty have been evident in its border territories to the south and east, this legislation may ease future attempts to expand controlled zones along the border in the Black Earth.

The creation of private property regimes in rural Russia and Ukraine did not guarantee stable or enforceable property rights for Black Earth landholders. Instead, redistribution of land continued after privatization had come to a close. Farmers who failed to satisfy local use requirements, or generate surplus production, lost their land, and it was recycled back into the pool of land resources at the district level. Privatization policy thus led not merely to weak land rights, but to dispossession and, in some cases, a form of renationalization. Local officials had wide discretion in their harassment of farmers and confiscation of land: zoning and other land-use legislation allowed, though did not necessarily require, the intensive regulation of private property after privatization.

Local officials wished to be seen as protecting the commons from the seemingly chaotic and maldistributive fate of many privatized industrial enterprises. This norm was manifest in the double standard that state officials initially enforced with respect to regulation of land use by private farmers and former collectives, as local officials privileged large-scale farming and insisted that land allotted for agricultural production be used as such. The implicit argument that proper use justified private ownership was not applied to former collectives, as their social utility as a form of production already had been demonstrated. Therefore, their use of land in the post-Soviet period was not subject to rigorous policing.

Land-use regulation, informal extraction of revenue, supervision of crop rotation and prescription of cultivation plans, and coercive attempts to ensure near monopsony kept many farms within the reach of the arm of the state. The selective application of techniques of control, exclusion, repossession, and harassment ensured that private farms would cleave to Soviet-era state–business relationships and that even after privatization, former collectives would remain under the thumb of district and regional authorities.

---

[102] Russian federal law #101 of 24 July 2002, "Ob oborote zemel' sel'skokhoziaistvennogo naznacheniia, June 2002. Also see Wegren, "Observations on Russia's New Agricultural Land Law," *Eurasian Geography and Economics* 43:8 (2002).

5

The Politics of Payment

After a decade of privatization, Black Earth villagers faced dwindling opportunities to gain access to the land that was rightfully theirs. In addition to the bureaucratic obstacles that stood in the way of land distribution, rural people faced a hostile economic environment and a local political landscape that prevented them from profiting from ownership. On most farms, labor payments and membership entitlements diminished over time, and ownership-based incentives were minimal. Amidst deepening poverty, villagers saw their chances ever of acquiring land or making a decent livelihood recede into the distance.

Farming land required start-up capital, and villagers had few ways to get it. Wegren et al. write, "While it was hardly the intent of market reforms to impoverish millions of rural Russians, this is exactly what has happened."[1] That the future held few prospects for most rural people became clear early in the process. In 1995, A. Rud'ko, a Kharkiv pensioner, expressed a common sentiment when he observed in a letter to the regional newspaper that "now, no honest villager can afford to buy land for himself, much less a combine or tractor. And without machinery, what can be grown today?"[2] For most farms, amidst continuing political uncertainty, chances for capital investment from within or outside of the Black Earth countryside were slim.

Employment outside of reorganized collectives was scarce. Villages far from cities had a few non-agricultural jobs: in a clinic, a school, or in one

---

[1] Stephen K. Wegren, David J. O'Brien, Valeri V. Patsiorkovski, "Why Russia's Rural Poor Are Poor," *Post-Soviet Affairs* 19:3 (2003), 266.
[2] A. Rud'ko, "Ie taka dumka. Zemlia – ne tovar," *SK* 8 June 1995, 2.

of a handful of village kiosks that sold beer, ice cream, soap, matches, and instant noodles to villagers and summer visitors. A small number of farms sought hired hands for wage labor, but their numbers were far from sufficient to generate a significant local labor market. Local entrepreneurs struggled in the face of extortion from local rackets, fire inspectors, and tax collectors who, in the words of one rural small business owner in Kharkiv, "come every day like the sunrise."[3] In theory, people in villages near urban areas could find work in city markets or factories, but in practice the cost of transportation could consume 80 percent of a typical salary.[4] Some young men became migrant laborers, traveling to Crimea and Poland to work in construction, while their female counterparts took jobs in Italy and Portugal caring for other families' homes and children.[5]

After privatization, most rural people in the Black Earth had little choice but to remain on reorganized collectives, where housing, primary education for their children, and rudimentary social services continued to remain available to them, where their wages would help sustain modest homesteads, and where the social networks they had developed over decades would carry them through difficult times. In places, official or *de facto* rules also prevented change in residence. Staying on the former collective usually meant leasing land to the former chairman, who remained as director of the reorganized enterprise. While some farm directors tolerated competition from private farmers and other former collectives, others threatened to withhold essential social services from employees who dared use their land or lease it to someone else.

Policy makers had envisioned land reform as a reversal of the collectivization drives of the 1920s and 1930s,[6] but privatization did not change rural built environments. Collectivization had not only forced privately owned goods into collective ownership, but had also restructured

[3] OT, Kharkiv women's organization meeting, March 2000. Caroline Humphrey, *The Unmaking of Soviet Life: Everyday Economies After Socialism*. Ithaca: Cornell University Press, 2002.

[4] OT, former poultry plant worker, XK, 15 April 2000. Interview, head accountant, Fatherland, LV, 8 May 2000.

[5] Natalka Patsiurko, "Multiple Responses to Economic Uncertainty: Migration and Entrepreneurship as Substitutes for the State Employment in Ukraine," paper presented at the annual meeting of the Association for the Study of Nationalities, Columbia University, 16 April 2005.

[6] S. A. Nikol'skii, "Kollektivizatsiia i dekollektivizatsiia: sravnitel'nyi analiz protsessov, posledstvii i perspektiv," in V. Danilov and T. Shanin, eds. *Krest'ianovedenie 1997: teoriia, istoriia, sovremennost'*. Moscow: Aspekt Press, 1997.

the physical geography of villages.[7] In the first decades of Soviet rule, rural buildings had been moved and people resettled, sometimes at great distances, to accommodate collective organization of agriculture.[8] Post-Soviet reform relocated neither populations nor buildings, and land privatization legislation made few provisions for altering the shape of rural settlements. Reorganized collective and state farms retained their former infrastructure, and villages remained located on the periphery of large tracts of farmland, sometimes miles from the fields in which land shares could be allotted. In their daily lives, rural people continued to trace patterns of movement that typified collective ownership and production.

Villagers who were able to obtain cadastral services to have shares allotted in the fields struggled as they sought access to their land. In addition to receiving sporadic threats of violence against them by directors of former collectives, villagers traveled long distances commuting between house and field.[9] Land shares were often far from roads and other infrastructure, and they were sometimes allotted from fields that had not been touched for years, making plowing and cultivation by hand a Sisyphean task.[10] Furthermore, cultivation of labor-intensive crops imposed a high physical cost on people compelled to walk miles every day, heavy farm implements in hand, over often uneven ground to reach their plots.

Rural people did not dramatically alter their daily routines as the years of reform wore on, but the compensation they received for their labor noticeably changed. After land privatization, worker-shareholders encountered incentive structures that were weaker and more impoverishing than those that had governed late Soviet agriculture. Without savings to pay for transportation and appropriate equipment, there was little reason to acquire land allotments during the first rounds of privatization: "If you don't have machinery, there's no sense in leaving."[11] Now, most were worse off than before, and formal ownership of land shares brought little tangible benefit. Villagers were unable to save

[7] *Sel'skoe zhilishche.* Kyiv: Budivel'nyk, 1976; James C. Scott, *Seeing Like a State: How Certain Schemes to Improve the Human Condition Have Failed.* New Haven: Yale University Press, 1998.

[8] Kate Brown, *A Biography of No-Place: From Ethnic Borderland to Soviet Heartland.* Cambridge: Harvard University, 2004 and Pavel Polyan, *Ne po svoei vole. Istoriia i geografiia prinuditel'nykh migratsii v SSSR.* Moscow: OGI-Memorial, 2001.

[9] V. Ivaniukovich, Conference "Legal protection of farmers and the fight with corruption in the implementation of land reform," 2–3 August 1999. Ukrainian Academy of State Management, Kharkiv.

[10] Interview, former collective farm worker, UZ, 19 May 2004.

[11] Ibid.

enough to make efficient use of their land share ownership, and opportunities to accumulate capital were thin. In such an environment, those who were unable to profit during the first rounds of land privatization are now unlikely ever to find material benefit from ownership of land.

Only Enough to Feed the Chickens

In midsummer, vast fields of sunflower blanket the Black Earth in gold. Their beauty belies their social meaning, for they signal economic distress. In the years following land privatization, struggling farms replaced fields sown with alfalfa and perennial grasses with ecologically unsustainable crops easily sold to extinguish debt and purchase spare parts.[12] Sunflower has many industrial uses and is easy to market, but it leaches nitrogen from the soil. Without the soil additives that cash-strapped Black Earth farms cannot afford, it should be planted only once every several years (Illustration 6). The "barbaric cultivation of sunflower"[13] was of concern to Black Earth officials who observed such abuses of the land: "Some 'uncle' comes along and rents land shares for a year, plants sunflower, and washes his hands of it. The following year, the same thing happens."[14]

Payment that rural people received in exchange for labor and ownership depended on the economic success of agricultural collectives, which began a slow decline with the fall of Soviet power and did not begin to recover until a decade had passed. Many collective and state farms had been weak, lumbering institutions ill-suited to the challenge of operating without subsidies. The obstacles posed by the economic environment of the privatization period tested the limits of what even healthy farms could withstand.[15] Successful farms that had managed to

---

[12] Interview, head accountant, Fatherland, LV, 8 May 2000; statistics obtained from district division of economics, LV; *Goroda i raiony Voronezhskoi oblasti*. Voronezh: Goskomstat, 1996; *Pokazateli ekonomicheskogo i sotsial'nogo razvitiia gorodov i raionov Voronezhskoi oblasti 1998. Statisticheskii sbornik*. Voronezh: Goskomstat, 1999; *Sil's'ke hospodarstvo Ukrainy. Statystychnyi zbirnyk*. Kyiv: Derzhkomzem, 1997; statistics obtained from Kharkiv regional division of private farms; *Ukraina u tsyfrakh 2002*. Kyiv: Derzhkomzem 2003.

[13] Interview, district administration, CK, 21 July 2006.

[14] OT, land tenure office, L'viv district, July 2006. The expression used here for "washing" also suggests money-laundering. For a similar account in Voronezh of carpetbaggers "from Moscow, from Petersburg, from Belgorod," who plant hundreds of hectares of sunflower and are "gone by fall," see S. Burdykin, "Poslednaia krepost' poka ne vziata,"*Bereg* 19 April 2002.

[15] David Stark and László Bruszt make a similar argument regarding industrial enterprises in eastern and central Europe. *Postsocialist Pathways: Transforming Politics and Property in East Central Europe*. Cambridge: Cambridge University Press, 1998.

ILLUSTRATION 6. Sunflower fields, Kharkiv, 2006. Black Earth agricultural enterprises increasingly turned to soil-depleting cash crops in the post-privatization period.

survive the first difficult years of independence were unable to improve their efficiency. Even in relatively prosperous Liski, where reorganized collectives had managed to retain an astounding 90 percent of their cattle during the first decade of reform, the volume of milk production dropped by one-third between 1989 and 1999, and milk production per hectare of land remained level during that period.[16] A prolonged scissors crisis, limited credit, the dissolution of Soviet-era trade ties, and a spiral of attendant problems limited farm profits and thus the ability of farms to pay worker-shareholders.

Rural enterprises throughout Russia and Ukraine battled price scissors both during and after privatization. Exposure to world markets drove down local prices on agricultural commodities and led to higher prices for agricultural inputs, particularly for machinery. Meanwhile, European Union and North American agricultural producers, fed by comfortable subsidy regimes, could afford to sell their harvests at low prices. Toward the turn of the twenty-first century, low agricultural labor costs in Asia

[16] Calculations based on statistics obtained from district division of economics, LV.

and the southern hemisphere put Black Earth producers at a further competitive disadvantage.

The initial lifting of price controls, followed by selective regulation of prices for some agricultural products, meant that no matter how well former collectives functioned, harvest sales could not cover costs. Rural homesteads suffered along with former collectives, unable to obtain production factors at affordable prices. Villagers summed up the situation in an oft-articulated complaint: a liter of milk cost less than a liter of gasoline and, worse, less than a liter of mineral water.

Long-term credit at reasonable rates was virtually unknown in the Black Earth. Lenders seeking to minimize risk turned to local officials to evaluate the credit worthiness of agricultural enterprises, and farms were unable to make credit arrangements directly with banks. Instead, creditors distributed loans through state administrations, which passed on the fees for their services to borrowers in the form of higher interest rates. State administrations thus acted as guarantors for farms; few banks were willing to risk lending without a buffer between often insolvent enterprises and themselves. The director of a former collective in Liski collective put it this way:

They don't give collectives direct credit, regardless.... We got credit at twelve percent interest, but the administration took on some expenses, so interest was thirty two percent. And if you don't take credit, it's difficult to seed. No one gives out fuel without cash.[17]

With the introduction of middlemen, interest rates on the ground were even higher than those set by banks, and access to credit was limited to a narrow range of farm managers on close terms with local state officials. In Kharkiv, district administrations kept priority lists for credit; those lists were targeted toward former collectives and included very few private farmers.[18] One Kharkiv farmer recalled that when he inquired about a loan, "they looked at me as if I were on temporary furlough from the nuthouse."[19] Access to credit, a necessity for modern commercial farming, was often available only to well-connected members of the collective farm elite.[20]

[17] Interview, director, Sil'nyi, LV, 8 May 2000.
[18] OT, Center for Rural Sociological Research, Kharkiv State Technical Agricultural University, 30 March 2000.
[19] A. Reshetov, "Fermer Anatoliy Usik: Veriu v uspekh," *TT*, 19 January 1991, 1–2.
[20] Interview with farmer, XK, 12 April 2000.

For much of the 1990s, farms that did receive credit paid between 40 percent and 100 percent interest on one-year loans.[21] Interest payments came due monthly, and so a portion of the loan had to be kept out of the production cycle in order to make those payments.[22] Except during the hyperinflation and currency devaluation of the early 1990s, farmers faced an uphill battle repaying their debts. Principal could be repaid in grain, but interest was paid in cash.[23] The prices used to calculate volumes of grain for repayment gouged producers, who were compelled to sell most of their harvest to service debt.[24]

This arrangement posed a particular problem for farms with inadequate storage facilities, which had no choice but to sell immediately after the harvest.[25] Grain prices fluctuated from month to month and were lowest at harvest time, when creditors expected to be repaid.[26] In 1999, producers in Voronezh received 1,900 rubles per ton of third-class wheat. Three weeks after the harvest, the price would rise to 2,500 rubles, but collectors used the 1,900 ruble rate to calculate debt repayment.[27] Furthermore, without liquid capital to purchase fuel during the growing season, Black Earth agricultural enterprises were compelled to mortgage future harvests against the cost of fuel.[28] Such arrangements typically involved the promise of 20 percent of the harvest to a middleman each time machinery went out into the fields. Given the low prices for agricultural commodities in general, few enterprises could generate enough profit from the sale of harvests to subsidize the following year's cultivation. Often, by the time land had been sown, cultivated, and harvested, nothing of the

---

[21] This varied by year, location, and the social status of the borrower: "We have something to impound... They just won't give it to others. There's nothing to take there." Interview, head economist, Il'ich kolkhoz, SV, May 2000. The highest rates encountered by my interlocutors ranged to 200%; a few farmers described loans at a low of 28% annual interest.

[22] Interview with farmer Chernets'kyi, ZK, 3 January 2000.

[23] Interview, district farmers' association, SV, May 2000.

[24] Interview, head accountant, Fatherland, LV, 8 May 2000.

[25] Interview with farmers, BK, 27 May 2000; Interview with farmer, ZK, 31 May 2000; Interview, director of grain elevator, VV, 16 May 2000; Interview with farmer, VV, 16 May 2000; Interview with farmer, PK, 7 June 2000; Interview with farmer, XK, 17 December 1999.

[26] This was also the case for all service contracts. OT, regional deputy head of agricultural management at meeting of Kharkiv regional farmers' association, 14 December 1999.

[27] Interview, district farmers' association, SV, May 2000. He added that those who engaged in such practices were "communists."

[28] OT, district farmers' association, LK, 30 March 2000.

harvest remained to sell,[29] and "afterwards we only have enough to feed the chickens."[30]

Many former collectives were unable to replace combines and tractors when they broke down beyond repair. Prices on imported machinery were prohibitively high, and former trade ties had dissolved, for under Soviet power,

> We lived stifled, and then we were given a bit of opportunity. Then, we were absolutely cut off in all respects.... The thing is, ties are a big deal for us. After all, Belarus supplied us with tractors, and Ukraine supplied us with tractors.... All international relationships collapsed together with the union.[31]

Even relatively successful farms saw their machinery deteriorate during the privatization period: a persistent lack of cash left farms unable to maintain their machine fleets. Machinery loads had increased dramatically since the late 1980s,[32] and as a consequence, crop yields were low even under favorable growing conditions. During harvest season, field-workers had a small window of time in which to conduct the intensive labor that would determine the survival of the farm for that season. Frequent machinery breakdowns and repairs caused massive crop losses: at the height of the harvest, a delay of even a few hours could have far-reaching consequences.

Farms with working machinery were sometimes unable to use it. Like their urban counterparts who put automobiles on blocks in the early 1990s because they could not afford gasoline, increased fuel prices increasingly compelled some farms to depend on manual labor for cultivation.[33] In Liski, when private farmer Tatiana Ankina first received three hectares of land in 1991, she acquired a new T-40 tractor. By 1992, her cash flow limited and compelled to find another solution, she turned to her three-year-old horse: "A horse is more reliable. I prepare hay, and I don't need to think about fuel for the tractor."[34] But the horse did not perform all farm labor: when it came time to thin sugar beet, Ankina headed for the

---

[29] The same conditions governed processing and storage on both sides of the border. Interview, chief accountant of Voronezhsky collective farm, SV, May 2000.

[30] Interview, farmer, MK, 6 April 2000.

[31] Interview, head agronomist, Chayanovskoe, August 1998.

[32] Statistics obtained from division of economics, LV.

[33] This is part of broader process of "de-development" in the post-socialist world. Mieke Meurs and Rasika Ranasinghe, "De-Development in Post-Socialism: Conceptual and Measurement Issues," *Politics and Society* 31:1 (March 2003).

[34] V. Ivanov, "'Vetla' po imeni Tat'iana," *LI*, 25 June 1992, 3.

fields herself, *tiapka* in hand. In the meantime, her tractor stood in the yard, awaiting a future when she could afford fuel to use it.

By the end of the 1990s, agriculture had been demechanized in some areas of the Black Earth, and it was not uncommon to witness people, rather than draft animals, pulling wooden plows and engaging in man-ual cultivation on former collectives. Some of the most profitable farms in Kharkiv were able to maintain surplus production by contracting out multiple smaller plots to families who would cultivate the soil by hand. Former collectives sold the food grown in these fields, and families who labored in them received a small portion of the harvest for household use or sale.[35] In the absence of fuel for tractors and combines, a successful manager could ensure cultivation of hundreds of acres. Former collec-tives, and family homesteads without draft animals, survived this way from season to season. Struggling to stay afloat in global markets, former collectives increased demands on rural people's labor, replacing animals and machinery with women and men. Even as workers became sharecrop-pers on their own land, payment diminished near to a vanishing point.

A "Wretched" Payment

Author:	How did people respond [to reorganization]?
Farmer Didenko:	Where could they go? They have nowhere to go ... The chairman said, I have a share and you have shares. I'm putting in my share. I'm join-ing. He says 'I'm a farmer ... '
Author:	Do you know what the conditions of leasing are?
Farmer Medvedev:	The conditions are such that you'd think they wouldn't accept them. They're wretched for those who lease their shares....[36]

Private ownership of land shares provided two benefits: rents and div-idends. Both were limited by the solvency of the farms to which shares were leased, and both were subject to farm directors' considerable discre-tion. Under the terms of reform legislation in Russia and Ukraine, land shareholders were to receive not less than 1 percent of the assessed value of their land share as yearly rents. In practice, 1 percent was the standard

---

[35] Interview, director, Red Partisan KSP, XK, 23 July 1999.
[36] Interview with private farmers, BK, 27 May 2000.

for many years. Intended as a floor, 1 percent became the ceiling, for in the absence of developed land share and labor markets, most worker-shareholders were unable to negotiate the terms under which farms used their shares and paid for their labor.[37]

For years, most shareholders had no allotments in the fields and no choice but to lease their land share to the former collective: a study in Nizhny Novgorod, where pilot programs of enterprise reorganization in Russia were conducted, showed in 1997 that "the bulk of owners... believe that they have been deprived of the opportunity to choose how their share would be used."[38] Competition drove rents up to 2 percent only where private farmers competed for land with local collectives and there had been "powerful investment" in large-scale agriculture.[39]

In Kharkiv, farm heads "paid pennies" to lease land shares,[40] and "the vast majority settle up in grain"[41] rather than cash. For years, share ownership yielded no obvious benefit: in 1998, 94 percent of shareholders surveyed in the region reported receiving no profit from their land share.[42] By 2006, increased demand for land around the city of Kharkiv increased annual share payments in peri-urban areas to between 500 and 800 UAH, more than 100 US$.[43] Such an improvement, however, was accompanied by a steep rise in the cost of goods and services, including plowing of garden plots.

Directors' control over the timing of price agreements decreased the value of land share rents. In Kharkiv, a typical land lease at the turn of the millennium annually provided owners with 600 kilograms of wheat per share.[44] The market value of that wheat at the time of contract was

---

37 On land markets for household plots, see Wegren, "Russian Peasant Farms and Household Plots in 2003: A Research Note," *Eurasian Geography and Economics* 45:3 (2004).
38 V. Uzun, ed. *Sotsial'no-ekonomicheskie posledstviia privatizatsii zemli i reorganizatsii sel'skokhoziaistvennykh predpriiatii (1994–1996 gg.).* Moscow: Entsiklopediia rossiiskikh dereven', 1997, 35. See also Chapter 2.
39 Interview, district head, CK, 21 July 2006. Although many shareholders spoke of higher rents "across the river," "in the next village," or "on a neighboring collective," I found no one who reported receiving two percent.
40 OT, farmer, ZK, 19 July 2006.
41 Interview, district administration, CK, 21 July 2006.
42 Report of State Committee on Land Resources. Kyiv: Derzhkomzem, 1998.
43 Interview, pensioner, VK, 18 July 2006. Interview, former state farm worker, VK, 18 July 2006. Interview, pensioner, PK, 18 July 2006. Interview, district head, CK, 21 July 2006. Interviews, pensioners (former milker and driver), PK 18 July 2006. Interview, pensioner, VK, 18 July 2006.
44 OT, Kharkiv regional farmers' association meeting, 14 December 1999.

150 UAH, or 32 US$.[45] However, at the time of harvest, when rents were paid, it was worth only 75 UAH, or 16 US$.[46] Leasing contracts that specified in-kind arrangements calculated grain amounts based on their market value at the time of signing, not during payment at harvest time, when prices were at their lowest. The actual value of rents thus was significantly reduced, at times by as much as half.

Land rents in Voronezh were even lower, and some farms stopped paying rents because "the contract conditions are unfeasible."[47] In 2003, the Voronezh regional newspaper observed that, "Last year, for the first time in ten years they distributed two hundred kilograms of grain, five liters of vegetable oil and fifteen kilograms of sugar for each share."[48] The value of even such a windfall could do little to feed a family for the year – 200 kilograms of grain was worth at most 600 rubles at the time, about ten days' pay for one person, or 20 US$.[49] In Liski, the situation had become so dire by the following year that the district council found it necessary to issue a recommendation on the value of land rents. According to the recommendation, for each share, the leaser should provide 500 kilograms of grain, 15 kilograms of oil, 15 kilograms of sugar, free plowing of household plots, and "household" and funerary services.[50] Such direction "from above" on the size of land lease payments later occurred elsewhere, as the governor of nearby, prosperous Belgorod region ordered farm directors to pay 600 kilograms of grain per share, or 830 rubles per year – about 5 percent of the harvest from that land.[51]

The low value of land share rents did not come about by accident. In the face of crushing economic pressures, reorganized collectives had achieved varied degrees of success. Many determinants of success were structural, but "a great deal depends on the leader" of the enterprise.[52] Some problems arose because of "unconscientious farm leaders"[53] who

---

[45] At January 2000 prices of 500 UAH per metric ton of third class wheat.

[46] At harvest 2000 prices of 250 UAH per metric ton of third class wheat.

[47] Interview, head accountant, Fatherland, LV, 8 May 2000.

[48] Mikhail Nikonov, "V partiiakh i dvizheniiakh. SPS – na pul'se krest'ianskogo interesa," *KO*, 21 August 2003.

[49] Aleksandr Marochin, "Pochemu v Voronezhe podorozhal khleb?" *Komsomol'skaia Pravda v chernozem'e* 5 February 2004.

[50] Kardashov, "Raionnye budni. 'Glavnoe dlia nas – eto stabil'nost'" *KO*, 22 June 2004.

[51] Y. Chernichenko, "Burov mgloiu nebo kroet. Kak novyi predsedatel' kolkhoza Burov dovel starikov do ubiistva korovy," *NG*, 25 April 2005.

[52] Interview, department of agricultural management, NK, July 2006.

[53] Interview, district administration, CK, 21 July 2006.

used land and labor "for their own selfish aims,"[54] while other farm directors, struggling to keep enterprises afloat, economized on lease payments. Whether their ultimate aims were illicit personal enrichment or business development, directors deployed a variety of strategies to withhold or minimize lease payments.

Some directors distributed rent payments in a familiar guise that added no new value for shareholders. The Soviet-era practice of providing symbolic payments in grain to collective farm members, a traditional harvest-time bonus, continued on reorganized collectives. After privatization, directors re-categorized such payments as land rents. During the last years of Soviet power, their value routinely had equaled or exceeded the amount now offered to worker-shareholders. In this sense, land ownership at best merely formalized existing practices.

Other directors found ways of reducing payments at the margins, either minimizing rents with "a little bit of underpayment" or reducing share sizes to accommodate requests of higher-ups. If the daughter of a local boss, for example, asks for land, "they cut a little bit off" for her.[55] Direct evidence of the latter strategy appears only in the narratives of shareholders; it is evident indirectly in the shrinking size of shares for workers on some farms.[56] In thin years, some farms "didn't settle up with people."[57] Even if the reason was genuine financial pressure, as in the summer of 1998, "people stopped trusting" farm management.[58]

Finally, directors who wished to avoid paying rents often targeted pensioners. Unable to leave the collective, but no longer in a position to withhold labor in response to poor treatment, pensioners had little control over the use of their land shares. A director faced few obstacles if, as in the case of a former state farm in Vovchans'k, he wished to "seize the shares of all the pensioners."[59] In the same district, one farm administrator excluded 247 pensioners from a land share list during the early 1990s, leaving the farm head with *de facto* ownership of over 90 percent of its land. Many of the aggrieved did not live to see the error corrected; by 1999, 100 of

[54] Y. Chernichenko, "Burov mgloiu nebo kroet. Kak novyi predsedatel' kolkhoza Burov dovel starikov do ubiistva korovy," NG, 25 April 2005.

[55] Interview, pensioner, PK, 18 July 2006. These strategies echo those identified by Verdery in Transylvania. "Seeing Like a Mayor, Or How Local Officials Obstructed Romanian Land Restitution," *Ethnography* 3:1(2002), 19.

[56] Interview, pensioner, VK, 18 July 2006.

[57] Interview, director of grain elevator, VV, May 2000. Interview, department of agricultural mangement, NK, 21 July 2006.

[58] Interview, director of grain elevator, VV, May 2000.

[59] Interview, pensioner, VK, 18 July 2006.

those omitted from the list had died.[60] Meanwhile, some managers saw
no reason to allow pensioners control of their land: in Semiluki, one farm
economist asked, "Why do pensioners need that land? The collective farm
helps them, and that's it."[61]

Shareholders generally received only rent payments, for even wealthy
farms largely paid "no dividends at all."[62] Reorganized collectives could
pay dividends only in profitable years, and only when farms did not
require reinvestment of profits in enterprise infrastructure. The absence
of dividends undermined the social meaning of new property rights, for,
as Koznova notes, "for the majority, ownership means the materially
expressed condition, 'I am an owner, because I receive dividends on my
share.' If there are no dividends, people do not consider themselves owners."[63]

In practice, the dividend system bore a strong resemblance to material
incentives used just after collectivization. Before Khrushchev introduced
advance payments as material incentives, or Brezhnev allowed cash payments,[64] the residue principle dictated that the produce that remained
after farms fulfilled their obligations to the state would be divided among
farm households. Under such an arrangement, households benefited only
if production exceeded state demands. After privatization, farms struggled
to repay creditors and obligations to shareholders likewise were rarely
met. Reformers believed land privatization would create a new system
of incentives, but in important respects, post-reform incentives came to
resemble most what they were designed to overturn: incentives under
Stalinist forms of collective production.

No Salary, No Incentive

Most worker-shareholders fared no better in obtaining payment for their
labor. Even in districts with strong farms, wages lagged behind inflation
and workers waited months for their salaries. In less prosperous districts,

---

[60] OT, Kharkiv regional farmers' association, 14 December 1999. The story was repeated
with some variation (one quarter of the pensioners had died in this telling) at a 13 January
2000 meeting in L'viv district.
[61] Interview, head accountant, Il'ich kolkhoz, SV, May 2000.
[62] OT, Il'ich, kolkhoz SV, May 2000. This farm director was the brother of the vice governor
of the region.
[63] Irina Koznova, "Traditsii i novatsii v povedenii sovremennykh krest'ian," in *Identichnost'
i konflikt v postsovetskikh gosudarstvakh, sbornik statei.* Moscow, 1997, 364–5.
[64] See Zhores Medvedev, *Soviet Agriculture.* New York: Norton, 1987, 345–6.

directors sometimes chose between paying for labor and ownership. As one Kharkiv agricultural management official explained, "I try to convince [farm] leaders that pay *either* for labor *or* in exchange for shares should be more or less within the bounds of the law."[65]

In Liski, where collective farms had been selected for the first rounds of farm organization in Voronezh,[66] and which the deputy governor of the region had designated as having excelled in economic reform,[67] officials kept careful farm salary records. Among Black Earth districts, conditions in Liski were relatively favorable for economic improvement, and the district should have been a place where property rights reform could improve labor incentives. However, salary records show some differentiation but improvement only for a small number of highly skilled male professionals. For most workers, privatization did not produce a clear link between productivity and salary. For women, salaries declined in both relative and absolute terms after privatization.

In late Soviet rural society, tractor and combine operators had been the most publicly celebrated and well-paid members of agricultural collectives.[68] In 1989, the average tractor operator in Liski made one and a half times as much as the average agricultural worker in the district.[69] By the 1990s, work with farm machinery had become an almost exclusively male profession. Sporadic shortages of machine operators during the twentieth century were followed by attempts by the Soviet state to recruit women to these positions, but at the end of the twentieth century, gender defined labor was a rule honored, and entered into the documentary record, in the breach.[70] Women who drove farm vehicles were rare enough to rate articles about them in the local press. One interview with

---

[65] Interview, department of agricultural management, NK, 21 July 2006.

[66] V. Chernyshov, "APK: v novykh usloviiakh khoziaistvovaniia. Rozhdenie kollektivnogo khoziaistva," *LZ* 26 June 1991, 3 and V. Ivanov, "Privatizatsiia – eto...spasatel'nyi krug kolkhoznoi sistemy, schitaet spetsialist rossiiskogo ministerstva," *LZ* 17 October 1991, 3.

[67] N. Ia. Averin, at conference "Problemy sovremennogo upravlenija v APK," Voronezh Agricultural Institute, 26–27 May 1998.

[68] A few of hundreds of examples of machinist hagiography include: "Pervyi vsegda pervyi," *TT* 13 April 1991, 1 and N. Skudnev, "Lider opredelilsia," *RV* 18 July 1991, 1.

[69] This had been occasion for public concern at the time, as local press drew attention to an accounting "disbalance" in wages. See A. Vakhtin, "Ser'eznyi razgovor sostoialsia na otchetnom sobranii v kolkhoze imeni Sverdlova," *RV* 21 February 1991, 3.

[70] Susan Bridger, "Soviet Rural Women: Employment and Family Life," in Beatrice Farnsworth and Lynne Viola, eds. *Russian Peasant Women*. New York: Oxford University Press, 1992.

members of a farm family in Kharkiv reported that the female head of household had been driving a tractor for nearly fifteen years "and doesn't plan to change her profession under any circumstances, no matter what idle tongues chatter about whether it's feminine or not."[71]

In Liski, only highly skilled tractor drivers saw their relative salary levels increase after privatization.[72] That highly skilled men should be the primary beneficiaries of transformed wage structures did not itself represent a change in the social order of agricultural collectives. Farm directors continued to draw salaries approximately twice those of average workers, and the salaries of livestock workers did not increase relative to other workers. Milkmaids and tenders to livestock received proportionally less compensation for their work as the post-Soviet decade wore on. Even for relatively high-status rural female professions, labor incentives did not improve significantly with privatization: in 1989, highly productive milkmaids received salaries that were, on average, 45 percent higher than those of average milkmaids. By 1999, that ratio had risen by only 3 percent.[73]

This lack of improvement in incentives for milk production is all the more surprising given the increasingly important role played by milkmaids on reorganized collectives, for "the sale of milk pays for diesel."[74] Without revenue from dairy production, many farms would have been unable to purchase fuel needed for plowing, seeding, cultivating, and harvesting crops in the fields. Women did the work that enabled farms to survive, but over time they were rewarded less and less for their efforts compared with other employees.

Finally, female workers on the vast majority of Liski farms experienced a decline in wages relative to male employees. By the end of a decade of reform, for people working in relatively prestigious, gender-defined agricultural professions, women made on average seventy-five kopeks for every ruble earned by a man. This represented a decrease from 1989, when women had earned eighty-four kopeks to the ruble.[75] In a district likely to provide the benefits that privatization was intended to generate, there was no constant association between improved individual productivity

[71] A. Khokhlov, "Ne dumai o mgnoven'iakh svysoka..." *TT* 11 July 1991, 3.

[72] Annual salaries in 1989 for best and average machinists were 5,826 and 3,957 rubles, respectively. By 1999 they had risen to 24,356 and 11,785 rubles. Calculations based on statistics obtained by author from district division of economics, LV.

[73] 1989 annual salaries for best and average milkmaids were 4,430 and 3,059 rubles, respectively. By 1999 they had risen to 13,127 and 8,846 rubles. Ibid.

[74] Interview, director, Chapaev, LV, 8 May 2000.

[75] Calculations based on statistics obtained from district division of economics, LV.

TABLE 5.1. *Milk production and wage ratios in Liski, 1999*

Relative Strength of Agricultural Collectives[a]		Kopeks Earned by Milkmaid per Ruble Earned by Machinist[b]		Metric Tons of Milk per Cow, 1999[c]
		1989	1999	
Strong	SkhA Davydovskaia	95	66	2.55
	SPK im. Tel'mana	78	65	2.00
	SPK Novyi mir	72	62	4.21
	SPK Rassvet	92	87	4.44
Average	SkhA im. Kirova	71	52	2.16
	SkhA Tikhii Don	84	63	1.98
Weak	SkhA Rossiia	53	63	1.16
	SkhA Divnogor'e	67	63	1.29

[a] Designations of farms given by the deputy head of agricultural management, LV, 8 May 2000. There were twenty-seven former collectives in Liski at the time.
[b] Calculations based on statistics obtained from district division of economics, LV.
[c] Ibid.

and relative earning power, or between enterprise strength and relative earning power (Table 5.1).

The relative success of former collectives in Liski likewise did not protect worker-shareholders from continual delays in receiving their wages. Some directors raised livestock workers' salaries in order to compete more effectively in a thin labor pool,[76] and one farm director claimed to have offered an advance to milkmaids, paying them monthly and in cash in order to raise productivity.[77] However, most worker-shareholders did not receive regular payment for their work. Five years into the period of liberalizing economic reforms, a nine-month delay in distribution of wages on Kolybel'sky state farm led milkmaids to slow production,[78] while livestock workers on the Petropavlovsky collective farm refused to feed or milk cows to protest unpaid wages.[79] The situation escalated to the point of open conflict by December 1998, when the milkmaids of the "40 years

[76] V. Kolodezhanskii, "Khoteli kak luchshe. Poluchilos'...kak nikogda!" *LI* 4 April 1996, 2. Some Kharkiv officials observed a similar dynamic at work. Interview, department of agricultural management, NK, 21 July 2006.
[77] Interview, director, Chapaev, LV, May 2000.
[78] G. Aleksandrov, "S chego zakrugliaetsia 'Rodina'. O kakom moloke govorit', esli doiarki s sentiabria bez zarplaty," *LI* 10 June 1997, 2.
[79] Aleksei Salchikov, "Kar'era pervoi v raione zhenshchiny-predsedatelia rukhnula. Kto ostanovit razval v 'Petropavlovskom'?" *LI* 23 January 1997, 1.

of October" collective farm "literally assaulted" its head, threatening to stop milking the cows if he did not release their wages for October and November.[80]

Even after wage arrears had been addressed in industrial sectors in Russia and Ukraine, agricultural enterprises continued to withhold wages from worker-shareholders. In Khava, a private farmer commented in 1998 that "with every year the situation on the agricultural enterprises becomes more troubled. In places people haven't seen their salaries for years."[81] Even in Liski, where workers received higher wages than nearly any other district in Voronezh, the situation only worsened over time.[82] In May 2000, strong enterprises were withholding wages for three months,[83] and other large agricultural enterprises in Liski had not paid their workers for six to seven months.[84] As the head economist of the Fatherland collective farm described the situation at the time, "There's no salary, no incentive...People have nowhere else to go."[85]

By the summer of 2003, wage arrears had skyrocketed. Agricultural production in Liski had increased, but enterprises in the district had an outstanding wage bill of over 446 million rubles, and Liski worker-shareholders on average had not received payment for their labor in well over a year.[86] Wage arrears removed a stimulus for work and created a widespread sense that work in the countryside had become more difficult – an assessment that Koznova describes as "defined not only by the traditional complaint of fathers to children, but a consequence of the situation into which the village has been placed."[87]

[80] Leonid Vybornov, "Zybkoe ravnovesie," *LI* 13 January 1998, 2.
[81] Interview with farmer Maria Nikolaevna Kur'ianova, "Est' u nas takie fermery. Dat' uma zemle neprosto, esli netu sredstv dlia rosta," *VR* 24 December 1998, 3.
[82] *Pokazateli ekonomicheskogo i sotsial'nogo razvitiia gorodov i raionov Voronezhskoi oblasti*. Voronezh: Goskomstat, 2003, 35.
[83] Interview, head of Pavlovskoe, LV, May 2000.
[84] Interview, head economist, Fatherland and interview, farmer, LV, 8 May 2000.
[85] Interview, head economist, Fatherland, LV, 8 May 2000.
[86] Aleksandr Iagodkin, "Vzgliad na doklad ministra iz Voronezha. U kogo chto vyroslo i komu pora obrezat'," *NG*, 9 February 2004. Agricultural workers in the district made, on average, 1,563 rubles a month that year. The official Liski administration website reports that the district was home to 8,319 agricultural workers in 2000. http://www.liski.infobus. ru/agriculture.html (accessed 29 May 2006). This number has declined each year (in 1999–2000, for example, the agricultural labor force decreased by four percent).
[87] Koznova, "Traditsii i novatsii v povedenii sovremennykh krest'ian," in *Identichnost' i konflikt v postsovetskikh gosudarstvakh, sbornik statei*. Moscow, 1997, 374.

Everything Up Through Burial

In addition to paying land rents and wages, agricultural enterprises provided a set of entitlements to worker-shareholders. Farms plowed household gardens, sold agricultural goods at discounted prices, offered transportation, health and education-related services, and paid for weddings and funerals: "Everything up through burial rests on the farm."[88] In the past, people who received such goods had earned them through investment in the community, both through past service and the expectation of future labor. Agricultural collectives functioned as social institutions that would require replacement where they broke down or were dismantled.[89]

After privatization, farm directors made services available only to those from whom they leased land: "I took land. They don't help me. But those who kept their land share documents and leased their land, they get plowed."[90] Those who chose to farm land themselves lost the benefits of community membership, and worker-shareholders who sought more profitable leasing contracts could find themselves homeless, their children kept out of kindergarten,[91] or their family members without transportation in times of emergency. Others risked losing their employment: "Nikolai and Anna Popovy decided to take their land shares from the agricultural enterprise. That intention led them to lose their jobs."[92]

A few farm directors in Kharkiv were reported to keep lists of pensioners who had leased their shares outside the former collective. Those pensioners were blacklisted from ambulance and other services.[93] In Liski, a resident of a village near the private farm Rus' (formerly the agricultural collective Daybreak) noted that "At one time we received an apartment in the collective farm, they won't let us privatize it, and now it's used as a method of pressure – if you don't like life in the village, vacate the apartment."[94] On occasion, farms used their control of social infrastructure to

---

[88] Interview, department of agricultural management, NK, 21 July 2006.

[89] Myriam Hivon, "The Bullied Farmer: Social Pressure as a Survival Strategy?" in Sue Bridger and Frances Pine, eds., *Surviving Post-Socialism: Local Strategies and Regional Responses in Eastern Europe and the Former Soviet Union.* London: Routledge, 1998.

[90] Interview, former collective farm employee, UZ, 19 May 2004.

[91] Interview, farmer, DL, 15 February 1998.

[92] M. Nikonov, "V partiiakh i dvizheniiakh. SPS – na pul'se krest'ianskogo interesa," *KO* 21 August 2003.

[93] OT, Kharkiv regional farmers' association council meetings, 28 March 2000 and 23 May 2000.

[94] Nikonov, "V partiiakh i dvizheniiakh. SPS – na pul'se krest'ianskogo interesa,"*KO* 21 August 2003.

leverage a supply not only of land, but also of labor. In Liski, the Novy Mir agricultural collective demanded in 1996 that one person from each of seven families in a nearby village be sent to work on the farm. Otherwise, the families in question would lose their access to the water main that ran through the village.[95]

Some shareholders who left former collectives were able to successfully demand services from the private farmers who leased their land shares. In such cases, land lease arrangements implied more than a simple exchange for use rights. Instead, they implied a patronage relationship that included the provision of social welfare benefits.[96] Private farmers battled the disapproval of rural communities by offering more grain, more sugar, and more services than local collectives.[97] Agricultural enterprises that had preserved Soviet-era labor institutions also allowed worker-shareholders a measure of leverage, as rural trade unions signed collective agreements that specified lower funeral and other costs for their members. On other types of private agricultural enterprises, however, worker-shareholders "had no opportunity to seriously influence" entitlements, "only through the courts."[98] Whatever the gains shareholders might achieve at the margins, leasing was not profitable in comparison with the social entitlements that had been provided under previous arrangements between collectives and their members.[99]

Entitlements were expensive, and former collectives faced heavy financial obligations supporting aging village populations. Retired workers were often more numerous than current employees. In Semiluki, 75 percent of the members of the Il'ich collective farm were pensioners.[100] The director of the Chapaev cooperative in Liski put it this way: "There are very many pensioners. We can't do what we want because we have to service them. Of 1,200 people, only 340 are workers. The rest are pensioners."[101] On nearby Fatherland, 260 workers maintained an enterprise that served 400 pensioners.[102]

[95] T. Zenina, "'Kollektivizatsiia' po-ermolovski: ne idesh' v kolkhoz – otrezhem vodu," *LI* 27 August 1996, 1.

[96] OT, Kharkiv regional farmers' association meeting, 20 March 2000.

[97] OT, Kharkiv regional farmers' association meeting, 23 May 2000.

[98] Interview, department of agricultural management, ZK, 19 July 2006.

[99] Nearly all of my interlocutors emphasized this point. Interview with farmers, BK, 27 May 2000; interview with director of former collective, VV, May 2000; interview with farmer, KK, 22 February 2000.

[100] OT, head accountant, Il'ich kolkhoz, SV, May 2000.

[101] Interview, director, Chapaev, LV, May 2000.

[102] Interview, head economist, Fatherland, LV, 8 May 2000.

Shareholders shouldered the cost of many such entitlements. In legal terms, agrarian and administrative reform shifted the burden of social service provision from farms to local government. At the same time, the economic environment in which farms operated led to low tax revenues for local government offices, which could not afford to support new social expenditures. The state externalized costs, and farms picked up the slack, providing social services but passing costs onto worker-shareholders. Directors deducted the cost of services from land rents and salaries, and worker-shareholders often ended the growing season with little or no income remaining from the use of their land or labor.

However They Arrange It

Farmer Medvedev:	Let's say, if a land share costs ... this is also an agreed-upon price. Each good is worth whatever is offered for it, or for however much you can sell it. And let's say that the price of seven hectares of arable land is fixed at 28,000 UAH. One percent of that is 280 UAH. [The leaser] will receive goods for what he lets, but that's the minimum price. 280 UAH. That's not money, of course. What is that, sixty or seventy dollars?
Author:	And the leaser receives that in kind?
Farmer Medvedev:	It'll be in kind or in cash, however they arrange it.
Farmer Didenko:	And sometimes it happens that they plowed or cultivated the garden ... or brought something in [from the fields], or removed something, or they settled accounts. Everything goes into that sum.[103]

Land rents, wages, and entitlements were negotiated between worker-shareholders, accountants, and farm directors, but farm directors set the terms of negotiation. Some farms included rents in an overall *quid pro quo* that provided basic services to shareholders and supplied farms with land and labor.[104] In practice, apparently discrete categories of compensation for ownership, labor, and membership overlapped, and no single payment

---

[103] Interview with private farmers, BK, 27 May 2000.
[104] OT, head accountant, Il'ich kolkhoz, SV, May 2000.

or benefit could always be ascribed to a particular category. Depending upon farm managers' preferences, grain that worker-shareholders received at harvest time could be categorized and entered into enterprise accounting records as rents on land shares, payment for labor, or simply as yearly "bonuses." Meanwhile, the economic vulnerability of villagers in the absence of developed labor or leasing markets left many in no position to complain if they were unsatisfied with the arrangement in question.

Furthermore, directors controlled the cash value of rents and salaries by pricing goods and services. It was common for rural people to have their household gardens plowed "at the expense of my salary" or pension and land share rent.[105] Rural families usually did not have access to appropriate machinery for plowing household plots, so farms typically performed this work, driving tractors through backyard allotments to prepare the soil for the following season. The cost of plowing household plots varied, with "different prices for different people."[106] In Kharkiv in 2006, it typically cost anywhere from two to six UAH per *sotka*. A garden of fifty *sotok* thus could consume anywhere from 15 percent to 60 percent of an annual land share rent.[107] Though "each enterprise allots a tractor for the season when plowing begins,"[108] in areas where farms did not provide this service, private companies did it, charging higher prices for the service.[109]

Homesteads required this service in autumn, after the harvest but before the ground froze. In addition to variation in price, the service varied substantially in value according to when it was delivered. There was constant competition among villagers for a place in the queue, and early plowing did not necessarily correspond to a higher price. Social standing and a good relationship with the farm director, or with tractor operators who had access to machinery, tended to determine the timing of plowing, and by extension, the fate of an extended family for the following year.[110] Urbanites with summer cottages and gardens paid higher prices, but "they plow for *dachniki* earlier."[111] Households last in line for plowing had to wait until spring, when farms would have less cash available to purchase

---

[105] Interview, pensioners (former milker and driver), PK, 18 July 2006.
[106] Ibid.
[107] Ibid, Interview, pensioner, PK, 18 July 2006.
[108] Interview, department of agricultural management, NK, 21 July 2006.
[109] Interview, department of agricultural management, ZK, 19 July 2006.
[110] Many of my interlocutors mentioned this issue. Interview with farmer, MK, 6 April 2000.
[111] Interview, department of agricultural management, NK, 21 July 2006.

fuel and when tractor operators would be forced to battle the prodigious mud that slows vehicles to a halt after the first thaw. Spring plowing meant sowing crops late; if seeds did not go into the ground during the correct week of the season, crop yields could shrink substantially. A household's ability to feed itself, or to produce any surplus for market, thus depended in part on the discretion of the farm director and the arrival of a tractor.

The method of calculating wage and rent payments also determined their value. During the critical early years of land privatization, and long after urban and industrial economies in Russia and Ukraine had moved away from barter as a mode of exchange, Black Earth village economies were predominantly cashless. Farms often paid worker-shareholders in goods, primarily inputs for household production and food conservation: "grain, sugar, oil...in particular quantities,"[112] flour, seed, the use of machinery or draft animals for cultivation, manure for fertilizing the soil, and young animals to be fattened for market. Farm accountants arrived at the kind and amount of goods to be paid in two ways. Many reorganized collectives used cash proxy payments, which were subject to negotiation, rather than outright payment in-kind, which generally was not.[113] Outright payment in kind consisted of a set amount of goods, often a few sacks of grain, received at a fixed interval, usually once each year at harvest time. In contrast, the cash value of proxy payments was fixed, but the amount of goods that worker-shareholders received could fluctuate. A milkmaid in Voronezh who took home 100 rubles worth of goods each month might receive one piglet in lieu of wages, or, depending on whether state or market prices were used, or on which market prices were used, she might receive two piglets. When workers received commodities in lieu of cash wages, they did so at reduced prices but at the discretion of enterprise managers, who struggled to cut costs. Wage values thus could vary depending upon personal relationships between an individual employee and enterprise managers.[114]

Some workers did receive outright in-kind payments. The standard accounting forms used by Ukrainian agricultural enterprises at the end of the 1990s included a page devoted to recording such payments, and the economics divisions of district state administrations kept track of

---

[112] OT, head accountant, Il'ich kolkhoz, SV, May 2000.

[113] Enterprise accountants' records distinguish between these two types: in Russian, *v rasschete na oplatu truda* and *naturoplata*.

[114] OT, Chayanovskoe, August 1998. Caroline Humphrey has found a similar relationship between dividends and status in Buryatia. Humphrey, *Marx Went Away But Karl Stayed Behind*. Ann Arbor: University of Michigan Press, 1998.

both cash proxy and in-kind payments. Directors varied in how they paid their employees, but even farms that made very few in-kind payments usually distributed some grain this way.[115] In 1998, for example, the worker-shareholders of the Novolypets'kyi collective agricultural enterprise in Kharkiv received no in-kind payments,[116] while employees of a nearby farm, Karl Marx, received sixty-three metric tons of grain, a metric ton of sunflower, five metric tons of melon, two and a half metric tons of meat, and one and a half metric tons of hay.[117] That year, one of the most successful former collectives in Kharkiv, Red Partisan, distributed eighty-four metric tons of animal feed to its employees as payments in-kind but only three metric tons through cash proxy payments.[118] Thus, the method farm managers chose for calculating and distributing wages and rents determined how negotiable payment for labor or ownership would be and, accordingly, how well some worker-shareholders would fare.

Half Starved and Dressed Almost in Rags

As we have seen, households as well as farms depended on a variety of informal exchange mechanisms after privatization: barter, payment in-kind, cashless accounting and other forms of reciprocity. Such practices strengthened local officials' resolve to act in response to local incentives as opposed to national ones: as Woodruff has shown, the use of barter "promotes subnational integration."[119] The time horizons for such exchanges, in which the terms of the *quid pro quo* were left unspecified, were long and embedded in complex networks of local transactions that created new obligations as they discharged old ones.

Cashless systems diffused the social tensions produced by protracted wage payment delays and minimized the amount of cash former collectives needed to obtain in order to pay their employees. However, when

[115] Bukhhalters'kyi zvity s-h pidpryiemstva 1995–1999 for Bezliudivka, Berezivka, Rassvet, Peremoha, Liptsy, Kolos, Komunar and others, 23. On some enterprises, in-kind payments tended to increase as the decade progressed.
[116] Bukhhalters'kyi zvit s-h pidpryiemstva za 1998 rik, KSP Novolypets'kyi, 23.
[117] Ibid. Karl Marx KSP.
[118] Ibid. Red Parstan KSP. The same enterprise paid its workers eighty-five metric tons of vegetables in-kind and twenty-nine metric tons as cash equivalents.
[119] David Woodruff, "Barter of the Bankrupt: The Politics of Demonetization in Russia's Federal State," in Michael Burawoy and Katherine Verdery, eds. *Uncertain Transition: Ethnographies of Change in the Postsocialist World*. Lanham: Rowman and Littlefield, 1999, 5.

former collectives were not able to allocate goods to employees immediately, delays could create a dangerous gap between allocation of wages in theory and receipt of goods in kind. With a short growing season, the timing of payment was of paramount importance, for the absence of appropriate and timely inputs could limit the productive capacity of village households.

In some cases, employees could wait months for cash payment, only later to have to accept their payment in another form. When prices rose and theoretical wages remained constant, as during the inflation that followed Russia's currency devaluation crisis of August 1998, wages lost value, even if that loss were measured in grain, livestock, textiles, or building materials. Inflation thus effectively could liquidate the unpaid wages that employees had come to regard as savings, making eventual acquisition of land an unattainable goal. This precarious situation was exacerbated by the fact that villagers had little opportunity to provide insurance against devaluation by acquiring other currency or durable goods.

Despite the physical absence of cash in Black Earth villages, however, farms and households did not operate entirely outside of the cash economy. Some understandings of informal exchange conjure an image of insular, independent rural communities protected from the vagaries of global economic change in part by virtue of their very backwardness.[120] In the post-Soviet Black Earth, the opposite was the case. Barter exchanges, including the payment of wages in goods, bypassed the physical presence of currency but were dependent upon relative commodity values established within cash markets.[121] Quantities involved in such exchanges were neither arbitrary (a factory furnishes each employee with fifteen kilograms of sausage monthly in lieu of wages) nor necessarily determined by surplus and interpersonal comparisons of utility (the October collective farm exchanges its extra two tons of sugar for the sunflower oil that the Kirov state farm does not need). Instead, market prices governed transactions: in the payment of wages in-kind and in barter, the current cash value of the goods offered was equal to the current cash value of the goods received. Transactions took place on a market model, with reference to but without the actual exchange of cash.

---

[120] Kate Brown, *A Biography of No-Place: From Ethnic Borderland to Soviet Heartland.* Cambridge: Harvard University, 2004 and Margaret Paxson, *Solovyovo: The Story of Memory in a Russian Village.* Washington and Bloomington: Woodrow Wilson Center Press and Indiana University Press, 2005, 4.

[121] Clifford G. Gaddy and Barry W. Ickes, *Russia's Virtual Economy.* Washington, D.C.: Brookings, 2002.

This "virtual cash" pricing arrangement provided individuals and farms with a common measure of value. However, it tied exchanges in goods to the cash economy's pricing system without providing an obvious reciprocal mechanism for influencing price levels. Informal economies were subject to market forces but had no direct means of influencing cash-based markets, other than to limit expansion of the cash economy. The viability of barter hinged on a stable parallel cash economy, and financial instability on a society-wide level upset the delicate balance of price relationships upon which barter-dependent communities relied. Currency devaluations, currency depreciation, and inflation affected Russian and Ukrainian village economies primarily through declines in the value of wages paid in-kind and through relative price fluctuation.

Households that survived primarily on labor and ownership-based compensation from a former collective found that price fluctuations were disastrous for both short-term solvency and long-term planning. Without stable relationships *among* prices for goods, it was difficult for individuals and enterprises dependent on wages paid using cash proxies to know what the surplus value of their production would be. A family that accepted piglets in lieu of cash wages could not determine in advance if the price a pig would bring on the market in the spring would exceed the cost of feeding the animal through the winter.[122] This problem of unpredictability is by no means unique to cash-poor economies, but in Black Earth villages, the results of most transactions were not convertible into a more flexible medium for further investment. In this respect, conditions of financial instability in the cash economy decreased the efficiency of barter-based economies and placed cash-poor communities of worker-shareholders at special risk.

Instability in relative prices not only led to unpredictability and inefficiency in wage distribution, but also inhibited entrance into cash markets, capital accumulation, and acquisition of land. From the fall of the Soviet Union until the end of the 1990s, it was profitable for rural people in parts of Voronezh to transport milk to district centers for sale. However, when the price of milk suddenly dropped to eighty kopeks per liter against one ruble thirty kopeks per liter for gasoline, such trade was no longer profitable: for low-volume sales, the added cost of transporting milk to an urban market caused the cost of producing milk to exceed its asking price. Structural economic change, prompted by factors beyond the influence of

---

[122] My thanks to V. I. for this example, drawn from her family's dilemma in 1997. OT, Chayanovskoe, August 1998.

village communities, resulted in an environment hostile to rural producers and to entrepreneurship that could lead to a demand for land.

The principle of cash equivalence placed communities dependent on barter transactions at the mercy of currency and price fluctuations, but wage payments in goods were an efficient response to an absence of cash markets. By widespread tacit agreement to conduct transactions according to market prices, individuals and enterprises circumvented some local power discrepancies, temporarily solved the problem of cash shortages, ensured a necessary level of trust among contracting parties, and minimized transaction costs.

These in-kind transactions may have represented nothing more than a transitional equilibrium. They together constituted an efficient and in many cases ingenious adaptation to some of the problems of survival that rural people faced in the post-Soviet decade, even as they remained far from the ideal of an ownership society. Nonetheless, observers warned early on of the dangers of reliance on cash equivalence: "It's become absurd. You give me meat, butter, vegetable oil, vegetables, and I'll give you spare parts. It's a faulty path. If we continue to treat village workers this way, we'll end up half-starved and, possibly, dressed almost in rags."[123]

Conclusion

The broader economic environment limited the profits agricultural enterprises could pass on to worker-shareholders, and the power that farm directors gained through the privatization process further diminished the meager payments that worker-shareholders received. Land ownership tied rural people to specific locations and communities without providing new labor or ownership incentives. The goods that worker-shareholders received in return for the use of their land, labor, and participation in community life made household production possible, which itself made movement less likely.[124] After land privatization, the material needs of household production continued to bind worker-shareholders to former collectives. In a direct sense, the word that many people in the Black Earth

---

[123] N. Solontsevoi, "Razgovor s chitatelem. Barter! Barter?" *TT* 7 November 1991, 1.

[124] Such risk-minimization may be understood in terms of a moral economy framework. See E. P. Thompson, "The moral economy of the English crowd in the eighteenth century," (1971) reprinted in *Customs in Common*. London: Penguin, 1993; James C. Scott, *The Moral Economy of the Peasant: Rebellion and Subsistence in Southeast Asia*. New Haven: Yale University Press, 1976.

chose to denote "land share" – *dolia*, rather than *pai*, the word widely used in land reform legislation in both Russia and Ukraine – suggested an ineluctable binding of people to land. Despite a lack of improvement, and in many cases, a distinct decline in material living conditions in the Black Earth as a result of privatization, economic circumstances continued to root rural people in the soil of former collectives. In Black Earth villages, where many people are bilingual, *"dolia"* carried a double meaning: in Russian, it meant a parcel of land; in Ukrainian, it was one's lot in life.

If local officials, responding to discretion, norms, and local incentives, stood in the way of partition of the commons by creating informal barriers to land distribution, sudden exposure to global markets created an environment in which most Black Earth villagers could ill afford the risk and expense of demanding that partition, either at that time or in the future. Both informal local politics and national economic liberalization thwarted property rights development beyond a paper facade of ownership. Meanwhile, administrative hierarchies on former collective farms, now even further embedded in village networks of economic interdependence and in the continuing importance of collectives as social institutions, entrenched the power of farm directors. Increasingly, poverty and inequality ossified many villagers' economic status and limited opportunities for improvement in the material quality of their lives.[125] As owners of land on paper alone, and unable to garner the economic and political resources necessary to make use of their property, many worker-shareholders saw their opportunities recede into the distance, eclipsed in the bright future of capitalism.

[125] David O'Brien, Valeri Patsiorkovski, and Larry Dershem, *Household Capital and the Agrarian Problem in Russia.* Aldershot: Ashgate, 2000. Future legislation would be inadequate to meet such challenges, despite a shift in intention under Putin. Wegren writes, "Whereas Yeltsin was satisfied to put land deeds in the hands of land share holders, the law on turnover of agricultural land is an attempt to allow land share holders to convert their land shares to actual land parcels." Wegren, "Observations on Russia's New Agricultural Land Legislation," *Eurasian Geography and Economics* 43:8 (2002) 657.

6

The Facade

By July 2005, Ukraine's national newspaper *The Day* had described Ukraine as a "country of nominal owners." The director of Ukraine's Koretsky Institute of State and Law observed, "Farmers are merely nominal owners of their plots. Neither domestic nor foreign investors will want to do business with such bogus landowners."[1] Only a few months earlier, across the border in Russia, a pensioner by the name of N. Volkova wrote to the newspaper *Krest'ianskaia Rossiia* asking, "Explain to me, please, how I can get rid of my land share." The Russian tax inspectorate had demanded a 1,500 ruble payment on her land share. Like so many other landowners in Russia and Ukraine, Volkova had never learned the location of her share and received no profit from the land. She continued:

Here's the thing. In 1993 our collective farm distributed land as property shares to the workers. Each received a certificate of land ownership. Then in the course of several years the former collective farm leased the shares and gave out feed grain, at first two hundred kilograms, then one hundred. Now the enterprise has finally fallen apart.... But where is my land? Maybe someone is sowing it, maybe there's already a mansion built on it.[2]

Volkova was far from alone. The paper records of results in Ukraine and Russia emphasized the distribution of land share certificates and the opportunity to allot land, thus confirming the existence of private ownership, but observation of changes on the ground told a far different story.

[1] Petro Izhyk, "A Country of Nominal Owners," *The Day Weekly Digest* No. 23, 12 July 2005.

[2] K. Nikolaev, "Zemel'nye doli naviazali, a brat' nazad ne khotiat," *KR* No. 13 (March 2005) 4.

Fifteen years into the process of reform, titling was far from complete and land rents minimal to non-existent, but the state still took its share in taxes. For many landholders, ownership was literally a losing proposition.

Rather than creating improved labor incentives within a framework of secure private property rights, land reform in Russia and Ukraine severed any clear link between ownership categories and economic production. Legal categories of ownership did not reliably predict either actual rights or modes of production. Some collective farms became private farms, changing only their legal status, and some private farms resembled household plots in their land holdings and scale of production. Reorganized collectives that registered as joint-stock companies, private farms, or other types of enterprises retained their former management structure and organization of production and labor. Other reorganized collectives operated only as shell firms holding enterprise debt. And all forms of agricultural production existed in a web of symbiotic relationships, in which private farms, household plots, and former collectives depended on one another for their continued existence.

In his introduction to *The Post-Socialist Agrarian Question*, Chris Hann proposes a shift in analytical focus from property rights to property relations, noting that the "juridical dimension cannot be read simply from the appearance of the landscape, and knowledge of legal rights may in turn offer little guidance into living standards, work patterns, group relations, inequalities, and notions of belonging to a community."[3] Beyond the subtleties of social organization that ordinarily underpin arid legal categories, however, the privatized terrain of post-communist Eurasia conceals an even deeper disjuncture between official narratives of an ownership society and the availability of rights in practice. In the Black Earth, legal categories of ownership not only fail to capture the rich variety of meanings people attach to property, they also mislead. Paper rights very often suggest the very opposite of what exists on the ground, allowing some observers to infer that private property rights have themselves produced broad opportunities for agricultural entrepreneurship in the countryside.

What does it mean to speak of a modern Potemkin village? Advocates of land reform in post-communist states sought to move rural regulatory institutions from one end of the public–private spectrum to the other. Property rights development thus was intended to transform Soviet-era state solutions to land use problems into market solutions.

---

[3] Chris Hann and the "Property Relations" Group, *The Post-Socialist Agrarian Question: Property Relations and the Rural Condition*. Münster: Lit Verlag, 2003, 1.

Reformers argued that partitioning and distributing the land formerly under the stewardship of agricultural collectives would allow smallholders to resolve resource use problems independently and more efficiently. But the political and economic incentives that accompanied land reform in Russia and Ukraine were not sufficient to generate changes in beliefs about optimal solutions to the "tragedy of the commons."[4]

As local state officials sought nonetheless to produce a record of successful reform, rights typically associated with resource ownership developed on paper alone, and farm directors jumped into the breach. Private ownership failed to change forms of production, and local networks of interdependence rendered many private farmers powerless without former collectives and the support of state institutions. Worker-shareholders found their rights in practice crushed under the weight of local political and economic interests, and property relations shifted dramatically as creditors and villagers with no apparent stake in privatization dismantled and carted away the remnants of the Black Earth's once modern agriculture.

The Same Old Collective Farm

Legal categories of enterprise organization and ownership were meant to mark variation in land tenure practices in both Russia and Ukraine, but new ownership structures and new names for rural enterprises did not correlate with *de facto* modes of production. In most districts, private farms with large landholdings functioned as collective farms. In Kharkiv, private farming had met with relative success in Bohodukhiv district, which at the end of the 1990s was home to approximately 10 percent of all of the private farms in the region.[5] Among the farmers of Bohodukhiv were several former farm directors who had converted collectives into private farms. Two members of the district farmers' association described the resulting companies:

Farmer Didenko: We have three collective agricultural enterprises in the district that were made private farms. They leased all of the shares.

---

[4] See Elinor Ostrom's critique of Hardin's (1968) "tragedy of the commons" as an idée fixe in Ostrom, *Governing the Commons: The Evolution of Institutions for Collective Action.* Cambridge: Cambridge University Press, 1990.

[5] Calculated from statistics obtained by author from Kharkiv regional division of private farming, 1999.

Author:	All of the shares?
Farmer Didenko:	All of the shares. That's not even practical.
Farmer Medvedev:	That's not the issue. The issue is that that's not a private farmer.
Farmer Didenko:	That's understood. It's a change of signboard. A change of signboard.... They changed the name and that's it.
Author:	It was the directors who did that?
Farmer Didenko:	Yes, yes.
Farmer Medvedev:	And they stayed principally just the same.
Author:	But they're legally registered as private farms.
Farmer Didenko:	Yes, yes. That is, the same old collective farm.[6]

The reregistration of former collectives as private farms was an ongoing process, and by the end of the decade in Ukraine, "Every chairman with a brain became a private farmer."[7] According to the head of the Kharkiv regional private farmers' association, between three and ten private farmers in each of the region's twenty-five districts were poised to take over entire collectives by spring 2000. Eight farmers created private enterprises, leasing the land shares of as many as 1,000 worker-shareholders[8] and creating what one state functionary described as "small collective farms."[9] This type of isomorphic development, which has been observed in other post-socialist contexts, reestablished social and economic relations characteristic of Soviet agriculture.[10]

Some such private farms continued to function as agricultural collectives within the economic fabric of their communities, receiving directives as well as subsidies from the state. These enterprises differed from other private farms in not only in the scale and organization of their production, but also in their relationship to local state regulatory institutions:

Author:	And nevertheless, these so-called private farmers who are chairmen of collective agricultural enterprises have come to you...

[6] Interview, district farmers' association, BK, 27 May 2000.

[7] OT, farmer Chernets'kyi, ZK, 19 July 2006.

[8] OT, Kharkiv regional farmers' association meeting, 14 December 1999.

[9] OT, Kharkiv regional division of private farms, 20 March and 4 April 2000. Also see Yu. Kryklyvyi, "Kolhospiv uzhe nema, ale ikhni problemy zalyshylysia," *SK* 4 April 2000 and M. Khablak, "Zatsikavlenist' u reformuvanni velychezna," *SK* 11 January 2000, 1.

[10] Jean C. Oi and Andrew Walder, eds. *Property Rights and Economic Reform in China.* Stanford University Press, 1999 and Verdery 1999.

Farmer Didenko:	To the association? No, no. I'll tell you how it is. Just as they were chairmen of collective farms...
All in unison:	So they've remained.
Farmer Didenko:	They're summoned, the administration head calls them in:

"You plant something." Yes, they get called in... to the administration.... I said to the head of administration, "How is that? Kyryl Dmytrovych, former collective agricultural enterprises became private farms. Why do you call them in?" And he says, they won't ever be private farmers: "You're not understanding me correctly. You started from zero, you risked your life, risked your assets. You acquired things yourself. They came already provided for (*nagotovye*)... Now they'll steal everything, they'll do something for themselves, but... they'll abandon people. They'll never be farmers. Therefore they need to be controlled at every step.... How do I understand you? I don't touch you and I don't call you in. Although I don't offer much because there's no currency, no money." The chair of the collective gets allotted seeding material, and so on. But for us: nothing.[11]

Across the border in Voronezh, a similar phenomenon unfolded as powerful directors of former collective farms reregistered their collectives as private farms and compelled shareholders to lease their land to the newly constituted enterprises. The two largest private farms in Semiluki district were just such enterprises. Directors of former collectives headed both farms, both of which were massive, encompassing more than 1,200 hectares each.[12] In this and other cases, members of the collective typically continued to work on the farm as before:

Author: And is it a collective farm now, or a cooperative, or something else?

Director of 'Sil'nyi': We're a cooperative, but you know, there's no difference, they way people worked before is the way they'll continue to work. Every year on the contrary, there are fewer people and they work more, more, but of course people think we don't work. Peasants work. We have no emigrants from the farm, it's just that now they come in from the field and go to their garden to harrow. The guys, even as tractor operators, sit all day at the levers, ten or twelve hours, and then there's your own garden and weeding, you have to help your wife, and the livestock... Those who say that peasants only drink are gravely mistaken.[13]

---

[11] Interview with farmers, BK, 27 May 2000.
[12] Interview, district land tenure office, SV, May 2000. According to the district farmers' association, these two enterprises covered more than 1,800 hectares each. The legal ceiling for land allotments of pasture was fifty hectares. Land Code of Ukraine (1991) S2/Ch7/A52.
[13] Interview, director, agricultural artel Sil'nyi, LV, 8 May 2000.

Here, the legal status of farms as private companies obscured the continuity with Soviet-era labor practices, even as the labor burden associated with household production increased the hours that rural people spent in the fields.

The language that worker-shareholders on former collectives used to talk about land privatization provides one indication of the frequency with which rights in law departed from rights in practice. Despite formal changes in the legal status of collective and state farms, and despite changes in the ways that reorganized collectives operated in markets, people who worked on these farms emphasized that little had changed in their own work lives. Over and over again, members of former collective farms, farm directors, private farmers, and district state officials conceptualized reorganization and privatization as transformation in name only:

... See how things have turned out... "Comrade Tel'man" stood around a long time before he became a "Farmer" [*Zemledelets*]. There's no reason, really, to object to that. Comrade Tel'man, of course, was a good person, but the *kolkhoz* in his blessed name somehow didn't look too good.... By the way, other farms named after very good people – Frunze, Michurin... and even very good events – "Twentieth Congress of the Communist Party" are no longer collective farms. "Progress" has become a branch "shell" [*podsovka*]. But so that everything's clear, we're publishing today on page one the new "agricultural map" of the district. In a word, two comrades have remained: Gorky and Kirov.[14]

As agricultural collectives officially became known as joint-stock companies, limited liability companies, and other types of enterprises, the meaning of reorganization to worker-shareholders appeared no different from that of the cities, urban streets, and metro stations across Russia and Ukraine that shed their Soviet-era names to adopt new or historical nomenclature.[15] Farm employees continued to use the old names in daily conversation, consistently referring to the enterprises as *kolkhozy* and *sovkhozy*.[16] This choice sometimes was made explicit: during an interview in a remote district of Kharkiv, two farmers provided instructions on how to record their speech: "We'll say 'collective farm,' but you write

---

[14] "Nastroenie nedeli. Vy chto – 'TOgO'? ili Kak Vas teper' nazyvat'," *LI* 4 April 1992, 1.
[15] It is possible that the preservation of old names in speech is less a signifier of stasis than an assertion of local identity through the articulation of local historical knowledge, as in the directions visitors to Boston still receive to "turn right after the Sears Building" (which Sears vacated in 1988) to reach Jamaica Plain.
[16] Ukrainian speakers in Kharkiv also referred to the collectives using the Russian terms, which are associated with Soviet rule.

'partnership' (*tovarystvo*)."[17] Others expressed less patience with the new taxonomy: as one local land tenure official put it, "Let's not call it a partnership or a company. It's a collective farm."[18] Some state officials – in this case, a people's deputy who was also a former collective farm chairman – went even further, arguing against changes in nomenclature in the absence of other improvements. The Lenin collective farm in Kharkiv kept its name, he said, because "we haven't found any innovations or reformation. It's necessary to fundamentally change state policy on the village, and not signs on offices."[19]

Some apparent privatization success stories depended on directors' successful manipulation not only of language but also of farm liability. As others have found in numerous other post-socialist contexts, some Black Earth directors managed enterprise debt by dividing their farms into two separate companies.[20] Under such an arrangement, one company held most of the land shares, machinery, and other assets, while the other held the debt of the former collective. This strategy allowed former collectives to shed their debt and improve their performance. One Kharkiv director described his strategy: "Liquid assets wouldn't have been enough to pay off the debt. Our liquid assets were the machinery, livestock, seed.... So in consultation with Ronco [a consulting corporation] we decided to form a private agricultural enterprise" – in this case, a private farm. Meanwhile, people "left the ... collective farm and started to work on the private agricultural enterprise ... in their same positions, on the same land, and they started to produce. In a word, they kept the assets and started to live normally."[21] Here, reorganization entered the documentary record as the creation of two companies. In reality, only one of these companies continued

[17] Interview, farmer, KK, 6 April 2000.
[18] Interview, village council land tenure office, XK, 31 March 2000.
[19] M. Mel'nyk, "Chyia zelmia v Rokytnomu?" *SK* 25 December 1999, 1–2.
[20] István Harcsa, Imre Kovách, and Iván Szelényi, "The price of privatization: The post-communist transformational crisis of the Hungarian agrarian system," in Iván Szelényi, ed. *Privatizing the Land: Rural Political Economy in Post-Communist Societies.* Routledge: 1998, 226; Katalin Kovacs, "The transition to Hungarian agriculture 1990–1993. General tendencies, background factors and the case of the 'Golden Age'," in Ray Abrahams, ed. *After Socialism: Land Reform and Social Change in Eastern Europe.* Providence: Berghahn, 1996; Martha Lampland, "The advantages of being collectivized. Collective farm managers in the postsocialist economy," in C. M. Hann, ed. *Postsocialism: Ideals, Ideologies, and Practices in Eurasia.* London: Routledge, 2002; David Stark, "Recombinant Property in East European Capitalism," *American Journal of Sociology* 101: 4 (1996) 993–1027; Katherine Verdery, *The Vanishing Hectare: Property and Value in Postsocialist Transylvania.* Ithaca: Cornell University Press, 2003, 296.
[21] Interview, head of PSP Progress, XK, 14 January 2000. A similar strategy in Russia is reported in Mikhail Nikonov, "V partiiakh i dvizhenniiakh. SPS – na pul'se krest'ianskogo interesa," *KO* 21 August 2003.

to function as an agricultural enterprise. The other existed only as a vessel for enterprise debt. This strategy did not usually have the sanction of local officials; instead, collegial relationships among directors provided a mechanism for its diffusion. In the course of one conversation between the Kharkiv director mentioned above and a farmer facing a similar problem in a neighboring district, the former left the room to make copies of his papers for the farmer, noting that he had found a solution to this problem.[22]

The relationship between ownership, organizational form, and mode of production was just as difficult to discern among private farms that were not simply renamed collectives. A large proportion – by most estimates, as many as half of all enterprises legally registered as private farms – were widely believed to be fronts for non-agricultural businesses.[23] Scholarship on Russia likewise has asserted that "private farms sometimes exist only on paper,"[24] or that under a third of enterprises registered as private farms functioned as such.[25] In 1995, the head of the regional farmers' association in Kharkiv had remarked that "there are a total of 1,002 private farms in the region. However, I'll say openly that only about half of them are real. The rest are a fiction...."[26]

It is not possible to know exactly how many private farms fell into this category. Even in districts where state regulatory institutions remained relatively strong during the 1990s, complete information about land use was not always available, and documenting the precise extent of such distortions poses enormous logistical challenges. Surveillance is comparatively simple within the compact confines of a town or small city, but large areas of the countryside remained illegible from the outside.[27] At the local level, official records of land allotments were known not to match

---

[22] OT, Kharkiv regional farmers' association council meeting, 8 February 2000.

[23] All the state officials and academics in Voronezh and Kharkiv regions whom I asked gave this figure. None was willing to go on record as having done so. When I inquired about this phenomenon among agricultural economists in Voronezh in 1998, I was warned that such questions "could end badly" for me.

[24] Max Spoor and Oane Visser, "The State of Agrarian Reform in the Former Soviet Union," *Europe-Asia Studies* 53:6 (2001) 898, summarizing Wegren, "The Politics of Private Farming in Russia," *The Journal of Peasant Studies* 23:4 (July 1996) 113.

[25] V. Vinogradsky and O. Vinogradskaia, "Obnaruzhivaetsia li kapitalizm v rossiiskoi derevne nachala XXI veka?" in T. Vorozheikina, ed. *Puti Rossii: sushchestvuiushchie ogranicheniia i vozmozhnye varianty: Mezhdunarodnyi simpozium, 15–17 ianvaria 2004 g.* Moscow: MVShSEN, 2004.

[26] M. Mel'nyk, "'Nas zlamaty uzhe neprosto,' – hovoryt' holova Kharkivs'koi assotsiatsii fermeriv S. V. Tsvetkov," *SK* 2 February 1995, 2.

[27] James C. Scott, *Seeing Like a State: How Certain Schemes to Improve the Human Condition Have Failed.* New Haven: Yale University Press, 1998.

actual land use, leading administrators in some districts to examine allotments personally.[28] Because of their smaller size and, frequently, distance from main roads, private farms in particular were notoriously difficult to enumerate with any accuracy.

The size of land holdings, however, can indicate the type of production – commercial or household – in which private farmers were engaged. Farms of under twenty hectares, often headed by marginalized members of rural society, rarely functioned as commercial agricultural enterprises.[29] In the Black Earth, holdings with such limited acreage generally are regarded as too small to observe crop rotations independently.[30] Such farms were common, including 148 of the 233 private farms in Semiluki district of Voronezh in 2000[31] – even as the head of that district's farmers' association described only fifty of the district's private farms as "serious," or engaged in profitable commercial production.[32] Likewise, in Bohodukhiv district of Kharkiv, where private farming was relatively well developed, 35 of the 115 private farms in the district were less than 20 hectares in size.[33] Such farms supported household economies, without necessarily marketing surplus production. One Ukrainian state official, in referring to the activities of a farmer in Krasnokuts'kiy district, described the phenomenon: "That's not a private farm...that's a peasant homestead."[34]

We're Fated to Live Together, Inseparably

New ownership categories not only obscured the reality of land tenure practices, but also provided an ill-fitting taxonomy for enumerating the success and failure of specific types of enterprises. Records produced by state statistical agencies in Russia and Ukraine aggregate production figures by form of ownership and provide separate records for the output of former collectives, private farms, and households. In Voronezh and Kharkiv, these categories not only fail to capture the reality of rights and land use, but also convey the impression that discrete and independent

---

[28] N. Fedina, "Samyi nadezhnyi kapital. Interv'iu s predsedatelem komiteta po zemel'nym resursam i zemleustroistvu g. Liski A. A. Batsunovym," *LI* 27 April 1993, 2.

[29] See Chapter 3, p. 111.

[30] "Fermerstvo rastet i chislom, i gektarom," *SZ* 16 January 1999, 1.

[31] Interview, land tenure department, SV, May 2000.

[32] Interview, district farmers' association, SV, May 2000.

[33] Statistics obtained from district farmers' association, BK, May 2000.

[34] OT, Kharkiv regional division of private farms, 2 March 2000.

forms of production now exist in the Black Earth countryside. In truth, the neat columns of statistical yearbooks belie the interdependence of forms of production that developed on privatized soil. In post-Soviet space, as in post-socialist Europe, the tripartite structure of agricultural production is molecular in form: household, former collective, and private farm sectors are held together by covalent bonds in which tractors and other inputs, rather than electrons, are shared.[35]

After privatization, reorganized collectives depended on the labor of worker-shareholders, who in turn used their wages and entitlements to support household-level production,[36] which accounted for an increasing share of total agricultural output during the 1990s in both Russia and Ukraine.[37] Collectives had encouraged such a relationship since before the fall of the Soviet Union: during the mowing season in 1991, the Friendship collective farm in Khava had advertised the good quality of hay in its ravines and allotted plots in hayfields for villagers with their own livestock. While recognizing the need for an organized approach, lest it be left with too little hay for its own needs, the collective farm encouraged people to gather hay for private use themselves, warning them not to expect "charity" from the collective later in the year.[38] A decade later, some privatized collectives still encouraged worker-shareholders to use the commons, now legally owned by worker-shareholders but held by farm directors, for household dairy production. Around 2000, at certain times of day in warm weather, even farm economists and accountants could be found outside, using the commons to graze their families' livestock.

The relationship between household production and former collectives was a fragile symbiosis. The wage and land-share rents that workers received were often "not enough for household gardens,"[39] and changes

---

[35] See Gerald W. Creed, "The Politics of Agriculture: Identity and Socialist Sentiment in Bulgaria," *Slavic Review* 54:4 (Winter 1995) 843–868.

[36] Gavin Kitching, "The Revenge of the Peasant? The Collapse of Large-Scale Russian Agriculture and the Role of the Peasant 'Private Plot' in That Collapse, 1991–97," *Journal of Peasant Studies* 26:1 (1998); Jessica Allina-Pisano, "Reorganization and Its Discontents: A Case Study in Voronezh oblast'" in David O'Brien and Stephen Wegren, eds. *Rural Reform in Post-Soviet Russia.* Washington and Baltimore: Woodrow Wilson Center Press and Johns Hopkins University Press, 2002; Peter Lindner, *Das Kolchoz-Archipel im Privatisierungsprozess: Wege und Umwege der russischen Landwirtschaft in die globale Marktgesellschaft.* Bielefeld: transcript Verleg, forthcoming.

[37] *Sil's'ke hospodarstvo Ukrainy. Statystychnyi zbirnyk.* Kyiv: Derzhkomzem, 1997, 79 and *Sel'skoe khoziaistvo Rossii. Statisticheskii sbornik.* Moscow: Goskomstat, 1995, 47.

[38] N. Krestnikov, "Kak idut senozagotovki," *RV* 11 June 1991, 1.

[39] Interview, department of agricultural management, ZK, 19 July 2006.

in either could seriously damage household production. A journalist describes the predicament of a household in Nizhegorodskaia region of Russia that held a nineteen-hectare share in the Red Star collective farm:

> Voronin, the chair before last, each year gave (specifically "gave," not "paid"!) a ton of grain.... The last chair lowered the lease to five hundred kilograms, but aunt Lida nonetheless kept a cow, there was some kind of [income] stream. Buyers... paid eighteen rubles for three liters [of milk], a great price. The little cow... brought home sometimes eight hundred, sometimes a thousand rubles a week. The grandchildren wore new sneakers.

> Two years ago the district sent former mechanic V. A. Burov to "Red Star," with its eleven million rubles in debt. He cut rent payment to one hundred kilos... It became expensive to keep the cow: ninety each month to the shepherd, that's in addition to the usual feed and potatoes, they cut their own hay, and there's no combination feed. Their health has started to give out, and the Nikonovs... sold the cow.[40]

The precarious nature of agricultural production, particularly small-scale surplus production amidst difficult pricing regimes, requires a safety net, whether informally socially constituted or provided by the state. Reorganized collectives filled that role for years after reform, but ruined farms could eventually destroy household production. The death of such farms could be long in coming: "The thing is that those enterprises of this type in Russia, as on Voronezh soil, that have been abandoned, so to speak, to fate... in most cases have been 'sentenced to a long life.'"[41]

Just as there exist symbiotic relationships between reorganized collectives and household economies, private farmers and collectives depend on one another for labor and inputs. The legal line that separates former collectives from other private forms of production is not evident in practice. The direction of assistance varies: many private farmers rely heavily on the resources of collectives, while some collectives receive assistance from private farmers. The extent and duration of reciprocity varies from place to place, but growers with different property rights arrangements living in the same locality rarely work independently. In most cases, the fact of mutual assistance is not in doubt; what is contested is the truth about which form of ownership and production is doing more to ensure the survival of the other.

---

[40] Y. Chernichenko, "Burov mgloiu nebo kroet. Kak novyi predsedatel' kolkhoza Burov dovel starikov do ubiistva korovy," *NG*, 25 April 2005.

[41] N. Fedina, "Komandirovka v khoziaistvo. Paishchiki–ne pai-mal'chiki," *LI* 22 August 1996, 1.

The chairman of a former collective farm in Liski district thus articulated a common belief when he explained, "Farmers will never get on their feet without the collective farms. We're fated to live together, inseparably...."[42] Another Liski director similarly observed: "We help the private farmer – we do everything 'from A to Z.' If there's no help for farmers, private farming will be condemned to extinction."[43] A member of a farmers' organization delegation in the district agreed: "The peasant, venturing out on his own today, risks finding himself face to face with his own problems. It's a paradox, but the private farmer is capable of surviving [only] close by a strong [collective] enterprise with its infrastructure."[44]

Conversely, the head of the Semiluki district farmers' association described leasing land from a collective farm with which he had a "friendly, mutual relationship": "We help the collective farm. They don't have enough pairs of hands." He emphasized the mutuality of the arrangement and the understandings that underlay it, "What belongs to the collective, what belongs to the farmer – it's all the same."[45] Across the border in Kharkiv, a local newspaper reported that "there is no small number of cases where it's not the farmer turning to the collective farm for assistance, but the collective farm turning to the farmer."[46]

Symbiotic relationships between different types of agricultural enterprises sometimes involved a single set of management personnel. In Semiluki, one former *kolkhoz* chairman also headed a private farm located on the territory of the former collective. The two companies were separate legal entities, but the chairman controlled all of the land involved, as well as other production factors of the collective farm. Such an arrangement allowed the chairman to use jointly held goods, as well as the land nominally owned by worker-shareholders, for private production–and for his own private gain.[47]

Everything Is Being Cleaned Out

Just as legal forms of enterprise organization did not predict modes of production, legal ownership did not guarantee real rights for worker-

[42] G. Aleksandrov, "Fermerskii 'lokotok'," *LI* 7 April 1994, 2.
[43] Interview, director, Chapaev, LV, 8 May 2000.
[44] V. Pleshkov, "Iur'ev den' pokhozhe, otmeniaetsia," *LI* 25 February 1992, 2.
[45] Interview, district farmers' association, SV, May 2000.
[46] L. Barkanov, "Za kem budushchee? Zametki s otchetno-vybornoi konferentsii fermerov oblasti," *TT* 25 March 1995, 2.
[47] Interview, district farmers' association, SV, May 2000.

shareholders. Years after reorganization, most rural people in the Black Earth found their ownership rights limited by political and economic constraints. In legal terms, landholders had only a narrow bundle of rights available to them. For more than a decade of reform, land was not fully commodified in either Russia or Ukraine: it could neither be freely bought and sold nor used as collateral. Instead, ownership conferred use and extraction rights – however restricted in practice – through the distribution of land share certificates.[48] Because directors of former collectives held *de facto* control of land shares, when there were third parties involved, they excluded shareholders from negotiations with potential leasers.

In Khava, one reorganized collective leased 3,000 hectares of land to a company that held a grain elevator, a private farm, and a machine-tractor station. The parties to this contract were not the shareholders of the collective and the management of the company. Rather, the director of the former collective negotiated with the company. The company paid the collective 300 kilograms of grain per land share and plowed the household gardens of shareholders, but the former collective passed on to shareholders only 200 kilograms of grain for each share.[49] Shareholders' exclusion from the bargaining table limited their extraction rights: they had no information about the terms of the agreement and no leverage in negotiating with the director of the former collective.

Some shareholders were prevented even from learning that third parties wished to lease their land. When a farmer in Zolochiv applied to receive land through a local reserve fund, he encountered resistance from the new director of a neighboring collective. The land in question had previously belonged to the collective, but it was now subject to distribution for private farming, so long as the members of the collective agreed to its alienation. The director of the former collective acted to thwart the presence of a competing farm:

That chairman ... it was his turf [*lit.* kitchen]. He didn't put this through the general assembly or the governing board ... he decided unilaterally. But you have to consult with the people. We have such a law. It's one thing that you can lead the people anywhere you want and have them raise their hands, but there wasn't even any of that, it wasn't recorded anywhere.[50]

---

[48] For a typology of ownership rights typically associated with common pool resources, see Edella Schlager and Elinor Ostrom, "Property Rights Regimes and Natural Resources: A Conceptual Analysis," *Land Economics* 68 (1992).
[49] Interview, director of grain elevator, VV, 16 May 2000.
[50] Interview, farmer Chernets'kyi, ZK, 3 January 2000.

Here, the director failed to perform the ritual of requesting the share-holders' consent. Even where that liturgy did take place, decision-making power about the disposition of property lay in the hands of enterprise managers, curbing the shareholders' choice.

An incident in Kharkiv illustrates the complexity of the problem and the obstacles shareholders faced in exercising their property rights. This particular dispute centered on the fate of a collective in a district on the Russian border, where in early 2000 a private farmer had attempted to lease the land shares of a bankrupt collective known as Victory.[51] The collective had been reorganized into a private leasing company earlier that year, and the land shares in question belonged to the members of the former collective. Forty-nine of the 180 members of Victory wished to lease their shares to the private farmer, but the director of Victory objected to the transaction.

To resolve the dispute, a group of officials gathered for several hours in the office of Taras Poriadnyi, the district head of agricultural man-agement. Present at the meeting were Sergei Ryzhkov, the director of the former collective; the chairman of the village council; the private farmer seeking to lease the shares; a representative of the district office of land resources; the deputy head of the regional land tenure office; the head of the regional technical resources division; and a representative of the Bank of Ukraine, which was seeking to repossess the harvest from share-holders' land as payment for the defunct collective's debt. No shareholder representative other than the head of the collective had been invited to the meeting. As in many other such instances, this was a case in which pow-erful local claimants trumped shareholders' legal rights in the disposition of land.

The farmer immediately voiced an objection to the fact that the director of the former collective spoke at all during negotiations: "This is the head of a collective agricultural enterprise which no longer exists. What right does he have to lecture us? He's no longer the head, he's simply a shareholder." The collective had been dissolved, though questions arose as to whether it still existed as a legal entity, and Ryzhkov had no legal right to represent the shareholders in negotiations. It was Ryzhkov's previous status that, in the eyes of those present, gave him the authority to speak on behalf of his former employees. That he arrived at the meeting late and visibly inebriated further weakened the already marginalized voice of shareholders in decision-making about their property.

---

[51] This section is based on my observations at the meeting in question on 31 May 2000.

The members of Victory had received land share certificates, which under the terms of existing legislation allowed them to lease their land. However, in order to lease their land to any entity but the collective, the shares would have to be located, divided, and allotted in the fields. Furthermore, land share certificates were valid for only two years, after which they had to be replaced by additional proof of ownership in the form of documents called "state acts." The villagers were running out of time, but the main issue being discussed by the opposing parties was the question of who would have access to shareholders' land. Ryzhkov and the farmer preferred to settle the question before people had received final legal title to it. Poriadnyi, meanwhile, was frustrated by this state of affairs, arguing that people should not be prevented from receiving state acts just because two leasers could not come to an agreement.

The representative of Victory's creditor threatened an impossible outcome if land were allotted to shareholders while Victory still owed the Bank of Ukraine money: "We'll requisition the harvest from both" the farmer and Ryzhkov. One of the regional officials present agreed that as long as there were outstanding debts on the part of Victory, land should not be allotted to anyone. Poriadnyi concluded that "the people who live in that village have become hostages."[52]

Those present at the meeting to discuss Victory's fate had difficulty agreeing upon a solution. The regional officials, who had attended many such meetings, seemed eager to arrive at even an interim agreement, so long as any compromise reached followed the letter of the law. One regional official suggested resolution through the courts, but all else present sought to avoid a court case. Such disputes could be decided through a judicial process, but local leaders with an interest in particular outcomes – the farmer wishing to lease the land, the former director hoping to prevent that, and the district head of agricultural management striving to satisfy everyone as well as protect the interests of the absent subjects in this dispute – were likely to intervene and make decisions themselves. Meanwhile, time was running out on shareholders' right to convert land title on paper to real access and permanent ownership. The longer the process dragged on, and the later shareholders were admitted

---

[52] The case of Victory was discussed at a meeting of the Kharkiv regional farmers' association earlier that year in reference to a similar debt problem at a former collective in Kharkiv district. A court of arbitration had required the issuance of non-land and land asset shares to pay off the enterprise's debts. Another local enterprise had been (illegally) selling off land shares to pay its fuel debts. OT, Kharkiv regional farmers' association council meeting, 8 February 2000.

to it, the less likely they would have any say in the matter. As one of the regional officials present commented, "We've all sat down together to make borscht. If someone arrives late, we'll have eaten it all already. The same thing goes with land." In the meantime, some villagers were finding ways to individually appropriate the non-land assets of the enterprise: "While papers are being processed, everything is being cleaned out."

And Where Will I Steal?

After privatization, worker-shareholders had negligible individual stakes in the short-term economic health of enterprises. With depressed production volumes and low prices on agricultural commodities, it rapidly became clear to worker-shareholders that there would be no profits forthcoming from the lease of their land shares. Non-land asset shares, meanwhile, were indivisible in practice, unobtainable, and, at first, impossible to liquidate. Over time, assets were sold off to redeem farm debt, and some farm directors, now founders of private leasing companies, purchased asset shares from worker-shareholders: "There's a buy-up of shares, a rather ugly [buy-up] of shares. They're sold for not more than ten percent of [their] value."[53] On such farms, "the founders bought up" everything, so people "don't stand in line for their asset shares."[54] Local influence and informal use rights drove distribution, as "the machinery was seized by those who were closest to the tractors."[55]

For some, economic pressure on their households, combined with an increasing certainty that privatization would benefit only the privileged, led to an intensification in pilfering and other, similar activity. A journalist in Kharkiv wrote at the end of the 1990s:

A critical situation has developed through the careless attitude of both heads and rank and file workers. The head of the collective farm, for example, has come to live much better than others. And in the village you can't hide anything – not the good, and all the more so not the bad (*ni, tym pache, z lykhym*). Power (*vlada*) in the village has lost its authority.[56]

With some local leaders' loss of social legitimacy, the built environment of Black Earth villages began to undergo a visible transformation. Like their counterparts elsewhere in the post-socialist world, villagers disassembled,

---

[53] Interview, district administration, CK, 21 July 2006.
[54] Interview, deputy head of district, L'viv district, 19 July 2006.
[55] Interview, pensioner, PK, 18 July 2006.
[56] Kryklyvyi, "Liudyna kriz' pryzmu reform," *SK*, 27 January 2000, 1, 2.

carted away, and sold off pieces of collective farm infrastructure.[57] The opportunity for informal liquidation of enterprise property was limited in time, for as farm infrastructure deteriorated, the assets of former collectives would lose value. Since individual worker-shareholders were unlikely to receive meaningful dividends on their ownership in shared property, and since the assets of reorganized collectives were widely understood as having been generated through the individual labor of community members,[58] it made short-term economic if not social sense to sell off property through informal channels before one's neighbors did (Illustration 7).

Warehouses and irrigation systems were sold for scrap metal, and building materials intended for ongoing farm maintenance began to disappear at record rates.[59] At Kalinin State Farm in Kharkiv, "... let's say they removed a rod (*tiaga*) from a unit and hid it in a warehouse under lock and key. In the morning, there's no trace of that rod in the warehouse. And the lock is still whole. It can only be a miracle."[60] Sometimes, whole structures vanished overnight. A prominent Kharkiv politician recounted how an intact warehouse had stood across the road from her summertime residence. When she awoke one summer morning, the warehouse was gone.[61] Collective farm directors in Voronezh articulated dozens of such stories, occasionally adding that directors of neighboring farms (in their telling, this happened only on other enterprises) had been compelled to install extra locks on warehouses to prevent their own employees from selling off the property used by the collective.[62]

The chief economist of a former collective in Anna explained the crisis of deconstruction not only as a reaction to deepening poverty and insecurity, but also as a consequence of changing understandings of ownership:

Today, the collective farm has exhausted land, which is destroying the production base. The productive life of the collective farm is in deep crisis. And it has arisen not only from the general economic and political situation in the country, but also

---

57 Gerald W. Creed, "The Politics of Agriculture: Identity and Socialist Sentiment in Bulgaria," *Slavic Review* 54:4 (Winter 1995) 860; Verdery, *The Vanishing Hectare: Property and Value on Postsocialist Transylvania.* Ithaca: Cornell University Press, 2003, 293.

58 Katherine Verdery, "Fuzzy Property: Rights, Power, and Identity in Transylvania's Decollectivization" in Michael Burawoy and Verdery, eds. *Uncertain Transition: Ethnographies of Change in the Postsocialist World.* Lanham, MD: Rowman and Littlefield, 1999, 53–82.

59 A. V. Zaburunov, "Malo zemliu liubit'. Ee nado pakhat'," *SZ* 21 September 1999, 2.

60 A. Reshetov, "Urozhai-91. V zharu s prokhladtsei..." *TT* 29 June 1991, 1.

61 OT, XK, 6 April 2000. More buildings in the area had melted into air by the time of my visit to the site six years later. Field notes, XK, July 2006.

62 OT, Il'ich kolkhoz, SV, May 2000.

ILLUSTRATION 7. Cowshed in Ukraine, 2004. In many areas, people dismantled collective farm infrastructure and used or sold the building materials.

from the changing attitude to collective property. Misappropriation and theft of collective farm property *by its very owners* is becoming widespread (*massovymi*). Losses from theft amount to millions of rubles.[63]

Eight worker-shareholders on the farm in question had recently stolen sugar beet, and the former collective took action to prevent such instances in the future by issuing a fine for stealing from the harvest. Punishment included withholding of grain and sugar payments in-kind, in full or in part, for a complete year.[64] Some former collectives did attempt to curb theft, and the fact that the situation required new rules to punish offenders suggested a problem that was systemic.

The dismantling of agricultural infrastructure intensified during the initial periods of economic liberalization, gaining even greater speed toward the end of a decade of reform. Reorganization had increased the power of farm directors on agricultural enterprises, but a variety of factors in the 1990s coalesced to damage the directors' authority in the eyes of

[63] "Khoziaiskii glaz vsego dorozhe," *AV* 17 July 1997, 1. Emphasis added.
[64] Ibid.

shareholders. Before this, the Soviet state had acted as the proxy owner for collective property that nominally belonged to "the people." The understanding that a powerful set of institutions stood behind collective ownership had protected farm property from large-scale, organized pilfering. When the command structure fell away, central state power no longer represented a credible threat to those on the farm. Meanwhile, the disjuncture between nominal and practical rights introduced a lack of clarity into local understandings of ownership. This, combined with worsened economic conditions, led to a free-for-all on some collectives and a generalized manifestation of the Soviet-era idea that *"vse vokrug kolkhoznoe, vse vokrug moe"* – "Everything around me belongs to the collective farm, so everything around me is mine."

The word "stealing" does not fully capture the social dimensions of this behavior. Pilfering and other informal methods of redistributing collective property had been practices deeply rooted in the property relations and inefficiencies of Soviet collectives. Such approaches to the exercise of property rights, however, were not exclusively Soviet. That is, they did not necessarily result directly from the existence of socialized property as such. Instead, they were a product of labor relations under rigid social hierarchy and as such can be observed elsewhere. In the post-emancipation American South, for example, "pan-toting" was the widespread practice of transferring food scraps from employers' ownership to household servants' ownership. Social historian Tera Hunter quotes one such servant's reflections on the meaning of this practice: "We don't steal; we just 'take' things – they are part of an oral contract, exprest [sic] or implied."[65]

The semi-contractual character of pilfering on reorganized enterprises in the Black Earth occasionally entered open discourse in a frank acknowledgement of the phenomenon and its likely causes. A Kharkiv farmer recounted one conversation with a prospective employee in which, during a tour of the farm and after he had explained his system of remuneration, he was asked, "And where will I steal?" (*A de ia budu krasty?*).[66] In the view of a village council official charged with overseeing land disputes in a nearby area, this particular understanding of pilfering as a right originated in the hierarchical character of the worker-manager relationship.

[65] Tera Hunter, *To 'Joy My Freedom: Southern Black Women's Lives and Labors After the Civil War*. Cambridge: Harvard University Press, 1997.
[66] OT, XK, 30 March 2000.

Even if workers received decent wages, she supposed, the right to steal would persist so long as managers received more.[67]

With increasing economic inequality and the growing sense that privatization would never improve the lives of villagers, attitudes toward property shifted. Amidst formal property relations that manifestly bore little resemblance to rights as they operated on the ground, criteria for assigning ownership lost clarity.[68] In Kharkiv, the district press complained, "One of the farmers of Vesele village sowed buckwheat, and the seeder was left in the field to rust in the bad weather. Now there's no way to tell whose seeder it is. Is it the property of the farmer ... or of one of the state farms closest to the field of the landholder?"[69]

This Was Done Deliberately

With every stage of privatization, rural elites consolidated their control over land and other farm assets. By the turn of the new millennium, *de facto* land markets had emerged. The beneficiaries of land markets were, increasingly, people who had held positions of power before the process had begun. As one Kharkiv district official described the situation in 2006, "The five 'godfathers' of the village – the chairman, the accountant, the veterinarian, the engineer, and the agronomist – accumulated capital during the barbaric period." Those five, wishing to work with only a few owners, rather than five hundred, "buy up assets from grandmothers." Next, "a banker comes and buys up all of it." If he offers a decent salary to the five founders, "no one at that level in his right mind will refuse." In this fashion, in a context of continuing low prices for agricultural commodities and "barbarians" who sowed sunflower in Black Earth fields year after year, depleting the soil for the sake of an immediate cash return, worker-shareholders were dispossessed of the land and farms they had collectively regarded as their own.[70]

---

[67] I communicated this exchange to the village official and asked her to interpret it. At the time, we were standing in the yard of a defunct shoe factory, waiting for her colleagues to survey it. OT, XK, 31 March 2000.

[68] K. Verdery, "Fuzzy Property: Rights, Power, and Identity in Transylvania's Decollectivization" in Burawoy and Verdery, eds. *Uncertain Transition: Ethnographies of Change in the Postsocialist World.* Lanham, MD: Rowman and Littlefield, 1999, 53–82.

[69] V. Petrenko, "U nas v raioni," *TT* 1 July 1995, 1.

[70] Interview, district administration, CK, 21 July 2006. In this official's view, Ukraine's "Orange Revolution" was meant to be the end of the "barbaric period."

From this perspective, private property rights in the villages of the post-Soviet Black Earth seemed to be a failed experiment. Rural people had little reason to believe that their land shares in former collectives would ever become a source of real revenue for themselves and their families, and life in the countryside continued to be a rough, difficult, work-filled daily challenge. A few enriched themselves, but not through ownership as such. Peter Lindner writes of former collective farms in Russia: "In fact, the often highly uneven distribution of income is usually less the consequence of property relations than of the differing possibilities to 'privately appropriate' or 'redirect' profits generated within the regular production process."[71] Amidst elite opposition to individuation of land, and without the opportunity to accumulate capital necessary for independent commercial farming or the requisite time and resources to do battle in the courts, rural people had little incentive to convert paper rights into actual allocation of land in the fields.

Meanwhile, urban populations continued to encroach upon farmland. By 1995, intimations of the future of farmland ownership were visible in the countryside, leading a group of rural "veterans of labor" in Kharkiv to lament:

> We asked the Frunze district committee to allocate a few small plots for us, but we were refused. Now, luxury homes (*kottedzhi*) are being built on that spot. Perhaps the poor are building them, who have nowhere else to live? We also have children, grandchildren, who really have no housing.[72]

As the decade wore on, rural people in villages near cities observed the fields and forest that surrounded them slowly replaced by the summer homes of the newly wealthy. Villagers, compelled by circumstance to work longer and harder than before and newly isolated in their daily lives as local transportation infrastructure deteriorated beyond repair, saw the land that had been promised to them occupied by others.

Fed by visible, growing inequality, the failure of land privatization to benefit most rural people, and the increasingly apparent fact that under such conditions, no amount of work would allow most to rise out of poverty, a dark suspicion emerged in the villages of the Black Earth.[73]

---

[71] Peter Lindner, "The Kolkhoz Archipelago. Localizing Privatization, Disconnecting Locales," Unpublished manuscript, Yale University, 2004, 25.

[72] M. Mel'nyk, "Z dumkoiu pro zemliu vse chastishe i chastishe pyshut' svoi lysty chytachi," *SK* 10 October 1995, 1.

[73] The widespread emergence of economic conspiracy theories in the wake of structural adjustment policies is documented in Harry West and Todd Sanders, eds. *Transparency*

Former members of collective farms began to wonder if the creation of new land rights had all been an elaborate ruse, yet another attempt to render the countryside legible in order to steal from it:[74]

> You know, maybe those who will be able to buy [land] later did that with the shares on purpose. For a thousand years no one needed them.... But without anything they handed out those certificates (*sviditel'stva*): "For God's sake, do what you want," understand? Who needed that? I've understood that in the future, land can be sold and maybe, of course, it's no difference to a pensioner, they'll give him 20,000, I'd give [my certificate] away right now, and why? Understand? This was done deliberately so that land would be sold.... They needed either to create suitable conditions, give out machinery, or why should I leave? As an agronomist, what would I grow on five hectares according to crop rotation? There's no machinery! And you can't dig a plot like that with a shovel.[75]

Resistance to individuation that ultimately led to rural dispossession was driven not only by personal ambition but also by sensible support for local economies of scale, given the structural constraints of the time. But many Black Earth villagers, for whom new property rights not only failed to offer improvement but, in many cases, brought economic loss, understood privatization as a conspiratorial fraud of massive proportions. Fifteen years after the beginning of privatization, the Voronezh regional press both asserted and seemed to encourage a new economy of dispossession, recognizing rural people's experience of deception and betrayal by the state while exhorting them to divest themselves of property:

> Pensioners on the farm received land shares. Owners! Masters! The majority saw no reason in those "innovations." Much became clear when the "scam" started to work. Land taxes sharply increased. The "owners" couldn't understand what for?! After all, with these virtual shares they have exactly nothing. And for that to hand over nearly half of a monthly pension, when there aren't enough resources for firewood, coal, electricity, medicine... We'll say no to those shares! It was not to be!"[76]

Like the hollow institutions that have resulted from electoral reform in some former Soviet states and administrative reform in new European

---

and Conspiracy: Ethnographies of Suspicion in the New World Order. Durham: Duke University Press, 2003.

[74] James C. Scott discusses Imperial Russian attempts to render communal property rights regimes "legible" (and provide for individual, rather than collective, accountability and taxation) in *Seeing Like a State: How Certain Schemes to Improve the Human Condition Have Failed*. New Haven: Yale University Press, 1998, 37–52.

[75] Interview, director, Sil'nyi, LV, 8 May 2000.

[76] E. Yefremov, "Zemel'nyi vopros. Bezzakonie...v zakone?" *KO* 17 March 2006.

Union member states,[77] land ownership provided a legitimizing facade that proclaimed to the world and, importantly, to international lending institutions, the existence of alienable private property in the Black Earth countryside, even as ownership threatened ruin for some Black Earth villagers.

If the Soviet system produced a facade of political rights, enshrined in its constitution but ignored or openly flouted in practice, land reform in post-Soviet Russia and Ukraine produced a new Potemkin village, easily visible from the windows of government offices in the capitals. This village is made of paper, and it records the recreation of a Eurasian steppe populated with independent landowners. But behind it stands the reality of the post-Soviet countryside. In that reality, rural populations on both sides of the border have become proletarianized and economically marginalized. Those who have prospered have done so either by capturing the privatization process for their own ends, or for reasons that have little to do with new rights in law. Most rural people's lives have not been noticeably improved by the emergence of private land ownership as such, and their grinding poverty is exacerbated by the retrenchment of state control at the local level and the newfound power of farm elites. The intended beneficiaries of privatization – the pensioners and worker-shareholders of reorganized collectives – now find themselves engaged in a daily struggle as they go about the hard business of working the soil, quietly awaiting the next repartition or, perhaps, the next revolution.

---

77 Andrew Wilson, *Virtual Politics: Faking Democracy in the Post-Soviet World*. New Haven: Yale University Press, 2005 and Wade Jacoby, *The Enlargement of the European Union and NATO: Ordering from the Menu in Central Europe*. Cambridge: Cambridge University Press, 2004.

Conclusion

Rural Proletarians in the Potemkin Village

A forest of high-rise apartment buildings now surrounds the Saltivka housing development where, in the twilight of Soviet power, the workers of the Ukrainka state farm had defended their farm territory. During the 1990s, Ukrainka's status as a research farm shielded it from privatization, but in recent years, amidst rising demand for land around the city of Kharkiv, Ukrainka's land was targeted for partition. The desks of the district cadastral office, where employees once had time for afternoon tea, are now piled high with seemingly endless mountains of paperwork.

The paperwork is not, in the main, for individual worker-shareholders seeking to allot their shares and lease them to the highest bidder. As the fortunes of the city improve, Black Earth villagers have seen their living standards continue to decline, for "life is improving everywhere but the village."[1] As Russian urban populations operate in an economy flush with oil revenue, and consumers in the city of Kharkiv patronize markets where they choose among "twenty-five different kinds of cheese," villagers "kill their cows because milk prices are so low."[2] Cadastral services, meanwhile, map land allotments for powerful local figures and interested corporate entities. A legal basis for private ownership thus established, the scramble for Black Earth land has begun.

Amidst the parceling of village land, particularly in districts near urban settlements, some villagers have begun to thrive. In certain areas, rural people have banded together to form vegetable growing cooperatives or engage in cottage industry. In Voronezh, casinos – and the temporarily

[1] OT, farmer Chernets'kyi, BK, 19 July 2006.
[2] OT, district land tenure office, XK, 20 July 2006.

lucrative but ultimately destructive trades that so often accompany them – have generated employment for some rural people. But the new forms of association and the profits they bring are usually not a result of private land ownership as such. More often, they are the fruits of *de facto* land use rights stemming from the decline of former collective and state farms.

Dispossession through Privatization

Land privatization in the Black Earth was a mechanism by which rural people were dispossessed of property they had built or maintained under socialism. This is not simply a matter of villagers' failing to gain through an ill-fated distribution scheme. Rather, in concrete ways, most Black Earth villagers face greater physical hardship, uncertainty, and poverty than at any time since after World War II.

Policy makers and villagers alike in Russia and Ukraine regarded allocation of farm assets as a partial return on their investment of labor during what Creed describes as "the heady days of building socialism."[3] This was clear in the rules used to calculate non-land asset shares on the basis of workers' salary levels for the past twenty years. As the head economist of a Voronezh collective farm explained to readers of a district newspaper at the time, "This number is direct evidence of how much each person invested in collective production during those years: the higher your salary, the greater your share."[4]

Additionally, members of reorganized collectives faced a choice under privatization that meant the loss of their investment of labor either way: they could remain on the farm and risk losing practical access to the land to which they had legal claim, or they could set out on their own and risk losing housing, transportation, access to informal distribution networks, and other goods and services that membership in the collective provided. In this regard, decollectivization resembled the post-war campaigns in East Germany to place "Junkerland in Bauernhand" (estate land in peasant hands). There, smallholder farming was a prelude to collectivization and was meant to fail. Households were allotted tracts of land without housing, infrastructure, or credit to support agriculture, and predictable disaster ensued.[5]

---

[3] Gerald Creed, "The Politics of Agriculture: Identity and Socialist Sentiment in Bulgaria," *Slavic Review* 54:4 (Winter 1995) 860.

[4] L. Dolgashova, "Gotovimsia k peremenam," *MP* 21 January 1992, 3.

[5] Arvid Nelson, *Cold War Ecology: Forests, Farms, and People in the East German Landscape, 1945–1989*. New Haven: Yale University Press, 2005.

Black Earth villagers retained neither right of withdrawal nor of management when they leased their land shares to former collectives.[6] Thus, in some areas, particularly those near large cities, villagers lost use rights to collective grazing areas when farm directors chose to reapportion fields for cash crops. This undermined households' income-generating capacity, for milk was the most important marketable commodity for many families. For this and other reasons, land privatization drew comparisons with industrial privatization in Black Earth and national opposition newspapers (Illustration 8). One Russian journalist argued: "The game of private property with citizens, with allotted land shares, apparently is ending just as it ended with citizen-owners of vouchers for the assets of industrial enterprises."[7] But industrial privatization did not itself divest the population of a means of production to which they formerly had individual use rights. With the capture of industrial privatization by a small handful of well-placed elites, workers lost income, and many lost their jobs. Those who received privatization vouchers in Russia lost potential revenue when they invested in pyramid schemes or exchanged their vouchers for more liquid assets.[8] Rural people, however, lost their only available means to make a living when land was alienated.

The combination of economic constraints on demand for land and the consolidation of power in the hands of local state and farm elites as a result of land privatization suggests that, contrary to the claims of those who argue that initial distribution is of minor importance, one should worry very much indeed about the first iterations of distribution. After privatization, transaction costs remain high, markets imperfect, and local parties are far from free to enter into contracts. Redefinition is thus largely a zero-sum game: those who lost in the first years of reform are unlikely ever to gain from it. The lack of actual land partition and distribution in the 1990s constrained the development of land share and labor markets in the Black Earth, limiting the capacity of rural shareholders to accumulate capital necessary for making future use of their rights. Future transfers are likely to continue to move land into the hands of powerful players

---

[6] Withdrawal refers to the right to subtractive use of a common pool resource, whereas exclusion is the right to allocate and establish rules for transfer of withdrawal rights. Management concerns improvement and regulation of use. Edella Schlager and Elinor Ostrom, "Property Rights Regimes and Natural Resources: A Conceptual Analysis," *Land Economics* 68 (1992).

[7] N. Kalinin, "Iz arendy – v doveritel'noe upravlenie," *KR* No3 January 2005, 4.

[8] Irina Kuzes and Lynn Nelson, *Property to the People: The Struggle for Radical Economic Reform in Russia*. Armonck: M.E. Sharpe, 1994.

ILLUSTRATION 8. "I'll buy land." The caption for this cartoon, printed in the Voronezh newspaper *Kommuna* 17 March 2006, read, "Land shares were treated like the distribution of [industrial privatization] vouchers had been at one time." The sight of people holding signs reading "I'll buy a voucher" were common in Russian cities during the early 1990s, when privatization checks [vouchers] could be traded for a small sum or a bottle of alcohol. Here, a pitchfork and *valenki* (felt boots) signify rural identity. Reprinted by kind permission of the editor-in-chief of *Kommuna*.

who create latifundia, leaving parts of the post-privatization countryside populated with landless peasants. Rather than preparing the ground for the free exchange of land as a commodity, land privatization in Russia and Ukraine seemed to foreclose future opportunities for rural people to own land.

Was dispossession a foregone conclusion? What would property rights in the Black Earth look like if there had been no venal farm directors, no state officials seeking to preserve collectives in order to maximize tribute from them? It seems likely that, given the economic environment into which policy makers introduced land reform, the outcomes might have been similar to those that actually transpired. Conscientious farm directors and local officials, and the villagers who chose not to seek land allotment, would still have encountered incentives that led them to try to preserve collective farms or to minimize personal risk. In the Black Earth, structural adjustment policies at the national level set the incentives faced by local state officials and villagers alike. Those incentives drove both demand for and supply of land, leading most villagers to choose to remain on reorganized collectives and officials to obstruct land distribution for those who tried to leave.

Even with more successful titling, Black Earth agriculture might have encountered the land fragmentation faced by Moldovan, Latvian, and Lithuanian farmers.[9] Widespread land distribution would still have disrupted already fragile production cycles, and even the healthiest of farms would have struggled with price scissors and the challenge of creating supply chains and distribution networks out of whole cloth. Under such conditions, post-socialist farmers elsewhere have recollectivized in order to survive.[10]

That policy failure was overdetermined in the Black Earth should come as no particular surprise to policy makers. Land privatization in Eastern Europe drew upon global boilerplate policies, explicitly mirroring policies in other world regions. In particular, successful land reform in certain areas with less heavily capitalized agriculture in China and Vietnam remained a touchstone and justification for land reform programs in post-Soviet space.[11] Scholars of Chinese land reform, meanwhile, documented regionally disparate outcomes of property rights development in rural China and argued that the existence of markets and private land tenure as such do not guarantee a particular economic, political, or social order.[12]

The policies implemented in the post-Soviet Black Earth also followed decades of efforts to create new property rights regimes in Africa and Latin

[9] Matthew Gorton and John White, "The Politics of Agrarian Collapse: Decollectivization in Moldova," *East European Politics and Societies* 17:2 (2003) 305–331; Junior R. Davis, "Understanding the Process of Decollectivisation and Agricultural Privatisation in Transition Economies: The Distribution of Collective and State Farm Assets in Latvia and Lithuania," *Europe-Asia Studies* 49:8 (December 1997) 1409–1432.

[10] Karen Brooks and Mieke Meurs, "Romanian Land Reform: 1991–1993," *Comparative Political Studies* 36:2 (Summer 1994) 17–32.

[11] This synecdoche may very well be an example of what Stein Rokkan called "whole nation bias." Rokkan, *Citizens, Elections, Parties*. Oslo: Universitetforlaget, 1970. On Asian models for land reform, see Max Spoor and Oane Visser, "The State of Agrarian Reform in the Former Soviet Union," *Europe-Asia Studies* 53:6 (2001) 885–901 and Zvi Lerman, "Does Land Reform Matter? Some Experiences from the Former Soviet Union," *European Review of Agricultural Economics* 25:3 (1998) 307–330.

[12] Jean Oi and Andrew Walder, eds. *Property Rights and Economic Reform in China*. Stanford University Press, 1999; Walder, "Markets and Inequality in Transitional Economies: Toward Testable Theories," *American Journal of Sociology* 101:4 (1996) 1060–1073.

America. Scholarly critique of those efforts suggests that formal property rights alone led neither to poverty reduction nor to more effective resource use. A large body of research in African states, for example, has shown that land titling not only did not improve efficiency, but also often led to increased social conflict and differential access to land for vulnerable groups.[13] Other research challenges a long-held assumption among development economists working in Africa that smallholder monoculture farming is more efficient than capitalized agriculture, showing that this maxim is at best, not proven, and at worst, untrue.[14]

The orthodoxy that privatization should be conducted concurrently with other elements of economic liberalization – lifting price controls and trade barriers, and enforcing of budgetary discipline by cutting spending rather than focusing on raising tax revenue – is not supported by the effect of economic incentives on Black Earth privatization. The economic conditions that kept Black Earth villagers from demanding land are likely to accompany all land privatization efforts conducted in the context of liberalizing economic reform. Farms face significant barriers to profitability when borders are open to international trade, when they are exposed to subsidized imports, and when price controls are removed. When enterprises continue to struggle, land rents shrink, salary payment becomes irregular, and worker-shareholders face limited opportunities to accumulate capital. Without access to capital, land acquisition is an unattractive prospect for individual households.

In the Black Earth, the local effects of economic liberalization and stabilization drove local responses to land privatization policies, which in turn shaped privatization outcomes. In this particular case, renovation of practices developed under communism allowed local actors to renegotiate the demands of the center. However, related strategies may emerge elsewhere, where commodification of land is contested and where surrounding economic conditions produce strong disincentives for the individuation and distribution of common pool resources.

Postponing land reform until more favorable conditions for agricultural production have been achieved could limit the potential for dispossession. Advocates of privatization ordinarily argue the urgency of property rights reform by asserting that delays will lead to large-scale

---

[13] See, for example, Pauline E. Peters, *Dividing the Commons: Policy and Culture in Botswana*. Charlottesville: University of Virginia Press, 1994.

[14] John Sender and Deborah Johnston, "Searching for a Weapon of Mass Production in Rural Africa: Unconvincing Arguments for Land Reform," *Journal of Agrarian Change* 4:1–2 (January and April 2004).

rent-seeking, but evidence shows this may also occur with rapid privatization. Furthermore, there is every reason to expect that agricultural collectives could have functioned in markets as public companies. The record of the late Soviet period shows that Black Earth collective and state farms had adapted to nascent markets before land privatization policy was introduced, and there were indications that they would continue to do so, regardless of their ownership structure.

Farm directors in Russia and Ukraine consistently identified weak supply chains and distribution networks as central problems plaguing agriculture; formal changes in ownership could do nothing to address those issues. If governments were to take seriously the proposition that ownership as such may be of less consequence than other market conditions such as competition, incentive structures, and regulation,[15] then privatization could be considered, planned, and executed in a judicious fashion, avoiding the disenfranchisement of workers who, in large enough numbers, have the potential to become a political problem.

Lessons from Post-Socialism

Land privatization in post-socialist countries has been conceptualized mainly as a feature of transition from state coordinated to market economies. Yet the reasons why land reform failed to bring benefit to rural people across Eastern Europe and Eurasia are linked to broader global conditions that will continue to shape the implementation of privatization policies. The lessons of post-socialist privatization may help other communities avoid similar problems in the future.

A vast volume of research worldwide has shown that privatization programs tend to benefit existing elites. Some have even suggested that elites may intentionally produce chaos to accomplish major shifts in property rights regimes that otherwise would not be accepted by the population.[16] Privatization is thus an instrument, in David Stark's formulation, by which debts and liabilities are socialized while assets are placed in private hands.[17] To the extent that privatization is a policy tool well-placed people use to enrich themselves, there is no reason to expect that large-scale

[15] See John Marangos, "A Post-Keynesian Critique of Privatization Policies in Transition Economies," *Journal of International Development* 14:5 (2002) 573–589.

[16] Joma Nazpary, *Post-Soviet Chaos: Violence and Dispossession in Kazakhstan*. London: Pluto Press, 2002.

[17] David Stark, "Recombinant Property in East European Capitalism," *American Journal of Sociology* 101: 4 (1996) 993–1027.

privatization should end with post-socialist "transitions." Instead, enclosure movements are likely to expand in scope. The current commodification of public goods such as water and cyberspace, and the rapid takeover of public sector institutions such as schools, prisons, and armies by private companies, are signs of this growth.

Furthermore, new frontiers of privatization may not be limited to public goods. The ideologies that ordinarily underpin privatization policy may be deployed to support not only initial enclosure, but also the transfer of assets from the relatively powerless to the powerful. The opportunity to extract rents can drive privatization, as in recent examples of water-table redefinition from India to Bolivia. Water beneath the land of some communities has been sold to buyers claiming that commodification will result in more efficient use. In such instances, rights are sold to apportion a good to which no one previously had imagined laying separate claims.[18]

How does land privatization in the Black Earth compare with other cases of dispossession through privatization in Eastern Europe and the former Soviet states? Despite fundamental procedural differences, in which land was returned to former owners through restitution in much of Eastern Europe and divided through distribution in post-Soviet states, outcomes are similar on a number of dimensions, as has been noted in this book. In some cases, as in Hungary, dispossession occurred with the stroke of a pen through legislation that allocated land to some categories of rural residents and not to others.[19] In cases from Transylvania to Siberia, local elites successfully consolidated control of land resources through the process of reform.[20]

However, the experience of people in the Black Earth differs from that of other post-socialist rural populations in significant ways. First, land privatization allowed Black Earth state officials to rearticulate their positions of power within rural society, as they not only became arbiters of land distribution, but also inserted themselves into old and new supply chains and distribution networks. With the apparent resurgence of authoritarian

---

[18] Vandana Shiva, *Water Wars: Privatization, Pollution, and Profit*. Boston: South End Press, 2002.

[19] István Harcsa, Imre Kovách, and Iván Szelényi, "The Price of Privatization: The Post-Communist Transformational Crisis of the Hungarian Agrarian System," in Szelényi, ed. *Privatizing the Land: Rural Political Economy in Post-Communist Societies*. Routledge: 1998.

[20] K. Verdery, *The Vanishing Hectare: Property and Value in Postsocialist Transylvania*. Ithaca: Cornell University Press, 2003; and Caroline Humphrey, *Marx Went Away, But Karl Stayed Behind*. Ann Arbor: University of Michigan Press, 1998.

forms of governance at the turn of the millennium in both Ukraine and Russia, local officials' rural networks helped reconnect the metropole with the village, delivering votes for incumbents and repairing links between levels of government that had been weakened following the Soviet collapse. This return of coercive state power (which should not be confused with the post-socialist state's radically reduced capacity to provide social services) contrasts with the receding role of the state elsewhere in Eastern Europe.[21] Second, as other parts of Central and Eastern Europe are absorbed into the agricultural subsidy regimes of the European Union, Ukraine and Russia will be left to their own devices. This may be of little concern to Russia, but it will mean that the common past of post-socialism in Europe will end at the door to the European Union for rural people. In other words, the future of Black Earth agriculture is likely to continue to diverge from that of its immediate neighbors to the west.

The Significance of the Facade

In recent years, scholars writing about property have attended to the many ways that communities engage and produce meaning around and through it. This literature "denaturalizes" property, revealing the architecture of its social construction and emphasizing the flexibility and negotiability of local rules governing property, whether those rules are rooted in socialist-era informal economies in Europe or "customary tenure" regimes in Africa.[22] It privileges local understandings and, in its implicit critique of land reform prescriptions, offers an additional analytical lens through which to view top-down approaches to social and economic transformation. The study of local responses thus may yield not only an alternative epistemology, but also an empirical correction to the story told by officialdom.

Such approaches illuminate the texture of rural life, including the ways in which economic inequality and social conflict may be reproduced or intensified through local adaptations to land policy.[23] This has been part

---

[21] David Kideckel, ed. *East European Communities: The Struggle for Balance in Turbulent Times.* Boulder: Westview Press, 1995.

[22] See the work of Sara Berry, especially "Debating the Land Question in Africa," *Contemporary Studies in Society and History* 44:4 (2002) 638–68.

[23] Pauline Peters, "Inequality and Social Conflict Over Land in Africa," *Journal of Agrarian Change* 4:3 (July 2004) 269–314; Aaron Bobrow-Strain, "Dis(Accords): The Politics of Market-Assisted Land Reforms in Chiapas, Mexico," *World Development* 32:6 (2004) 887–903.

of the task of this book. However, just as there is a danger of focusing exclusively on legal rights, paying attention only to local understandings of property can occlude broader processes at work.[24] It is thus important also to pursue the path of the parchment institutions that triggered local negotiation and resistance. Rights in law, even as they are not fully realized in life at one moment, may later prove to be a basis for further reconfiguration of power. If the past is to be any guide, this may mean enrichment for the powerful or dispossession for the weak. Like rural people in other parts of post-socialist Europe who lost their right to land when they failed to request it in good time, Black Earth villagers saw their opportunity to consolidate rights fade as farm directors collected shares for themselves.[25]

No matter how land is currently used in practice, all agricultural land in Kharkiv and Voronezh now has an owner. In future years, vast tracts of unused land in remote areas may, by law, be reclaimed by the state, while powerful landholders may at any time expel villagers who use it for hay fields, pasture, or gardens. Even as the politics of privatization at the local level shape the relationship between paper rights and rights in practice, it is the former that ultimately may matter most, whether for the benefit of villagers who managed to allot their land in the early years of privatization, or for the good of farm directors who seized and held certificates, or for the corporate entities that, understanding that most villagers were gaining little in rents but needed cash, purchased land shares at a low price.

A decade from now (2007), many of the pensioners who invested decades of labor in collectivized agriculture will have passed from the earth. Stronger farms will retain workers, but as the infrastructure of weaker farms deteriorates, younger people will have less reason to remain attached to them. Farm directors' intensification of control over people is likely to give way to a struggle for control over land. The potential for outside interests to intervene in that struggle has already been partly realized, and its significance is signaled by its banishment from discourse:

---

[24] Martha Lampland, "The Advantages of Being Collectivized. Collective Farm Managers in the Postsocialist Economy," in C. M. Hann, ed. *Postsocialism: Ideals, Ideologies, and Practices in Eurasia.* London: Routledge, 2002, 34; Louis Skyner, "Property as Rhetoric: Land Ownership and Private Law in Pre-Soviet and Post-Soviet Russia," *Europe-Asia Studies* 55:6 (2003) 889–905.

[25] For example, in Hungary see Harcsa et al., "The Price of Privatization: The Post-Communist Transformational Crisis of the Hungarian Agrarian System," in Iván Szelényi, ed. *Privatizing the Land: Rural Political Economy in Post-Communist Societies.* Routledge: 1998, 221.

in all of my time in the Black Earth, the only line of questioning I was ever cautioned not to pursue concerned people known in Voronezh as "white farmers" – absentee landowners who have made sharecroppers of the farm workers who saw themselves as building socialism.

Cows and Dispossession

Fifteen years after the fall of the Soviet empire, tethered cows began to appear along roads leading to the city of Kharkiv. The cows themselves signify the continuity of livestock husbandry in Black Earth villages, but their location speaks volumes about land ownership and agriculture. During the last decades of socialism, Black Earth cows lived in large sheds on agricultural collectives, grazing in open fields during summer. As dying farms failed during a decade of land privatization, cowsheds on many farms became empty ruins and cows lived in the yards of villagers who kept them for milk and cash. They pastured on the leased land of reorganized collectives, and at milking time, villagers went out to them in the fields, buckets and stools in hand.

Tethered cows are a sign of enclosure and dispossession. Tethering a large animal requires labor: the stake must be moved as the animal eats through fodder within the rope's circumference. A cow thus secured must be moved several times a day, and time spent in travel to and from the spot is labor lost. Compared with pasturing in open fields, tethering is an inefficient method of caring for an animal, and Black Earth villagers would be unlikely to tether a cow if there were common land available for grazing.[26] Livestock confined to the margins of well-traveled roads and highways is mute testimony that villagers have lost access to the fields of former collectives.[27]

Such scenarios are, for the time being, more common near cities than in more remote villages, where unused land is abundant and "the hares feel at home. It's steppe now."[28] But they suggest a problem likely to intensify as large-scale agriculture in the Black Earth recovers from

---

[26] David Kerans provides a helpful description of this problem, which is well known to farmers, in *Mind and Labor on the Farm in Black-Earth Russia, 1861–1914*. Budapest and New York: Central European University Press, 2001.

[27] Judith Pallot and Tatyana Nefedova address a similar problem in Russia. Pallot and Nefedova, "Geographical Differentiation in Household Plot Production in Rural Russia," *Eurasian Geography and Economics* 44:1 (2003) 40–64.

[28] OT, land tenure office, XK, 20 July 2006. Tat'iana Nefedova, "Nerusskoe sel'skoe khoziaistvo," *Otechestvennye zapiski* No. 2 (2004); Grigory Ioffe, "The Downsizing of Russian Agriculture," *Europe-Asia Studies* 57:2 (March 2005).

crisis. The growth of household production in the 1990s depended in part on the weakness of commercial farming, as households used the resources of reorganized agricultural collectives to produce a marketable surplus. As Moscow oil money trickles into the Russian periphery, and as Ukrainian agriculture attracts more investment, the large farms that continue to dominate the Black Earth are likely to regain their strength as parts of vertically integrated – and, in some cases, state-controlled – companies. Over time, those companies may have the incentive and resources to better surveil their land and labor resources. Competitive farms will not employ most rural people, but they may be less inclined than their predecessors to allow village households to pasture their animals or otherwise use the land over which farm directors gained control in the 1990s. In that case, rural people will have neither income from ownership of their land nor access to the means for a basic livelihood.

As such a world comes to pass, the collective farm members who became reluctant peasants in post-socialism will be poised, as twenty-first century rural proletarians, to greet the birth of a new economic liberalism, in which privatization is now the handmaiden both of monopoly capital and the resurgence of state power.

Index